John Inglis

In the New Hebrides

Reminiscences of missionary life and work, especially on the island of Aneityum,

from 1850 till 1877

John Inglis

In the New Hebrides
Reminiscences of missionary life and work, especially on the island of Aneityum, from 1850 till 1877

ISBN/EAN: 9783337314125

Printed in Europe, USA, Canada, Australia, Japan

Cover: Foto ©Andreas Hilbeck / pixelio.de

More available books at **www.hansebooks.com**

IN THE

NEW HEBRIDES

Reminiscences of Missionary Life and Work,

ESPECIALLY ON THE ISLAND OF ANEITYUM,

FROM 1850 TILL 1877.

By the

REV. JOHN INGLIS, D.D.,

Thirty-three Years a Missionary, first of the Reformed Presbyterian Church of Scotland, and then of the Free Church of Scotland, in New Zealand and in the New Hebrides;

Author of "A Grammar and Dictionary of the Aneityumese Language," etc.

London:

T. NELSON AND SONS, PATERNOSTER ROW.

EDINBURGH; AND NEW YORK.

1887.

Inscribed

TO THE MEMORY OF MY BELOVED WIFE,

THE PARTNER OF MY LABOURS, TRIALS, AND COMFORTS,

DURING ALL THE PERIOD COVERED

BY THIS BOOK.

PREFACE.

The literature connected with the New Hebrides is somewhat copious. We may pass over the "Memorial of Mendana to the King of Spain," which has been often quoted, more or less fully. The portion of Captain Cook's Voyages referring to the New Hebrides, published more than a century ago, is written in all the clear, graphic, and truthful style of the great navigator. When in 1850 I first sailed along the group, I read Cook's narrative in the large edition of his Voyages, and the accounts seemed as fresh and truth-like as if they had been written only a twelvemonth before. Captain (now Admiral) Erskine's admirable "Journal" refers only briefly to the New Hebrides; it has reference chiefly to the eastern islands. The second volume of the Rev. William Gill's fascinating work, entitled "Gems from the Coral Islands," contains some interesting details of mission work on the New Hebrides. In his "Nineteen Years in Polynesia," in a clear, methodical, and perspicuous narrative, the Rev. Dr. Turner has recorded the labours and perils of the first two mission families—his own and Rev. Dr. Nisbet's—settled on Tanna, and to which he added three voyages in the *John Williams*. The Rev. A. W. Murray comes next, with his "Missions in Western Polynesia," and in strong and earnest language relates what was done for the introduction of the Gospel by the agents of the London Missionary Society. The next two volumes are from a navigator's point of view, being Journals of Cruises in H.M.S. *Rosario;* the one by Captain Markham, R.N., the other by Captain Palmer, R.N., who were sent to examine into the labour traffic and report upon it. They are both well-written volumes; the authors were in deep sympathy with the greatly injured natives. The two volumes that followed those are deeply affecting biographies, the first of the Rev. J. W. Matheson and his wife, and the Rev. S. F. Johnston, by the Rev. Dr. Paterson; the second of the Rev. G. N. Gordon and his wife, by his brother, the Rev. J. D. Gordon. The life of the Rev. Dr. Geddie, by the Rev. Dr. Paterson, is to a large extent a collection of Dr. Geddie's journals and letters, and gives a full and interesting account of the commencement and early history of the New Hebrides mission, up to the time of our arrival in 1852. After that date the work connected with the mission increased so much, that it was in working, not in writing, that Dr. Geddie's time was chiefly occupied, and hence his journals and letters were for the most part brief. An excellent little volume, entitled "A Year in the New Hebrides," &c., by F. A. Campbell, 1873, gives a very good account of the islands and the mission up to that date, and is enriched by an appendix containing a "contribution to the phytography of the New

Hebrides by Baron Von Mueller," the plants having been collected by Mr. Campbell, but arranged and named by the learned Curator of the Melbourne Botanical Garden. But the Rev. Dr. Steel's volume, entitled " The New Hebrides and Christian Missions," is really the history of the New Hebrides mission. It contains a vast amount of valuable information, collected with much pains, patience, and discrimination. He records fully and faithfully the toils, trials, and triumphs of the missionaries; defends them ably, and vindicates them successfully, from the aspersions cast upon them and the misrepresentations made against them by such writers as Meade and Brenchley—able men, but prejudiced and misinformed, and who unhappily accepted their information from sources utterly unreliable. Dr. Steel is remarkably well informed on missions, knows everything about the New Hebrides mission, writes with extreme care and accuracy, and is in full sympathy with mission work to the heathen.

It is highly probable that some friends of the New Hebrides mission will be disappointed with this volume. It is not, as they may have expected it to be, a history of that mission. Dr. Steel's book rendered that quite unnecessary; but I never contemplated a history of the whole mission. When about to prepare his history, Dr. Steel consulted me, and would not have proceeded with it if I had thought of writing a history of the whole mission. But I urged him to go on with his work, as it would in no way interfere with mine. This is a history of the Aneityum rather than of the New Hebrides mission, and, furthermore, rather of my own station (and not all that I wished to say about it) than of the whole island; but as the work on both stations was carried on on the same lines, and with very much the same results, it so happens that what I have said about my own station will generally apply to the whole island. This volume is not written in chronological order; it does not record what was done year by year; it is a succession of subjects, but not a consecutive history; although, as far as practicable, I have arranged the subjects to follow each other in regular order. It is not autobiographical, but it contains almost nothing that has not come under my own personal observation, or been attested to me by eye or ear witnesses. I have to some extent copied from my own letters and journals published in the *Reformed Presbyterian Magazine* and elsewhere; but these extracts have all been rewritten and abridged or extended, as seemed to be required, and the information, where needed, brought down to the present date. There is nothing startling in the book, nothing sensational; it is not written specially for the learned or for the scientific, but for average Christian readers, who feel an interest in missions to the heathen; and I sincerely hope that those who come to its perusal with moderate expectations may not be disappointed. The elder Dr. M'Crie used to say, " A sermon is a sermon, but a letter is only a letter; " and on one occasion, at a meeting for Foreign Missions in Exeter Hall, the Chairman said, " Now let the missionaries give us their facts, and we will draw our inferences for ourselves." In the following pages

I have tried to avoid sermonising, and to allow my readers to draw their inferences for themselves. In a few cases the same idea or the same fact has been repeated in different chapters, but as seldom as possible, and only for the sake of connection.

I have still sufficient materials on hand to form another volume, which would contain biographical sketches of natives, both heathen and Christian,—chapters on the manners, customs, and traditions of the Aneityumese,— illustrations of Scripture through light supplied from the New Hebrides, and other aspects of missionary life and work similar to those given here. But the appearance of that volume will depend very much upon the reception given to this one. Publishers are extremely chary about running any risks with missionary literature; and hence the authors of mission books have to make strong and pathetic appeals, to secure the patronage of their private friends, as well as the support of the general public.

LINCUAN COTTAGE, KIRKCOWAN, N.B.,
November 13th, 1886.

CONTENTS.

CHAP.	PAGE
I. THE SOUTH SEA ISLANDS	1
II. THE NEW HEBRIDES	8
III. ANEITYUM	19
IV. THE ANEITYUMESE IN HEATHENISM	29
V. ORIGIN OF THE NEW HEBRIDES MISSION	37
VI. MISSION-HOUSES	55
VII. THE SABBATH ON ANEITYUM	63
VIII. THE SCHOOL ON ANEITYUM	74
IX. THE BIBLE ON ANEITYUM	89
X. THE PULPIT ON ANEITYUM	115
XI. THE SERVICE OF SONG ON ANEITYUM	136
XII. THE NEW HEBRIDES MISSION SYNOD	154
XIII. MISSION VESSELS—THE "DAYSPRING"	164
XIV. ASTRONOMY ON ANEITYUM—"ECLIPSES"	172
XV. EARTHQUAKES AND TIDAL WAVE ON ANEITYUM	183
XVI. THE LABOUR TRAFFIC IN THE NEW HEBRIDES	198
XVII. THE FRENCH AND THE NEW HEBRIDES	222

CHAP.				PAGE
XVIII. BIOGRAPHICAL SKETCHES—REV. JAMES M'NAIR				. 234
XIX.	.,	,,	REV. DR. GEDDIE .	. . 247
XX.	,,	,,	MRS. INGLIS .	. . 261
XXI.	.,	,,	SIR GEORGE GREY	. 295
XXII.	.,	,,	ADMIRAL ERSKINE	. . 301
XXIII.	.,	,,	BISHOP SELWYN .	. 309
XXIV. ANEITYUM IN 1876			. .	. 319
XXV. CONCLUSION .			.	. 344

MISSIONARY LIFE AND WORK.

CHAPTER I.

THE SOUTH SEA ISLANDS.

THE South Seas, or the Pacific Ocean, is the largest expanse of water on the face of the globe. Speaking in round numbers, it is 7000 miles square, or nearly fifty million square miles. It is studded with something like a thousand sunny isles, every one of them fair as Eden, and fertile as the garden of the Lord. If Homer had possessed our geographical knowledge, he would have made the 3000 Oceanides, the daughters of Oceanus and Tethys, not to be the goddesses of the rivers, but to be the goddesses of those beautiful, palm-crowned, paradise-like islands that stud the Pacific, and bask on its sunny bosom. But Oceanica, or the Island world, as it has been called, is perhaps the most imperfectly known of any portion of the earth's surface. It is invariably laid down in all our maps in such a narrow compass—on such small proportions—that the islands, and groups of islands, appear as indistinct as the star dust, or the nebulæ, in the Milky Way; so that nobody, to whom the subject has not been a special study, has any distinct conception of either the separate islands, or of the groups to which they respectively belong.

The name of the *South Seas* was given to this ocean by Balboa, the man who was the first to discover it; and it was discovered and named in this way. In 1513, the year in which the battle of Flodden was fought, when Vasco Nugnez de Balboa was governor of Santa Maria, in the isthmus of Darien, on one occasion while he was travelling inland exploring the country, his native guides informed him that the sea could be seen on the other side from the top of the mountain before him. Animated by a glowing hope, he proceeded alone to the summit, and there, to his surprise and delight, he saw the great expanse of ocean stretching away as far as he could see to the *south;* for from the bay of Panama to Mexico the coast-line is nearly west. He immediately fell on his knees and thanked God for this great discovery. Columbus, and nearly all those first great discoverers, were men of simple earnest piety; if not enlightened, they were devout, and recognised the hand of God as guiding them. Balboa no doubt felt at that moment, as Franklin felt when he discovered that the electric spark and the lightning were the same, that he had secured an earthly immortality. He hastened with all speed to the shore, and with sword and buckler in his hands, he plunged up to his middle in the waves, and took possession of the whole ocean in the name of his sovereign, Ferdinand, king of Spain, and from the direction in which the ocean lay from where he stood, not from its relative situation on the globe, he named it the SOUTH SEA.

How little did Balboa think, when he performed that symbolic act in the name of his master, that the ocean he had just discovered was of such enormous dimensions — was covered with such a multitude of islands—was to lie so long unexplored—was to be of so little benefit to his country; but was by-and-by to be the scene on which such triumphs of the Gospel were to be achieved—was to become one of the great highways for the commerce of the world—was, in these latter days, to create such an earth hunger among the colonising nations of Europe, and was to engender such a fever among them for the annexation of its islands!

It received the name of the *Pacific Ocean* in this way. In 1519, six years after Balboa's discovery, the year in which Charles V. was made Emperor of Germany, Ferdinand Magellan, a famous Portuguese navigator in the service of Spain, was despatched, in a vessel named the *Victory*, to discover the exact position of the Molluccas. He sailed along the east coast of South America till he discovered the two clouds—the two patches of nebulæ—that bear his name, and also the straits that are called after him, and through which he passed. He then sailed westward for 7000 miles, at first before the south-east and then before the north-east trade wind, till he reached first the Ladrone, and subsequently the Philippine Islands, where, after all this brilliant discovery, he was killed in a quarrel with the natives in 1521, just as Cook, after his world-renowned voyages, fell a victim to a native quarrel at Hawaii, in 1779. As the sea was remarkably smooth during this long voyage, Magellan naturally inferred that it must be always so, and called it the PACIFIC OCEAN; although at times it is swept over by tremendous hurricanes and is occasionally the reverse of pacific, which has led superficial critics and tyroes in seafaring knowledge to show off their feeble wit by speaking of it as the so-called Pacific, or the ocean that is non-pacific; but these cases of storm are simply like the exceptions that strengthen the rule. The late Admiral Fitzroy, who was well acquainted with this ocean, and one of the very highest authorities on such a subject, while urging the claims of the Panama route from London to Australia, gave as one of his principal reasons the extent of smooth sailing enjoyed on this ocean. There is so much of this ocean being within intertropical and subtropical regions, where the sea, as a general rule, is so much smoother than in higher latitudes, whether north or south, that Magellan, with the intuitive sagacity of a great man, rightly named it the PACIFIC OCEAN.

Exclusive of Australia and New Zealand, geographers have arranged the South Sea Islands under these three divisions, viz., *Polynesia, Melanesia,* and *Micronesia.* Polynesia, or the *Many Islands* (from πολυς, *polys,* many, and νῆσος, *nesos,* an island), was the name given at first, in a general way, to the whole of these islands; then they were divided into Eastern and Western Polynesia; but now Polynesia is restricted to the eastward islands, situated between long. 180 deg., the last meridian, and South America. Melanesia, or the *Black Islands* (from μελας, *melas,* black, and νῆσος, *nesos,* an island), so called from the colour of the inhabitants, comprises all the islands south of the line from long. 180 deg. and west to New Guinea, including the Fiji group, the New Hebrides, New Caledonia, the Loyalty Islands, the Solomon group, New Britain, New Ireland, the Louisiade Archipelago, and other islands. Micronesia, or the *Little Islands* (from μικρός, *mikros,* little, and νῆσος, *nesos,* an island), so called from the islands being little, comprises all the islands north of the line, from Hawaii on the east to China on the west, and includes the Kingsmill group, the Scarborough Range, the Radick and the Ralick chains, and a multitude of other islands.

The South Sea Islands are inhabited by two, and only two, races, viz., the Malay Polynesian and the Papuan, two races perfectly distinct, both in personal appearance and in language. The Malay are the descendants of Shem, or at least they are of Asiatic origin; the Papuans are the descendants of Ham, or at least they are of African origin. The Malays are by far the finest in personal appearance; they are tall and well-formed, their skin a light yellow, their hair a smooth glossy black. Their language is soft and mellifluous, rivalling, if not surpassing, the Italian itself. It is a peculiar but universal rule in all the dialects of this language, that not only every word, but every syllable, ends with a vowel; while of the consonants, it is the semi-vowels l m n r s, and the slender consonants k p t, that are most commonly used. There are no gutturals, and ng is the only double consonant; while even that, in some of the dialects, is softened into n—*tangata*, man, becomes *tanata* or *kanaka*. If on a map of the South Sea Islands a point is fixed upon at Easter Island, another at the north-west extremity of the Sandwich Islands, and a third at the south-west extremity of New Zealand, and if lines are drawn from these three points so as to form a triangle on the map, this triangle will include nearly the whole of the Malay Polynesian race. While the language spoken by all these Malays is one, the natives of nearly every group speak a different dialect of this one language. There are at least seven distinctly marked dialects of the Malay languages, viz., the Hawaiian, the Marquesan, the Tahitian, the Rarotongan, the Samoan, the Tongan, and the Maori or New Zealand. The Samoan is by far the softest and smoothest, the Maori is the strongest and roughest. The one is the Ionic of Polynesia, the other is the Doric. Climate, it is said, by affecting the muscles of the mouth, has a strongly modifying influence upon language. Certain it is that Samoa and the Marquesas, where the softest dialects are spoken, are the warmest localities; whereas New Zealand, where the strongest dialect is spoken, is the coldest. But the softness and liquid smoothness of their language brings one great disadvantage to the Polynesians, it renders them nearly incapable of pronouncing English.

Melanesia, or, as it is sometimes still called, Western Polynesia, is inhabited by the other distinct race, the Papuan, who take their name from the island of Papua or New Guinea, the largest island in Oceanica. They are also called Melanesians, from their dark colour, and Negritoes or Negrilloes, from their negro-like appearance. They have crisp hair of different shades, but never glossy black like the Malays. Their skin is dark, a kind of coffee-and-milk colour, and their features generally plain. Their whole appearance is unmistakably African, but without the prognathous, protruding jaws of the genuine negro. Their language is quite distinct from that of the Malay Polynesian; it belongs to an entirely different family of languages, and it is endlessly diversified. Not only on every group, but on every island, a different dialect is spoken; and so widely different are they as to be almost, sometimes altogether, unintelligible to the inhabitants of an adjoining island. It will be difficult to say, till the languages are more fully examined and compared than they have yet been, how far they are connected by a common paternity. On the south of the New Hebrides the dialects have evidently sprung from a common language. There are strong resemblances in grammatical structure, but the diversity in the vocables is very great. One would almost think that the whole race had come direct from Babel at the confusion of tongues, and that the inhabitants of one island had scarcely ever spoken one word to those of another, from that day to this.

CHAPTER II.

THE NEW HEBRIDES.

BEFORE proceeding to describe the New Hebrides, I may insert a short paragraph or two, to connect the early discoveries in the South Seas with the discovery of the New Hebrides. After Magellan the next great name that appears in this ocean is Mendana. Alvaro Mendana de Meyra, the nephew of the Viceroy of Peru, sailed on a voyage of discovery from Lima, in South America. He discovered the Solomon Islands in 1567, the year in which the Reformed Kirk of Scotland was established and endowed by the State. He called them the Solomon Islands, from a belief that they had supplied the gold and treasure employed in the building of the Temple. The minds of the early discoverers seem to have been constantly inflamed by the description of the wealth of Solomon. The land of Ophir was the object of continual research. Columbus, among his other dreams, believed that he had discovered this source of Jewish splendour in Hispaniola and Veragua. The Solomon group extends about 600 miles, lying N.W.W. and S.E.E., between 11 deg. and 5 deg. S. lat. and 163 deg. and 154 deg. E. long. Although this group was discovered more than three centuries ago, it was, till recently, one of the least-known groups in the world. It is not much more than a century since the very existence

NEW HEBRIDES &c.

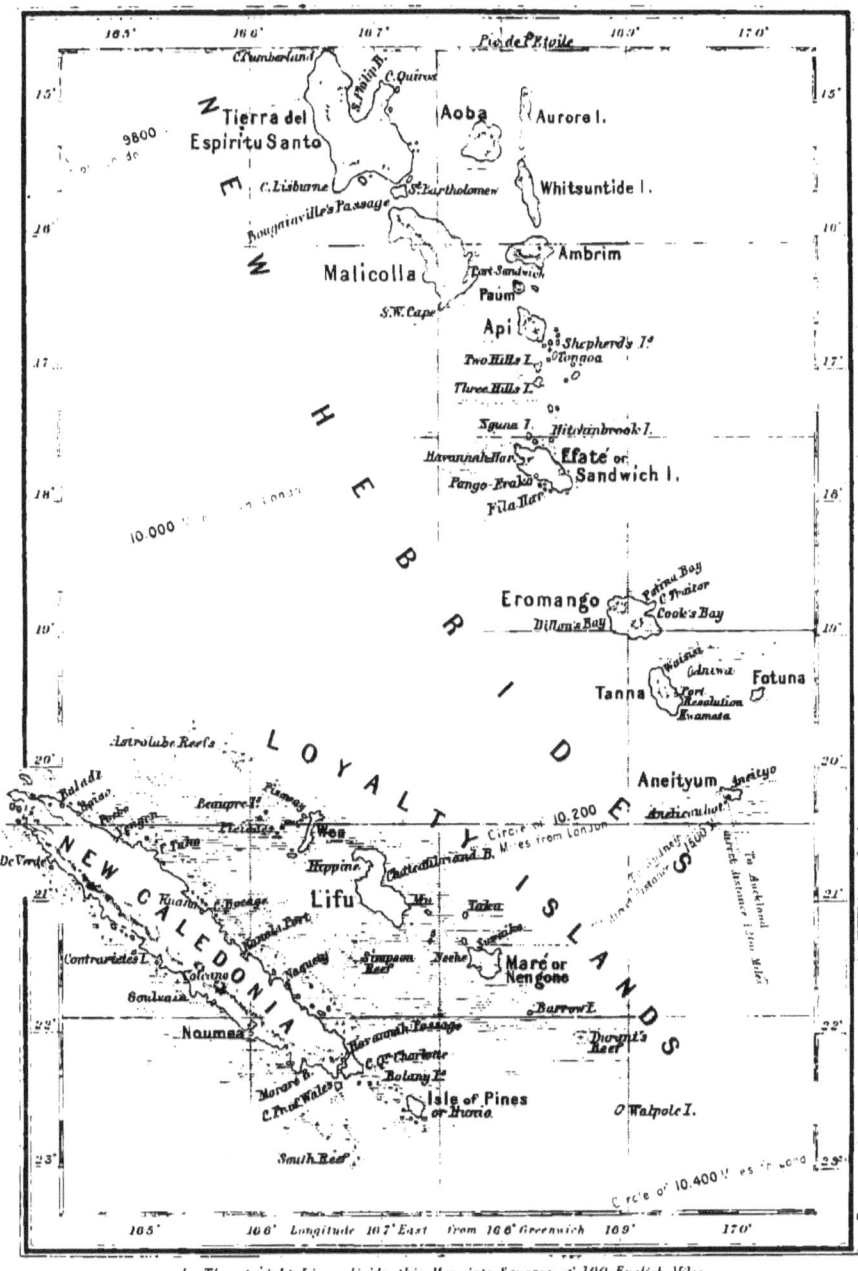

1 The straight Lines divide this Map into Squares of 100 English Miles.
2 The ordinary Degrees of Latitude and Longitude are given in the margin.

of this group was doubted. So little was then known of those seas, that one of the best hydrographers of that period, Dalrymple, removed them on his chart ten or twelve degrees to the west of their true position, under the belief that the Solomon Islands of Mendana were the same as New Britain. It was not till, by the elaborate disquisitions of the French, comparing and combining the early and later discoveries, that it was found that Mendana, Bougainville, Surville, Carteret, Shortland, and others, had all discovered the same group. The imperfect means in use for finding the longitude left the discoveries of the early navigators in much uncertainty. But with Australia, New Zealand, Fiji, New Caledonia, and other islands all rising to such importance, and lying in such near proximity, there is no fear of the Solomon group remaining much longer a *terra incognita*.

After the Solomon group, the next discovered was what are now called Queen *Charlotte's Islands*. Mendana was anxious to revisit the Solomon Islands, and found a colony there, but it was not till twenty-eight years afterwards, not till 1595, that he was able to make the attempt. He was accompanied by Pedro Vernandez de Quiros, a native of Portugal, and "an officer of known worth." They failed to find the Solomon group. They knew the latitude, but ship chronometers were then unknown, and their longitude was wrong. They kept too far to the east, and they came upon the Queen Charlotte's Islands, which they called Marquesas, but which must not be confounded with the modern Marquesas, which lie to the north-east of Tahiti. Queen Charlotte's group is small, and lies about 10 deg. S. lat. and 168 deg. E. long. It lies a little to the north of the New Hebrides. It was, as I have said, discovered by Mendana in 1595. He formed a settlement at Santa Cruz, and died there the same year. After his death the settlement was broken up. It was on Santa Cruz where the deeply lamented Commodore Goodenough was killed by the natives in 1876. This group was lost sight of for nearly two centuries, till it was rediscovered by Captain Carteret in 1767, and named after the reigning Queen. It was proposed by French writers to withdraw the name of Queen Charlotte, and to call it the Archipelago of La Perouse, in honour of that distinguished French navigator, who perished in one of them, called Vanikolo, in 1788. But this has not been done. The episode of La Perouse is the most thrilling event connected with the history of this group ; and all that is known of it has been told by Chevalier Dillon, an enterprising colonial captain, well known in Australia more than fifty years ago, who published, in two volumes, an account of his voyages to Fiji, the New Hebrides, &c., and after whom Dillon's Bay, in Eromanga, was named. La Perouse was sailing on a voyage of discovery ; the last place at which he was seen or heard of was at Botany Bay, in New South Wales. The account given to Captain Dillon by the natives of Vanikolo, in 1826, was, that one morning after a fearful hurricane, when they went out, they saw two vessels wrecked on the reef that surrounds the island : one of them sank outside the reef ; the other was driven over the reef into smooth water: a great number of the men on board were drowned, and their bodies devoured by the sharks ; others were killed by the natives, but a portion survived, who erected a stockade by the side of a stream, and out of the wreck of the large vessel they built a small one with two masts, in which they all sailed away but two. As this vessel was never heard of it must have been lost. The natives had never seen a ship or a white man before. They supposed them to be water or ocean spirits. They said, "A man stood at the gate of the stockade with an iron rod in his hand" (the sentry with his musket). "The men had long noses out from their heads" (alluding to their cocked hats). "They ate only little bits of food" (probably biscuits). "The chiefs kept looking through something at the sun and the stars. Of the two men who remained on the island, the one was a chief, the other a common man; the chief had died three years before Captain Dillon's visit; the other had fled away to another island with the native chief under whom he lived." Captain Dillon obtained a great number of articles belonging to the two vessels, so as to furnish abundant proof that La Perouse's vessels were lost there. He conveyed them to France, received the rewards offered by the French Government, and was honoured with the title of *Chevalier* by the French King. The group next discovered was the *New Hebrides*.

The New Hebrides were first discovered in 1606, the year after the Gunpowder Plot. Dynamite was then unknown, or the plot might not have been discovered. Torres Straits, between Australia and New Guinea, were discovered the same year by Quiros's second in command, Louis Varz de Torres, after whom they were named. Quiros had been major pilot to Mendana in his last voyage. He supposed the New Hebrides to be part of the great southern continent, the idea that filled the imaginations of all the early adventurers, and hence he called it *Tierra del Espiritu Santo*. He anchored in the large bay of St. Filip, in the north-east corner of the northernmost island, now generally called *Santo*. Here a large river runs into the sea, which he called the *Jordan*. He founded a town on its banks, which he called *Le Nuova Jerusalem*,

the New Jerusalem. The port he named *Vera Cruz*, the True
Cross. The Spaniards quarrelled with the natives, and soon
abandoned the settlement. Quiros returned to Mexico, but
Torres sailed west, and passed through the Straits that he
discovered, and which are rendered memorable by Commodore
Erskine's proclaiming there the British protectorate over
the south-east of New Guinea. Nothing more was known
of the New Hebrides till 1768, when Cook sailed on his first
voyage to the South Seas to observe the transit of Venus at
Tahiti; and, two years after, Wallis and Carteret had proceeded on a voyage of discovery in the same ocean : a period
brilliant with eminent men in pursuit of new regions.
This year Bougainville ascertained that the land discovered
by Quiros was not a continent, but a group of islands. He
sailed through the passage that bears his name, between
Mallicolla and Santo, landed upon what he misnamed *Lepers'*
Island (he had mistaken some skin disease for leprosy—
there is no leprosy on the New Hebrides), the correct name
of which is Aoba, and called the group by the name of the
Great Cyclades. In 1773 Captain Cook explored the entire
group, and thought he had done enough to entitle him to
name them anew himself, and called them *The New Hebrides*,
supposing them to be the most western islands in the Pacific.
In a subsequent voyage, however, he discovered another large
island, nearly 200 miles farther west, which he named *New
Caledonia*, and took possession of it formally in the name of
his sovereign, King George the Third ; but which was taken
possession of surreptitiously in 1854 by the French during
the Crimean war, when our Government could not afford to
have a quarrel with the French about such a paltry possession. Some writers, jealous for the honour of Quiros, have

strongly urged that the original name should be restored to this group. For the sake of distinctness and simplicity, the plain, common-sense plan of retaining or restoring the native names of places, wherever these can be ascertained, is now generally acted on. But as the natives have no name for the entire group, some foreign name must be adopted. The name given to them by Quiros, however, is objectionable. Sounding in grave sonorous Spanish, in Roman Catholic ears, there might appear nothing improper in *Tierra Australis del Espiritu Santo*. But translated into English, where sacred names are so carefully excluded from common objects, what would sound more harsh and profane in Protestant ears than the *Archipelago of the Holy Ghost!* Whatever opinion may be formed of Cook's procedure in rejecting the *Great Cyclades* and employing the *New Hebrides*, the latter name is now so firmly established, that it is certain to be retained permanently and employed universally.

The New Hebrides group extends to about 400 miles in length, lying N.N.W. and S.S.E., between 21 deg. and 15 deg. S. lat. and 171 deg. and 166 deg. E. long. They lie about 1000 miles nearly due north of New Zealand, about 400 miles west of Fiji, about 200 miles east of New Caledonia, and about 1400 miles north-east of Sydney. There are about thirty islands in the group; nearly twenty of them are inhabited, and the third of them are of considerable extent. It is their proximity to New Caledonia that is the only plausible argument advanced by the French to justify their desire for annexing the group. The French have no claim whatever upon the New Hebrides. The claim of the British is beyond dispute. Everything that has been done for the group, and for the natives of those islands, has been done by the British. Cook, as we have seen, partly discovered the islands; he fully explored them, surveyed the whole group, and laid the islands down in maps, with an accuracy that has never been surpassed. For about forty years they have been visited almost annually by a British man-of-war, to maintain law and order, and secure life and property. Nearly all that has been done to develop trade on the islands has been effected by British capital, skill, and industry. All that has been done to introduce Christianity, promote education, and advance civilisation has been done by British missions and British subjects. It was the British missionaries who were the first, and all along have been the most active and earnest, to oppose and repress kidnapping and slavery on the group. Our Presbyterian mission has expended £160,000 in their efforts to Christianise the natives: and we are not only maintaining, but we are extending and increasing our agencies to promote the highest interests of the natives. But what have the French done to promote any of these objects? They have done literally nothing. And judging from what they have done in the islands nearest to us, viz., the Loyalty Islands, they would suppress our mission as fast as they possibly could. Moreover, all the natives are eager to be under British protection. But they all dread any connection with the French. It is true there was a French mission for some years on Aneityum, but what were the results? They were equal to the means employed, but no more. The missionaries printed no books, opened no schools, and erected no churches. They held one short service in their own house on the Sabbath, and gave to the natives small brass medals with the image of the Virgin Mary on one side, and assured them that if they wore these medals she would protect them from all evil. After the priests left the island, a young lad who had lived with them went and lived with Mr. Geddie, and continued faithfully to wear the medal; but he attended church and school on the mission station. Mr. Geddie took no notice of the medal; but by-and-by it disappeared, the lad had ceased to wear it; and Mr. Geddie said to him one day, "Mataio, what has become of the medal of the Virgin Mary that you got from the priests?" "Oh," said he, "you remember that the other Sabbath day you read to us out of the book how Joseph and Mary lost little Jesus about Jerusalem, and they had to seek Him for three days before they could find Him; so I thought, if Mary knew so little about her own son, it was not likely she could know much about me. So I threw the medal away!" And so ended Mariolatry and the Popish mission on Aneityum. I have heard *Ave Maria* pronounced on New Caledonia, but never on Aneityum.

The New Hebrides may be looked upon as a continuation of New Zealand. The geological character of both is the same. The islands are volcanic, resting upon a basis of coral. The lava in its melted state has often run over above the coral. The islands constitute something like a range of mountains, covered largely with forests and deep valleys with steep water-formed ridges; and with blank spaces, of course, where the ocean rolls between. The west side of Santo, the largest and most northerly of the group, is extremely beautiful and picturesque. The island rises up out of the sea like a long, huge mountain. The ridges and valleys rise up one above another from the shore to the summit; and if presented in a picture, they would resemble the frontispiece of a geography, where the relative heights of the mountains on the globe are represented in a plate. I have not visited the north end, nor the east side, of Santo, but I understand they are beautiful. A few years ago the *Dayspring* sailed round the island, and anchored at the head of the great bay of St. Filip, where Quiros and Torres anchored their two vessels. One of our missionaries, the Rev. Mr. Neilson, was on board. He was much pleased with all that he saw, and supplied a very interesting account of the voyage. The natives were peaceable and kind, and gave them a good reception. Mr. Neilson strongly recommended that a mission station should be formed, and two missionaries should be settled, at the head of St. Jago Bay, at the port of the True Cross, on the banks of the modern Jordan, and on the very site of the New Jerusalem as laid down by Quiros; that so a reality might be effected, far nobler than the ideal contemplated by the courageous and devout, but ignorant and superstitious, adventurer of 1606. Want of men, rather than want of means, prevented the Mission Synod from carrying out this proposal. But we are creeping northward, and occupying one island after another as fast as we are able; and we trust that the day is not far distant when that suggestion will be an accomplished fact, and when it shall be said, "Behold Philistia, and Tyre, with *Ethiopia;* . . . the Lord shall count, when He writeth up the people, that this man was born there."

The New Hebrides, like New Zealand, have a moist, humid climate; they rarely ever suffer from drought. The islands are well supplied with streams of excellent water; there is generally a sufficiency of rain, and very seldom too much. As in New Zealand, the clouds are high, and the atmosphere is clear. Anything like a London fog is quite unknown. The climate is delightful, the range of the thermometer all the year round is only about 30 deg.; from 60 deg. up to 90 deg. The sea-breeze modifies the heat. The prevailing winds are from south to east. The public health is always best in summer during the warmest weather, while sickness prevails most in winter when the weather is coldest.

The volcanoes constitute the next point of resemblance. There are three volcanoes in the New Hebrides, one on Tanna, another on Ambrym, and a third on Polevi; all three are active. The volcano on Tanna is as active and conspicuous to-day as it was a century and more ago, when seen by Cook and the Forsters. Heavy earthquakes are felt in both groups. Both regions are to a large extent covered with forests, although necessarily different, the one being in the temperate and the other in the torrid zone. But the far-famed *damara*, or kauri pine, so plentiful and so prized in the north of New Zealand, is also found in the New Hebrides, though of a different species. In the forests of both there is the same dense undergrowth and the same profusion and variety of ferns: on Aneityum there are about a hundred species. In the shores of both groups fish are plentiful, but for the most part they are coarse and hard as compared with the fish in our northern seas. There are, of course, exceptions, for some are soft, tender, and delicious. Fifty years ago the coasts of New Zealand were among the best whaling grounds in the southern hemisphere, till the whales were either nearly killed out or frightened away from the shore. In the New Hebrides whales appear in large numbers during the calving season; and for the last thirty years there has been one, often two, whaling stations on Aneityum, and occasionally one on Eromanga. From £2000 to £3000 worth of whale oil has been obtained on Aneityum in one season. In both New Zealand and the New Hebrides the only indigenous quadruped is a small rat. In the New Hebrides there are four species of small lizards, but all of them are harmless; there are snakes of two feet long or more on the shore, and serpents of three feet long or so in the interior, neither of which are poisonous.

The New Hebrides are a valuable group of islands. Every tropical production can be cultivated there to perfection. If carefully protected and developed they may become to Australia and New Zealand what the West Indies have been to the mother-country. But if the so-called labour traffic is allowed to continue, or still worse, if they are allowed to become a French penal settlement, as the French Government has been straining every nerve to accomplish, then Ichabod may be written over every island, and the hopes of the missionaries and the philanthropists will be extinguished. Let the friends of those poor natives watch and pray; watch against the selfishness of man, and pray to the merciful and righteous God to defend these poor helpless aborigines.

The population of the New Hebrides has been estimated as low as 70,000, and as high as 150,000. The islands are not populous, and from various causes the population is rapidly diminishing; and nothing can neutralise these causes, and save the natives from extinction, except Christianity. It is the true Conservatism. The Wesleyans say that they are the friends of all, and the enemies of none, and certainly so is Christianity, and so is our Mission.

CHAPTER III.

ANEITYUM.

THE correct spelling of this word is A-neit'-yum, pronounced in three syllables, with the accent on the second syllable. But the word has struggled hard to secure the proper pronunciation, and still more to establish the correct spelling. In this group almost every island has two or three names; one given by the natives belonging to the island, and another or others by the natives of other islands respectively, and by foreigners. Captain Cook was the first to reduce the name to writing and publish it in print, and he wrote it Anattom. This is the way it is pronounced by the Tannese. Cook was never nearer Aneityum than Tanna, and he accepted the name which he heard there. The people of Futuna call it E-ki-á-mo, and here again the traders have corrupted it into Gama; and, not satisfied with this, they have Scotticised it into Campbell. On one occasion, in the first year of the Mission, the captain of a small schooner called on me, and was shown into my study. He told me that his object in calling at the island was to bring home half a dozen Campbell boys, who had been working for a white man on the Isle of Pines.

While this conversation was going on my wife came into the room.

When the trader had gone away, she said, " But who

are these Campbell boys that the man is speaking so much about?"

"Don't you know these?" I said; "they are your own Aneityumese."

The early traders gave another variation to Aneityum, and called it Anatam, with the accent on the last syllable, as if it had been an Indian word. This was the recognised form of the word in Sydney. When we first went to the Mission, one of our correspondents in Sydney addressed our letters to Aneityum (Anatam), the latter word being added to prevent mistake. Bishop Selwyn wrote it, for native purposes at least, Anaijom. The missionaries all pronounced it correctly, but the Samoan brethren fixed the spelling of it to be Aneiteum, which was caused in this way. In the Samoan alphabet as fixed by the missionaries there is neither *w* nor *y*, as these letters are not needed in the Samoan language. Mr. Geddie and I, however, introduced them into our alphabet when we finally fixed the number of letters for the Aneityumese. The Samoan missionaries spelled the word with Samoan letters only, but retaining the correct pronunciation. Mr. Geddie and I followed their example till 1860, when I came home to carry the New Testament through the press, and found almost every person mispronouncing the name of our island. Most of them called it A-nei-té-um, pronouncing it in four syllables, with the accent on the third. I took upon myself to change the *e* into *y*, so as to prevent this mispronunciation. The Rev. Mr. Copeland, who had charge of my station at the time, an exact scholar and an excellent orthoepist, wrote me suggesting the same change. His letter and mine on this subject must have crossed each other in mid-ocean. This spelling is now generally accepted.

The natives of Aneityum, following the genius of their own language, call Tanna *Anma*, and Futuna *Anhas ;* or more fully, *Inpekeranma*, the Land of Bread-fruit; and *Inpekeranhas*, the Bad Land, that is, the land where food is scarce; their own land, as I have said, being *Inpekeraneityum*. It was discovered, however, that *Ipari* was the proper name of Tanna. Tanna means land; the natives call it *Tanna asora*, the great land, as we speak of the continent or the mainland. But when Captain Cook, pointing to the ground, made signs as to what they called the island, the natives always said *tanna*, meaning *land* or *earth*, whereas he understood them to mean the name of the island, at least so we infer from similar experiences. Two of our young missionaries having discovered this, thought, in their youthful zeal, that they would put down the usurper, and reinstal the lawful owner; call the island Ipari, and discard Tanna. But, alas! the prescriptive right of a century held good against all comers. Max Müller tells us, in his "Lectures on Language," that on one occasion, when the Emperor Sigismund was delivering a speech, he mispronounced a Latin word. An old grammarian took the liberty of reminding him of the correct pronunciation. But the Emperor, conscious of his despotic power, spoke to the effect that the Imperial pronunciation must henceforth be accepted. But, alas! against the long-accepted pronunciation of the word the will of Cæsar was powerless. Our young friends, certain that they were right, and believing in the long-accepted axiom, "Great is the truth, and it will prevail," published their supposed discovery —although it had been known twenty years before to some of the older missionaries, who, however, were willing to let well alone—discarded Tanna, and dated all their letters from

Ipari, and concluded that the change was completed. But what is more obstinate than use and wont? So far as I am aware, Ipari has never been seen in print, except in connection with the published letters of these two brethren. By the way, some people spell this word Tana. This spelling would be correct if it were a Malay word, where every syllable ends in a vowel. But in this case it is incorrect. It is a Papuan word, and as you hear it pronounced, the first syllable ends in a consonant; it is not pronounced Ta-na, but Tan-na.

Aneityum is the most southern island of the New Hebrides. The harbour at Anelgauhat, on the south-west side of the island, is in lat. 20 deg. 14 min. S. and long 169 deg. 49 min. E.; the variation of the compass is 10 deg. 30. min. E. It is a small and, for a tropical, rather a poor island, about 35 miles in circumference. It consists of a congeries of mountains, the highest of which is nearly 3000 feet. These are intersected by three or four large valleys and a number of small ones. When we went to Aneityum in 1852, in the *Border Maid*, with Bishop Selwyn, the night before we reached the island, immediately after sunset, he called our attention to the first glimpse of land. About 50 miles west of our calculated position, on the extreme edge of the far-distant horizon, there rose up in clear and distinct outline, like two little knolls, the two round summits of *Inrero*, or *Saddle Back*, as it was afterwards called by the officers of H.M.S. *Herald*, who surveyed the island. The hills are steep, and the valleys for the most part deep and narrow. A small strip of alluvial land along the shore, where the shore is protected by a reef, with the lower part of the larger valleys, include the most of the cultivated land of the island,

and contain the principal part of the population. The lower and middle parts of the mountains next the sea are mostly formed of red ferruginous clay, and are scantily covered with herbage and brushwood. On the upper parts, the soil, though stony, consists of a rich black mould, and dense forests cover the summits of the mountains. The island, as might be expected, is well watered, and the ingenuity of the natives is seen in nothing perhaps so much as in the system of irrigation by which they water their plantation of taro and sugarcane. There are swamps in different parts of the island, which are extremely valuable as taro grounds, but, from being imperfectly drained, are also productive of ague and fever.

The principal fruit trees on the island are the cocoa-nut, the bread-fruit, the horse chestnut, and a few others of less value. Taro is cultivated largely, and may be considered as the bread of the land. Sugar-cane and bananas are equally plentiful. Yams are produced only to a very limited extent, whereas on Tanna they are a staple article of food. The sweet potato grows well, and so does arrow-root. Pine-apples, custard apples, the cape gooseberry, &c., have been introduced and grow well. Oranges, lemons, limes, and all that family grow exceedingly well. But the common fruits and culinary vegetables of this country come to no perfection there. Pigs and fowls are the only live stock that the natives possess, and these are not numerous. The cows and goats at the two Mission stations throve well, but sheep did not increase, and we ceased to keep them. Around the island, but especially at the principal harbour, fishing is one of the regular and almost daily pursuits of the natives. The fish, however, are not very plentiful, and are for the most part of an inferior quality. A good many turtles are caught from time to time. The island of Aneityum is one on which, by a moderate industry, an abundance of food may always be raised, but where the spontaneous productions of the earth and the ocean are much less abundant than they appear to be on some other islands, and on some other groups.

The island is divided politically into six principal districts, three on the south side, and three on the north. Aname, our station, is on the north, but the districts are of very unequal sizes : each of these again is divided into several sub-districts. In the days of heathenism there was a principal chief for each principal district, and an under chief for each sub-district. It is much the same still, only formerly the principal chiefs exercised the priestly rather than the kingly power, though both offices were frequently combined in the same person. The priestly office has now ceased. The power of the chiefs on Aneityum was very limited. Every man did very much that which was right in his own eyes. The men who were most distinguished as warriors or famed as disease makers, being most dreaded, possessed the greatest power. Under the reign of heathenism, both in civil and religious matters, fear and not love was the grand ruling principle by which obedience was secured.

There is neither a town nor a village in the whole island. The system of cottage farming is in a state of full development there. There is no large proprietor, no powerful or wealthy chief; every man sits proprietor of his own cottage, his own garden, and his own cultivated patches—you could not call them fields. The waste lands and the forests, to the summits of the mountains, belong to the tribe. They are a kind of crown lands, but what each man cultivates belongs to

ANEITYUM.

himself. But this system, so warmly advocated by many in this country, is not good as an exclusive system. There they have no capitalists and no division of labour : every man cultivates his own garden, builds his own cottage, hews out his own canoe : every man does everything, and hence he does nothing either quickly or well. The Mission stations, however, became the germs of villages, and the arts of civilised life have largely sprung up around them. In mechanical skill the natives of Aneityum and of the New Hebrides generally are greatly inferior to the Malays of Polynesia. Being evidently a much earlier migration than the Malays, they had brought less civilisation with them, and being longer dissociated from the civilised world, they had lost more of what they originally brought. Their houses, canoes, ornaments, and weapons of war showed the least possible skill in their form and workmanship. But they are quite an improvable race, and are eager to imitate their superiors. In their movements they are active and energetic; they work well at any kind of unskilled labour, and at what may be called native skilled labour, and when trained they evince a fair aptitude for acquiring a knowledge of European skilled labour. The women make excellent nurses and good domestic servants.

It was currently and extensively believed that the climate of the New Hebrides was extremely unhealthy. From what I saw and heard, when I first became acquainted with the group, I fully concurred in that view at the time. There were apparently good grounds for that opinion. I am now, however, fully certain that this is not the case. It would be foolishness in the extreme in that group to tamper with the laws of health. And no command in the decalogue requires to be more carefully obeyed than the sixth, which " requires all lawful endeavours to preserve our own life and the life of others." In regard to this commandment, on those islands retribution follows on the heels of disobedience both with swiftness and certainty. Still, as there are no examples of caprice, and as, by the dear-bought experience of the first missionaries and others, the causes and character of the diseases most prevalent on those islands are known, there is much less to be apprehended on the ground of sickness than was at one time believed.

For a number of years I kept a Meteorological Register of the winds, weather, and temperature; I insert that for 1853, which may be accepted as a fair average, and will convey the most distinct idea that I can furnish of the climate.

It will be seen from this table that the mean temperature in the shade, at my station, during that year was 76 deg. (in Samoa it is about 78 deg.); the highest was 89 deg. and the lowest 58 deg. The number of fine days was 251; and indeed the most of the eighty-seven showery days might be set down as fine, though not as fair days. On the wet days, however, the rain often descends in torrents. Thunderstorms are not frequent—not oftener than two or three times in the year, but they are occasionally violent, and sometimes bordering on the terrific. The nights are often clear and beautiful, and every part of the firmament is bespangled with stars. At one season or another every constellation in the heavens is visible, from the Southern Cross to the Great Northern Bear. I was quite delighted the first night that I saw the *Plough*. The Ursa Major is not visible in New Zealand, and hence I had not seen it for six years. But on Aneityum, when it is at its highest southern altitude here, it is seen in the north, a

METEOROLOGICAL REGISTER FOR 1853.—ANEITYUM, NEW HEBRIDES.

LAT. 20 DEG. 8 MIN. S., LONG. 169 DEG. 49 MIN. E.

Months	Average height in shade			Fahr. Thermometer						Winds							Weather		
	6 A.M.	2 P.M.	8 P.M.	Maximum height	Minimum height	Mean height	Maximum range	Minimum range	Mean range	S.E. Trades days	S. days	S.W. days	W. days	N.W. days	N.E. days	Variable days	Fine days	Showery days	Rainy days
January	77	84	79	88	72	80	13	0	7	19		2		3	5	2	13	16	2
February	78	85	79	89	72	81	14	1	8	18				2	6	2	20	4	4
March	75	84	78	89	68	79	18	2	9	18	1	4		3	3	3	24	5	2
April	74	81	76	84	64	77	18	3	7	24		2		2	2		19	7	4
May	74	77	75	85	66	77	13	1	6	25		1		2	2	1	17	13	1
June	69	75	71	82	62	72	15	1	8	15	6	5		3		1	25	2	3
July	68	75	70	83	58	71	15	2	8	11	8	5		3	1	1	25	4	2
August	68	77	70	80	62	71	11	3	7	11			2	6	1	1	21	9	1
September	70	78	70	82	60	72	17	3	10	10	11	2		8		1	26	2	2
October	73	82	72	84	60	73	10	2	9	20	8		1		1	1	22	8	1
November	75	84	75	86	72	77	11	4	9	21	7			5		4	19	9	2
December			77	88	70	70	12	1	8	24				2	3	1	20	8	3
Whole year	72	80	74	85	65	76	14	2	8	216	42	22	3	41	24	18	251	87	27

27

few degrees above the horizon, and night after night it keeps hovering, like a guardian angel, over the island of Tanna. While approaching Port Resolution I have seen it stretching across the mouth of the harbour, like the ancient Colossus at Rhodes. From the great breadth of ocean around and the general prevalence of the trade winds, the atmosphere is kept cool and pleasant; and during a great part of the year the salubrity of the island is secure.

CHAPTER IV.

THE ANEITYUMESE IN HEATHENISM.

THE Aneityumese, as well as the natives of the New Hebrides generally, are all, as near as may be, unmixed Papuans. They are of a distinctively African type, doubtless descendants of Ham. Their traditions are very vague, and of little or no historical value. Their mythology is equally vague and indistinct. So far as we could sift out from the most intelligent natives, their ideas about the unseen world were somewhat as follows:—*Inhujeraing* was the supreme deity. He was the maker of heaven and earth, and all things that they contain; he had many children and grandchildren, but nobody, say the natives, knows who their mother was. *Moitukke-tukke*, *Inbotheth*, *Naho*, and a host of others, were inferior or local deities. They appear all to have been deified men. *Natmas*, the name given to every deity, signifies literally a dead man, and they all dwelt in *Uma-atmas*, the Land of the Dead. Theirs was the Worship of their Ancestors. Prayers and offerings were presented to one when taro was planted; to another when a canoe was made; to another when war was undertaken; to another in time of sickness, &c. Like the ancient idolaters, one tribe were worshippers of one class of deities, another tribe of another class. There were no temples, but every little district had a piece of sacred ground that was never tilled, and on which all sacred rites were performed. At the Reformation in Scotland, Knox and the Reformers urged that the Church lands, when forfeited to the Crown, should be appropriated for the support of religion, education, and the poor. So there, when heathenism was given up, those Church lands, those untilled sacred grounds, were appropriated by public consent, and, so far as they went, for the support of education, and were passed over to the teachers for the time being, as gardens for the planting of taro, sugar-cane, and bananas. The popular belief was that earth, and air, and ocean were filled with *natmasses*, spiritual beings, but all malignant, who ruled over everything that affected the human race. There was a numerous and powerful priesthood, who, according to the popular belief, directed all the malignity of the unseen world, and whose exactions on the people were very oppressive. Stones were the chief *fetishes*, or representatives of the *natmasses:* these were of all sizes, from that of a pebble to blocks of some tons weight. About a mile inland from our station are two blocks each as large as the roof of a small cottage; both of them were recognized as *natmasses;* the one, the larger, was called the sun, and the other the moon. The sides of the larger rock are marked with some rude sculptured figures of fishes and birds; and as one of the best fishing grounds could be seen from these rocks, certain incantations performed on these were believed to affect the success or non-success of the fishing. Every family had a basket containing a collection of *natmasses* of their own—a sort of *penates*, or household gods, which they worshipped as a family. When they professed Christianity these were destroyed, or sometimes brought to the missionary; but in a few cases a portion of them were secretly retained, and for long afterwards, in time of severe sickness or on a deathbed, when they were pressed, as they often are by their friends, as Job of old was by his, to confess their secret sins, this secret idolatry was brought to light. Scarcely anything is so tenacious of life as superstition; witness the remains of it among the ignorant in our own land. The natives had a distinct belief in a future state, and in the efficacy of prayer and sacrifice to propitiate their offended deities. They never offered human sacrifices, although they were cannibals; and although their beliefs were in many respects exceedingly erroneous, yet they were of great use to us in helping to lead them to understand and receive the Scriptural doctrines on these vital points. But while they believed in the immortality of the soul, like the Greeks and Romans and our Pagan forefathers they had no idea of the resurrection of the body. The wife was strangled on the death of her husband, that her spirit might accompany his to the land of the dead, to be his servant there as she had been in this world. The entrance to *Uma-atmas* was in the west end of the island. Tradition said there had been a volcano at this place, but that in some period, of what we should call the prehistoric era, the *natmasses*, for some reason not known, had removed it to Tanna, and it has remained in the neighbourhood of Port Resolution from that time to this. *Uma-atmas* was divided into two regions, called the good land and the bad land, corresponding to paradise and gehenna; but their ideas of the rewards and punishments of the unseen world were extremely vague and indistinct; the sin that would be visited with the severest punishment there was stinginess or niggardliness in giving away food, and the virtue that received the highest reward was a generous hospitality and a giving liberally at feasts.

Their deities, like themselves, were all selfish and malignant; they breathed no spirit of benevolence, and the rewards and punishments of the future state were connected more with ritual observances than with moral character. Their religion contained no principle that could lead to a holy life; they certainly thought that their gods were like themselves, and that they approved of their sins. It would have been morally impossible on Aneityum for any man to have conceived of such a character, morally and religiously, as that of the man Christ Jesus. To have done so would have been a miracle as great as that of His resurrection.

I may here give a brief account of one of our *natmasses*, which may be accepted as a typical case. His name was Rangitafu; he belonged to Nohmunjap, a district to the west of our Mission station. Rangitafu was a block of whinstone, about five feet long, a foot and a half broad, and a foot thick. He was a sea-god, and presided over shipwrecks. He seemed to have been an Abaddon, not a Joshua; an Apollyon, not a Jesus; a destroyer of seamen, not a Saviour; and was thus in unison with the malignant divinities of the New Hebrides. No mariner saved from shipwreck ever hung up his dripping garments in the temple of Rangitafu, as a thank-offering to the god for his deliverance, as Horace represents them doing in the temples of Neptune at Rome. If a man went to sea in his canoe, his friends did not approach the shrine of Rangitafu with offerings and prayers, supplicating for his safety. He seems to have been powerless in this respect. But, on the other hand, his enemy went to the priest with a present; the priest then presented a piece of a broken canoe to Rangitafu, and offered up a prayer, in the belief or hope that the *natmas* would destroy the canoe and cause those on board to perish. One day, when we were preparing to erect our Teachers' Institution, without my knowledge, the chief and people of the land in which Rangitafu was worshipped made a frame of wood, placed the *natmas* thereon, and some thirty men carried him two miles on their shoulders, and brought him to the Institution, to be laid in the foundation. But we did not hide him away underground—I thought we could utilise Rangitafu to a better purpose. As the Roman generals of old were in the habit of augmenting the splendour of their triumphal entries into Rome by exhibiting as trophies the gods of the conquered nations, so we resolved to do something of the same kind with the rejected divinity of Nohmunjap. As the stone was admirably adapted for the front-door step of the Institution, so we set it apart for that purpose; and that it might remain as a perpetual trophy to the power of the Gospel, we laid the well-known *natmas*, with all needed Masonic honours, as the principal step before the principal door of this important building. At Ashdod, Dagon fell prostrate on the threshold before the ark of God. On Aneityum, Rangitafu, for about eight and twenty long years, has been trodden underfoot by every one that has entered into that temple of ours, in which the Word of God has been taught, and the elements of a liberal education have been communicated.

On Aneityum the idols were all, like the Jewish altars, of uncarved, unhewn stones. The only exception to this which we ever found was in the case of Tuatau, a *natmas* which I found at Anauunse and took home with me. Tuatau was of wood, a piece of a breadfruit tree. Like the idolaters mentioned by the prophet, the maker of this idol had chosen a tree that will not rot. It was a rudely shaped, uncouth figure, its countenance only very slightly resembling the "human face divine." I was struck with its being made of wood, and afterwards learned that it was not a native idol—it was of foreign manufacture. It had a little history of its own, which may serve to illustrate that of "the image which fell down from Jupiter" (Acts xix. 35). About the beginning of this century, as nearly as native chronology supplied me with the date on which to calculate, in the days of Tuatau, a great chief of Anauunse, this poor idol was one morning found drifted ashore by the north-east wind. How long it had been tossed upon the ocean nobody knew. But as it bore all the marks of a Malay idol, and was very like the fisherman's god of Rarotonga, as given in Williams's "Missionary Enterprises," and which, he says, "was placed on the forepart of every fishing canoe; and when the natives were going on a fishing excursion, prior to setting off they invariably presented offerings to the god, and invoked him to grant success,"—it seemed highly probable that this idol was a Rarotongan fisherman's god—that the canoe on which it was borne had been wrecked—that the poor fishermen had been drowned—and that the idol had been drifted along before the trade-winds till it was cast ashore on Aneityum. But, be that as it may have been, its subsequent history was well enough known. Among a people remarkably unskilled in the pictorial arts, its faint resemblance to the human form secured for it favour and veneration. The day on which it was found was one on which Tuatau was making a great feast. The *Natmasses* were always closely connected with the feasts. It was one of the fundamental articles in the creed of heathenism on Aneityum, that the man who made the largest feasts and who presented the most costly offerings to the *Natmasses* was the man that most effectually propitiated their favour. The sacred men all declared that the *Natmasses* had made this image and brought it to Tuatau; and the chief and the ignorant populace accepted the statement as readily, and believed it as firmly, as the Asiarchs and the idolaters of Ephesus believed that the ugly little statue, made of ebony or vine-wood by Canetias, was, as the priests of Diana affirmed it to be, "the image that fell down from Jupiter." The chief received it as a token of the special favour of the *Natmasses*, placed it within the sacred enclosure, and thenceforth regarded it as his tutelar divinity. After the death of Tuatau the idol received his name, and was supposed to be watching over his spirit; and it continued to be worshipped till Christianity was accepted in Anauunse.

Had the idol been a man—a shipwrecked sailor, or one of the poor fishermen on the prow of whose canoe it sat conspicuous, as Castor and Pollux did in the ship that carried Paul—to a certainty he had been killed, and most probably also eaten; at least a shipwrecked sailor met with this sad fate at Eromanga, within less than a twelvemonth of the time when Tuatau fell into my hands; but being a block of wood, shaped so as to have a faint resemblance to a man, it was set up and worshipped as a god. But this dumb idol, after a somewhat singular history, and after, through the deceit of Satan, it had got as it were a new lease of life, and its worship had been prolonged a quarter of a century longer than if it had remained in its own land, also fell before the Word of God. For "the idols He shall utterly abolish!"

But Tuatau still exists, and serves a purpose. When Mr. Geddie saw it, he was eager to send it on to Nova Scotia, and I at once gave it up to him. He forthwith made a suitable box for it, packed it securely, and shipped it by the *John*

Williams for Sydney, to be forwarded thence to Pictou, in Nova Scotia, for the Foreign Mission Committee of the Presbyterian Church of Nova Scotia. And, so far as is known to me, it continues to occupy a conspicuous place in the missionary museum of that church, just as a selection of Rarotongan idols, supplied by the apostolic John Williams, stand in the museum of the London Missionary Society, in the Mission House, Blomfield Street, London; and when some young natives of that island were in London a few years ago, those idols were the first Rarotongan gods they had ever seen, so completely has idolatry been swept away from Rarotonga. Now, as the Reubenites and Gadites continued to point to the altar Ed, that was reared on the right bank of the River Jordan, to prove to the Israelites that their ancestors had had a share in the wars and the conquest of Canaan as well as theirs, so future generations in the Presbyterian Church of Nova Scotia may point to Tuatau, to prove that their ancestors, as well as ours, had taken a part in the evangelisation of the South Seas.

There are various other things connected with the character of the Aneityumese, with their manners and customs, as well as their idolatry—of which alone I have spoken—to which I might here refer; but these will come in, and perhaps more appropriately, as I go on to narrate the progress of the mission, and the marvellous revolution which it effected, and to which I now proceed as the great outstanding fact of the island's history.

CHAPTER V.

ORIGIN OF THE NEW HEBRIDES MISSION.

THE New Hebrides Mission was commenced, and has been carried on, without any previously arranged plan. One chapter of its history has been developed after another, as God has opened up the way by His providence. He has originated movements and raised up agencies in such ways, in such places, and at such times, as clearly to demonstrate that the work has been His own. The London Missionary Society was the first to enter this field, as they were the first to carry the Gospel into the South Seas. The Presbyterian Church of Nova Scotia was the first to follow them. Next came the Reformed Presbyterian Church of Scotland; then the Presbyterian Churches of Australia and New Zealand; and finally the Presbyterian Church of Canada and the Free Church of Scotland. God in His providence brought all these agencies so gradually and so naturally into the work, that one cannot but believe that the New Hebrides Mission has a future before it greatly beyond anything that has yet appeared.

John Williams was the first missionary that landed on the New Hebrides. He visited Tanna, Futuna, and Eromanga; and, as the whole Christian world knows, he was killed by the natives of that island in November 1839.

Next, in 1842, Messrs. (afterwards Drs.) Turner and Nisbet were settled on Tanna; but after labouring with considerable encouragement for about seven months, an epidemic broke out. The missionaries were blamed for causing the disease; war ensued, and their lives were threatened. During this crisis a vessel appeared in sight, and after carefully weighing the prospects before them, they resolved to take advantage of this opportunity; they engaged a passage and returned to Samoa, leaving some native teachers behind them to keep the station open, their lives being less in danger than the lives of the missionaries. They said afterwards, however, that if they had known the character and customs of the natives as well then as they did subsequently, they would have remained on Tanna; but they acted according to the best of their knowledge.

The next agency that entered the field was, as I have already said, the Presbyterian Church of Nova Scotia. Their mission originated in this way. When, in 1838, the year before the martyrdom of John Williams, the late Dr. Geddie was ordained, and settled over a congregation on Prince Edward Island, the Presbyterian Church of Nova Scotia had no mission to the heathen. Mr. Geddie was no sooner settled than he began to agitate the question. He wrote on the subject in the local newspapers and in the denominational magazine. He brought the matter up, first in the Presbytery, and afterwards in the Synod. After vigorous and persistent efforts, Mr. Geddie and his friends prevailed. The Synod agreed to commence a mission to the heathen, and to support two missionaries. Missionaries were advertised for, but no one offered his services. Subsequently Mr. Geddie came forward and offered to go himself. Another missionary could not be found, but Mr. Isaac Archibald was engaged

ORIGIN OF THE NEW HEBRIDES MISSION. 39

as a lay Catechist. The South Seas were selected as the mission field, and on this account: When John Williams, the martyr of Eromanga, was in Scotland, the United Secession Synod gave him £500 to assist him in opening up some islands for their contemplated mission to the heathen. Afterwards, however, they abandoned this idea, and chose Old Calabar as their mission field. Meanwhile the Presbyterian Church of Nova Scotia, being an offshoot of the Secession Church, naturally entered into communication with the parent Church, to assist them in selecting a field for their mission; and the Secession Synod, on their part, frankly resigned to the Nova Scotian Church their claims on the South Seas, in connection with the London Missionary Society. In November 1846 Mr. Geddie and his party sailed from Halifax to Boston, in the United States. After difficulties and delays, they again sailed from Newburyport in a small whaler bound for the Sandwich Islands. After a long, perilous, and extremely uncomfortable voyage, they reached Honolulu. After staying there for about two months, and receiving no small kindness from the brethren of the American mission, they obtained a passage to Samoa in another whaling ship. They had to remain about eight months on Samoa, awaiting the return of the *John Williams* from England. During their detention, both at Hawaii and Samoa, they laid themselves out to become acquainted with the working of both these missions. When the *John Williams* reached Samoa in 1848, the brethren there made every arrangement for the speedy and satisfactory settlement of the mission party from Nova Scotia. One of the Samoan missionaries, the Rev. T. Powell, and his wife were appointed to accompany them for a year, to introduce them to their work, and a band of Samoan teachers was told off to go with them as helps. Messrs. Turner and Nisbet, formerly of Tanna, accompanied the *John Williams* as a deputation during the voyage; so counsel and experience were always at hand. No new missionaries should be settled in a new field without having, if possible, an experienced mission family to remain beside them for six or twelve months, to give them the benefit of their experience. The *John Williams* sailed for the New Hebrides. The five southern islands of the group had been for ten years more or less occupied by Rarotongan and Samoan teachers. The *John Williams* visited all those five islands at this time, and the missionaries examined them most carefully. Their choice finally lay between Efate and Aneityum, and at last they fixed upon Aneityum; and, as they afterwards discovered, a kind and merciful Providence had guided them in their choice, for the Efate natives had been laying plots for their lives.

But even here their prospects were anything but bright. Shortly before this a party of eight French Roman Catholic priests and lay brothers had settled at the harbour. They had erected an iron house, and mounted two small cannon on the roof; thus proclaiming themselves to belong to the Church militant. Here were religious opponents. Then there was a large sandal-wood establishment recently begun, also at the harbour. Here were secular influences all distinctly adverse to the mission. The natives, too, were all decidedly opposed to the settlement of the missionaries among them. At last, Nohoat, the principal chief at the harbour, got the matter compromised. "My brethren," he said, "let us allow the missionaries to stay; the teachers have been very quiet: there is no fear but the missionaries will be the same. You may steal from them as much as ever you like, only do not kill them, and do not hurt them. They are few, we are many: they are weak, we are strong: if they trouble us, we can send them away at any time." Nohoat continued to the end of his life the true and tried friend of the missionaries; and, what was better, his love and fidelity to the servants ripened, and that before very long, into love and fidelity to the Master. To these very easy conditions the natives assented, and the missionaries were allowed to remain. And certainly, for the first twelvemonth at least, the eighth commandment lay very much in abeyance. A piece of land was bought near to where the teachers lived, on which to build their houses, and the mission was commenced.

The Roman Catholic missionaries had selected, and purchased from the natives, a piece of the finest land in the harbour. They had enclosed, dug, and planted a fine garden; and it looked as if a second Eden was about to bloom around them. But, alas! although the natives were quite quiet, yet neither their iron house, their mounted cannon, nor the rifles they always carried with them wherever they went, could protect them from danger. There was a lurking enemy near them, which they did not suspect. There was a large swamp behind their house over which the trade-wind blew, and wafted the invisible and impalpable malaria into their dwelling. The result was that, in a comparatively short time, one after another of the party was laid down with fever and ague. In consequence of this, by-and-by the Popish Bishop came, and took them all away to the Isle of Pines. And, happily for our mission, such was the effect of this terrible scare, that from that day to this a Popish priest has not been seen on the New Hebrides. The Lord can bring good out of evil.

The traders bought the island of Inyeug, which forms one side of the harbour, and is the best sanitarium on Aneityum; on this little island malaria is unknown. But after a time, ignorant of their mercies, they removed their establishment to the mainland, drove the Samoan teachers off the place on which they had built their house, and took possession of the next best piece of land in the bay, and which was adjoining to the Roman Catholic mission property, forcing the Samoan teachers up to a narrow barren corner towards the head of the harbour. But Providence watches over helpless innocency. The portion selected by the traders was only a little less unhealthy than that selected by the priests, while the part left for the teachers, and subsequently for the missionaries, was the least unhealthy of the three. Both the other two stations have been abandoned, but this one is occupied still, and has been found to be, on the whole, one of the healthiest spots on the island.

At the end of the first year Mr. Powell and his family left Aneityum and returned to Samoa. About the end of the second year Mr. Archibald and his family left the mission and proceeded to New South Wales. After this, for nearly two years, Mr. and Mrs. Geddie toiled on alone. Near the end of the fourth year my wife and I arrived from New Zealand and joined the mission. Mr. Geddie's letters and journals, published in his Life, and other publications, give such a full and particular account of the history of the mission during these four years, as to render it superfluous for me to enter into details; suffice it to say, that these were years of hard toil and much suffering, but with not a little to encourage. With the exception of Mrs. Geddie, nearly every member of the mission had long and severe attacks of fever and ague, the one outstanding disease of Aneityum and of the New Hebrides. Our arrival was very opportune, and our reception was very cordial; but of this more by and by. I proceed now to explain how it came to pass, in the good providence of God, that the Reformed Presbyterian Church in Scotland was brought in to the New Hebrides Mission; for it was providential. "God is in history," says D'Aubigne, and certainly still more so in missions, as the history of every mission abundantly testifies.

In the end of last century and the beginning of this, when the missionary spirit awoke, missions were undertaken and carried on by societies, not Churches; but, as the missionary spirit increased and spread, the Churches were aroused to a sense of their duties and responsibilities, and missions began to be undertaken by Churches. Among the first in Scotland to recognise this duty was the Reformed Presbyterian Church. About 1828 the Rev. S. Bates of Kelso, afterwards Rev. Dr. Bates of Glasgow, preached the sermon at the opening of the R. P. Synod, and chose for his subject Christian Missions. The result of this sermon was the establishment of a mission to our fellow-countrymen in Canada, to whom in succession four missionaries were sent. In 1838, the year again before that in which John Williams fell on Eromanga, the Rev. Dr. Duff addressed a public meeting in Stranraer. His overpowering appeals on behalf of the heathen left such an impression on the mind of Dr. W. Symington, that, at the next meeting of the R. P. Synod, he brought forward a motion, which was cordially agreed to, to the effect that the Synod should not be satisfied with a mission to the Colonies, it should also undertake a mission to the heathen. A Committee was appointed, and, after careful inquiry, it was agreed to establish a mission among the Maories or natives of New Zealand. This mission, as we shall by and by see, was subsequently transferred to the New Hebrides. The R. P. Church, from 1842, when it ordained its first missionary to the heathen, till 1876, when it was united with the Free Church, sent forth to New Zealand and the New Hebrides no fewer than eleven missionaries and their wives, and since the union of the two churches the United or Free Church has sent forth other six, and of these seventeen missionaries and their wives, who have been sent out during these forty-two years, only one missionary and three missionaries' wives have died.

In 1842 the R. P. church sent out the Rev. James Duncan and his wife to commence their mission among the Maories. In 1844 my wife and I followed. We found Mr. and Mrs. Duncan fully engaged in mission work among the natives on the Manawatu River, in the north of Cook's Straits, some seventy or eighty miles from Wellington. We joined them at once. After the mission had been in existence for two or three years; after we had acquired a knowledge of the Maori language, and had become acquainted with the condition of the natives, we felt satisfied that the Church had committed a mistake in selecting New Zealand as their mission field. The natives were comparatively few; they amounted to only about one-half the number we had been led to believe that they were. We found only about 700 on the whole of the Manawatu. All the natives of New Zealand were claimed as belonging either to the Church of England or the Wesleyan Missions; and although we were forty miles from the nearest missionary,

ORIGIN OF THE NEW HEBRIDES MISSION. 45

yet he had native teachers settled in every village; so that we found ourselves to be simply interlopers. While there was ample room for more missionaries, there was not room for another mission to work advantageously. In these circumstances Mr. Duncan and I wrote a joint letter to the Committee, advising them to select another field for their heathen mission. By a singular coincidence, or rather an overruling Providence, on the very day on which our secretary, Dr. Bates, received our letter, he received one from the Rev. A. W. Murray of Samoa, one of the London Missionary Society's missionaries, an intimate personal friend of his own. In this letter Mr. Murray, who had had no communication with us, stated that when he first heard that we had gone to New Zealand, he was sure, from what he knew of the New Zealand missions, that we had made a great mistake; but if the Church would remove us, and send us to the South Seas, the Samoan brethren would do everything in their power to secure for us a suitable field of labour; that they were expecting two Presbyterian missionaries from Nova Scotia, and they would be glad to locate us all in the New Hebrides.

Dr. Bates at once put himself in communication with the Committee of the London Missionary Society, inquiring if the Society could provide a field for their two missionaries. The Committee answered that, as they were extending their operations in India and elsewhere, they could not at that time increase the number of their missionaries in the South Seas, and that they would gladly receive, not two only but twenty, if the R. P. Church could send them. The *John Williams* was in England at that time, and about to sail for the South Seas; and it was arranged conditionally that, after leaving Sydney, the vessel should call at New Zealand for us. But before these arrangements could be carried out the Reformed Presbyterian Synod held its annual meeting, and these arrangements required to be confirmed by the Synod. But the Synod, not so well informed on this point as their Committee, being also, like all larger bodies, more timid and more conservative than smaller ones, thought that these steps were too precipitate, and decided that a longer trial should be given to the New Zealand Mission. Meanwhile the Maori war had broken out, and all the settlers and missionaries on the north side of Cook's Straits were driven into Wellington. While thus detained there, Mr. Duncan and I employed our time in preaching to the Presbyterians in Wellington, who were at that time without a minister. When we received the answer to our letter, it was to the effect that we were to hold ourselves in readiness to proceed to the South Seas by the *John Williams*. The next mail brought letters countermanding these instructions, and informing us of the decision of the Synod, and that we were to return to the Manawatu as soon as practicable. As the Maori war was now over, Mr. Duncan, acting on these instructions, returned to his former station. But, acting on my own convictions of duty, I remained in Wellington for eighteen months or so ministering, under temporary arrangements, to the Scotch settlers, and being supported by them, but corresponding still with the Committee about a new mission field. The Nova Scotian Mission party were before this time settled in the New Hebrides, and I received a letter from Mr. Geddie, through Bishop Selwyn, inviting me to join him.

At the end of this time I paid a visit to Auckland. I was daily expecting a letter from the Committee. Postal com-

ORIGIN OF THE NEW HEBRIDES MISSION. 47

munication between the home country and New Zealand was at that date slow and irregular. At the end of two months a vessel arrived from London with a mail on board, and having letters for Wellington as well as Auckland. At my request the postmaster kindly looked over the Wellington letters, and found some for me; and one of them was from our secretary, Dr. Bates, authorising me, if a suitable opportunity occurred, to proceed to the South Seas, and confer with Mr. Murray or Mr. Geddie, or any of the Samoan missionaries, and select a field satisfactory to myself.

I was staying with the Colonial Secretary, Dr. Sinclair, and told him the purport of this letter. He told the Governor, Sir George Grey, who said that if a man-of-war were coming in soon, and sailing for the South Seas, he would gladly use his influence with the Captain to secure me a passage. At this juncture occurred a singular providence, which proved a turning-point in the history of the New Hebrides Mission. In less than ten days after I received my letter, H.M.S. *Havannah*, Captain Erskine, R.N., arrived in Auckland harbour from Sydney, about to proceed to Western Polynesia on a three months' voyage, and was to sail direct to Aneityum in a few days. Sir George Grey kindly applied to Captain Erskine, who very frankly granted the passage, and said he would either land me on Aneityum or take me on to Sydney, as I might require. They had taken Bishop Selwyn on to Samoa the year before, and what they had done for the Episcopal Mission they were equally glad to do for the Presbyterian. In a week or so we had sailed for Western Polynesia. We reached Aneityum. I consulted with Mr. Geddie, and made certain conditional arrangements. We then proceeded on our voyage, visited the other islands of the New Hebrides, also Queen Charlotte's group, the Solomon Islands, and New Caledonia, and at the end of three months we reached Sydney. This was a singularly favourable opportunity for carrying out my object. And, strange to say, that was the only instance, either before or since, in which a man-of-war sailed direct to Aneityum or the New Hebrides from New Zealand. Had I not been in Auckland at that time, and had I not received that letter at the time that I did, I could not have taken advantage of that opportunity, and there was no other practicable way I could have reached Aneityum. And had I not visited Aneityum, it is probable that I might never have joined the mission; and at the end of two years, when I did join it, Mr. Geddie told me that, had I not come at that time, he did not think that he could have held on much longer, as his health was so impaired by successive attacks of fever and ague. And had the mission been broken up, its future history would have been extremely doubtful. The knowledge I acquired during that voyage of the islands and of the natives was to me of great and permanent value. At the end of seven months I rejoined my wife in Wellington. I might have proceeded to the New Hebrides at once, but, acting on the principle of the Latin proverb, *festina lente*, "hasten slowly," I wrote a full report of my voyage in the *Havannah* to our Mission Committee, and awaited instructions from home. Meanwhile, as the Presbyterian congregation in Auckland was vacant, that I might neither be idle nor a burden upon the mission funds, I made an arrangement to supply their pulpit till I should receive an answer to my report. At the end of a twelve-month I received a letter from the Secretary, authorising me, on conditions that were satisfactory, to proceed to

Aneityum, and take up a station for myself in connection with Mr. Geddie.

When I communicated my intentions to Bishop Selwyn, he kindly renewed an offer he had formerly made, of giving us a free passage to Aneityum in his mission vessel, the *Border Maid*, in which he was shortly to sail to the islands, to his own mission field. This we gladly accepted, and had we been his own missionaries, he could not have treated us more kindly and considerately. He took all our supplies, our furniture, a whale-boat, the frame of a house, goats, pigs, and poultry, &c., so that we commenced our labours under great advantages. There was another special providence here, or another event providentially overruled in our favour. Had we not been in circumstances to take advantage of the Bishop's voyage at that time, instead of getting to Aneityum as we did without delay and without expense, we should have found it to be a matter of extreme difficulty and of very great expense.

In a few months after this the Bishop sold the *Border Maid*, returned to England, had a new vessel built at home—the *Southern Cross*—and brought her out with him to New Zealand; and it was two years before he again visited the New Hebrides. In these circumstances, it would scarcely have been practicable for us to have reached Aneityum at all. We arrived on the 1st of July 1852.

In the end we found that all the tantalising delays, and all the vexatious disappointments, that we had experienced were only parts of a gracious plan, wisely arranged to bring about an important end. The old divines used to say that "Heaven is a prepared place for a prepared people;" and so we found Aneityum to be a mission field prepared for us, who by a somewhat special training had been in some measure prepared for it. We arrived also, as I have said, at a most opportune time. But as the success of the mission on Aneityum during the following eight or nine years was so rapid, so much beyond anything that has ever occurred since on any of the other islands, I think it necessary to state what appears to me to be, under God, some of the principal causes of that remarkable success. When we took the first census the population of Aneityum was 3500. We may assume that it continued stationary till the measles were brought in 1861. When Mr. Geddie settled on the island in 1848, the natives were all heathen, with a few exceptions. When we arrived in 1852, there might be 400 professedly Christian, the rest were all heathen. When we left the island in the end of 1859, to carry the New Testament through the press in London, the whole population had professed Christianity; and what was perhaps more remarkable, there was never afterwards any going back to heathenism; except once or twice, and that for only a very short time and to a very limited extent. One obvious cause was this; on the year that we arrived the last of the outside opposition disappeared. The Popish opposition had never become formidable. It was more feared than felt, and it was not long till it entirely ceased, by the removal of the French priests. The sandalwood establishment during the first four years of the mission was an active and unscrupulous opposition. The leading persons among them employed every means in their power to put down the mission. This establishment was removed first to Tanna, and finally to New Caledonia. Moreover, the gold discoveries in Australia drew off all the floating white population from the islands to the gold-fields, and for some years

ORIGIN OF THE NEW HEBRIDES MISSION.

we had the natives entirely to ourselves; and the new religion was almost the sole object that engrossed their attention. And before the return of the traders the work of the mission was so far advanced that they were unable to retard it. In the next place, during these eight years both the mission families enjoyed remarkably good health, which greatly promoted our mission labours, whereas during the first four years of the mission all the mission families suffered severely from fever and ague, and the experience of the Samoan teachers as to health was relatively the same. Moreover, both Mr. Geddie and I had each of us some special, though different, qualifications for the kind of mission work that required to be done on Aneityum. Mr. Geddie had been some years a minister in a settled charge, and well acquainted both with preaching and pastoral work. I had had a somewhat similar experience both at home and in New Zealand. Mr. Geddie, during his stay at Hawaii and Samoa, had had the best opportunities of becoming acquainted with the missionaries of both the American and London Societies, and also with the way in which the work was carried on in both these missions. He acquired also a considerable knowledge of the Samoan language.

During my eight years' connection with New Zealand, I had become acquainted with the leading missionaries in both Societies, and with their modes of conducting their mission work, and had gained a tolerably minute acquaintance with the Maori language. In mechanical, medical, and educational knowledge and experience both of us were, I believe, above the average of those commencing a new mission. And coming from different countries and different Churches, and approaching the mission field from opposite points and by totally different routes, and having come in contact with totally different sections both of religious and general society, and having each seen so much, but yet totally distinct portions, of the South Sea Mission field, when we met we brought together, without any merit of ours, an amount, especially of extra-professional, but withal of valuable knowledge, rarely combined in the case of two missionaries entering a new field. Yet our views and principles in all the essentials of mission work were singularly alike. It was notable, also, that on those points in which we were constitutionally different, the one was generally found to be the complement of the other; where the one was weak the other was strong, and *vice versâ*. Hence the one was no drawback to the other, and the work went smoothly on. Furthermore, the natural condition of the island was favourable for our work. The island was moderate in size and very compact. The language was everywhere the same. The localities were accessible and not difficult to work. We were able to visit the whole island, and occupy it with native evangelistic and educational agencies, as soon as we had these trained, which we superintended and directed. And there were no contiguous outlying masses of heathenism to resist our operations and make counter aggressions. In our approaching the New Hebrides, Mr Geddie and I, as I have said, became acquainted with the agencies and appliances employed by the four great Societies carrying on missionary operations in the South Seas. Our field was in many respects different from theirs. We never slavishly copied any of their modes of working. But whenever, in our altered circumstances, we could adopt any of their plans, we availed ourselves of their experiences, and frequently with great advantage. Hence I used often to say to our young missionaries, after I had explained to them our modes of working, "This is the way we do. It is very well for you to know how we do things here, but it is not necessary that you should do always as we do. Your circumstances may be so different from ours, that were we in your situation we might adopt some totally different course."

I have said that our arrival was very opportune. Mr. Geddie had struggled away, and that successfully, in the face of many difficulties and much opposition; but the state of the island and the mission was such that, even had we arrived sooner, we could have rendered him but very little help; but had we been much longer in arriving a great opportunity would have been lost. About the time of our arrival, in the good providence of God, the chief difficulties were being removed, and as a feeling favourable to Christianity had set in among the natives, by our coming at that juncture, that feeling was utilised, and those favourable circumstances were taken advantage of. It was a striking example of the truth of the poet's well-known lines—

"There is a tide in the affairs of men
Which taken at the flood leads on to fortune."

Had this opportunity been lost it might never have returned. Our arrival, too, had a wonderful effect on Mr. Geddie's health and spirits. Up till the arrival of the *John Williams* and the deputation of the Samoan missionaries, three weeks before our arrival, he had been suffering almost daily from fever and ague; but the first day after the vessel came in, the excitement caused by the arrival of the brethren completely stopped the fever and ague. Our settlement so shortly after, and the new departure taken in the mission, acted like magic, and effected a complete cure. New and congenial company, encouraging prospects, and abundance of work, put new life into him; he felt himself like another man. He was naturally a man of action, and his hands were now full—full of work entirely to his mind.

CHAPTER VI.

MISSION HOUSES.

IN order to work, and work successfully, it is necessary, in the first place, that we should live and be in good health. This holds specially true of mission work in the New Hebrides. Hence health must be secured at whatever price. Owing to my visit to the New Hebrides before I went thither to reside, I had obtained a much better idea of the climate, and of the conditions under which health could be enjoyed, than I should otherwise have had. From my youth I had studied more or less carefully the laws of health. When a mere boy I had read "Buchan's Domestic Medicine," and studied carefully the first part, which relates to the prevention of disease, and I continued to read popular works on the same subject as they came into my hands. After my ordination I attended medical classes for six months in Glasgow. When I was in New Zealand I became acquainted with several medical gentlemen connected both with the army and the navy; some in active service, and some retired from active life, but who had had extensive experience in tropical climates. From these I got many useful hints, which proved of great benefit to me during my residence on the islands. At that time the New Hebrides islands had a pre-eminently bad character as regards health, and not without good cause.

The French priests and lay brothers, as we have seen, succumbed to the malaria, and left the island. Both the white men and the natives of other islands, connected with the sandal-wood establishment, suffered very severely from fever and ague, and a good many of them died. A medical gentleman from Sydney, who resided for some months with the proprietor of the above establishment, and who had the best opportunities of studying the diseases of the island, told Mr. Geddie that he observed not only the island fever, but also the jungle fever of India. The missionaries and the Rarotongan and Samoan teachers had also been severe sufferers. When I visited Aneityum in the *Havannah* in 1850, Mr. Geddie came on board, accompanied by a Rarotongan teacher. He had been suffering for some months from fever and ague, and was very much reduced, and was looking very ill; the teacher was still worse, and died a few weeks thereafter. I used afterwards to say to Mr. Geddie, that if he had on set purpose intended to deter me from joining the mission, he could not have taken a more effectual method to accomplish his object. He and the teacher, with their pale faces and sickly, haggard appearance, were such a contrast to the fresh, vigorous-looking men on board the man-of-war, that it looked as if we had been boarded by Death and his body-servant the moment we came to anchor, and as if both were saying to me, "If you stay here this is what you may look forward to." When we went north to Efate we found two Rarotongan teachers, both of whom had suffered severely from fever and ague. As we sailed up Havannah Harbour we saw two or three beautifully whitewashed houses belonging to the Samoan teachers. The teachers were all dead; their houses were empty, and their canoes were lying rotting on the beach. The sickness and mortality among the teachers up to that date had been very great. In short, they could not stand the climate at all. Frequently they got away by some trading vessel to the Loyalty Islands, where, there being no malaria, they soon regained their health and strength. Bishop Selwyn said to me that we might possibly find some elevated, healthy spot near the centre of the island so free from malaria that we might be able to live on Aneityum all the year round, and yet enjoy good health; although he admitted that this was doubtful.

In these circumstances, how to be able to live at all on the islands was the first question. Were these diseases preventable, or were they inevitable? Therefore, before we left New Zealand, we made every effort in our power to secure the preservation of life and health. Our friend Dr. Logan, who had served his full time as a surgeon in the royal navy, told me that when cruising on the west coast of Africa, they often, when lying at anchor, covered the port-holes of the vessel at night with woollen netting, to keep out the damp and protect themselves from fever; and that in the morning every net was wet as Gideon's fleece, when the dew lay on the fleece alone, and the whole earth around was dry. He advised us, therefore, to provide something of this kind, with which to cover our windows in the hot and rainy season of the year, as often as we had to keep them open, whether by day or by night. We did our best to prepare for those conditions of life. My wife fell in with a job lot of thin net-like woollen shawls, which she bought, and took with us to Aneityum. However, happily for us, we never found it necessary to use these precautions.

In addition to maintaining in as high a state as possible

the general health, the most important sanitary improvement that I introduced related to the construction of our dwelling-house. In Tahiti, Rarotonga, Samoa, and elsewhere the missionaries, for the most part, had simply earthen or lime floors in their houses, covered with native mats for carpets, and as there was little or no malaria in those islands, they found these houses healthy enough. Mr. Geddie brought the frame of a house with him from Samoa, and erected his house on the same principles as the brethren did in Samoa. Instead of covering the wooden frame with weather boarding, between the studs the walls were wattled outside and inside, and plastered with lime prepared by burning the live coral. The house, when plastered and whitewashed, was clean, neat, and beautiful. The earthen floor, when covered with native mats, was comfortable, tasteful, and elegant. This did very well during the day, when the sea-breeze blew in at one window and out at another; but at night, when doors and windows were shut, when the malaria rose from the floor, and was confined inside the house by the lime walls, and was also breathed and breathed again by the inmates, sooner or later fever and ague was the result.

I took with me from Auckland materials prepared for two weather-boarded rooms, and flooring for other three rooms. I built a foundation of stone two feet high, inserting under each room two little windows of perforated tin or zinc. On this foundation I set up the frame and constructed the house. This plan secured a free circulation of air underneath the floor; so that the connection with the earth beneath the floor, and hence with the malaria, was completely cut off during the night. And we were living to all intents and purposes, as far as sanitation was concerned, not on the ground floor, but on the first floor, or in an upper storey. I had no fever and ague for seven years; and even then, it was caused more by exhaustion from continuous overwork than from climatic influences. My wife suffered sooner than I did, though only slightly, but it was from the same causes—from over-exertion rather than miasma.

I introduced another principle, borrowed from some of the Samoan brethren, and that was, to have the house single or only one room in breadth, with a window on each side, having two sashes, and hinged, so that the windows could be thrown open whenever it was desirable, and a free circulation of air from side to side established.

At the end of six months, when our dwelling-house and some outbuildings were completed, Mr. Geddie, seeing the manifest advantages of these arrangements, resolved to erect a new house for himself on the same principles. He had not wood, but suitable stones were available; and I assisted him in marking off the site of the house, and in laying the foundation. At the end of a twelvemonth, notwithstanding a heavy pressure of mission duties, the house was completed, and Mr. Geddie and his family took possession of the building. Up to this time his youngest daughter, a child of four years of age, had been suffering continuously from fever and ague. She had a fit every day, and, during the continuance of the fit, she shook and became delirious. But they had not been six weeks in the new house till the ague left her, and she had not another fit for the following six years, when she left the island to go home for her education. Mr. Geddie himself, too, was all but completely free from fever and ague for many years.

In after years, when new missionaries arrived, in some

cases they could not be provided with boarded floors, even if anxious to get them; in other cases the new arrivals were sceptical as to the necessity for such precautions. But the result was, that, as a general rule, the absence or presence of fever and ague was dependent very largely on the presence or absence of house-building on these principles. We lost several of our missionaries, because the health either of the missionary or of his wife had given way, owing to the bad site or the defective construction of their houses. And the greatly superior health, enjoyed as a whole in the families of the New Hebrides Mission in recent years, is owing, more, perhaps, than to anything else, to the greater care that has been taken to carry out these principles in the building of their houses.

The conditions of a healthy dwelling-house on the New Hebrides are these: the selection, if practicable, of an elevated, dry, and open site for the house; a closely jointed, boarded floor, raised two feet above the ground; the foundation completely closed all round, to prevent rubbish of any kind from accumulating beneath; with small windows of perforated tin or zinc to secure a free circulation beneath. The house must be only one room in width, with a window on each side, with double sashes, and hinged so as to open on each side, and allow the air to circulate freely from side to side of every room during the day. To prevent a draught, the window on the weather or windy side of the room can be closed, and the other left open, and the fresh air can thus be enjoyed, without any danger from the current or draught. If these precautions be observed, fever and ague will not be troublesome, the general laws of health being, of course, carefully attended to and faithfully observed.

MISSION HOUSES.

When the Livingstonia Mission was commenced on Lake Nyassa, I wrote a letter to the Rev. Dr. Goold of Edinburgh, who, along with Dr. Duff, was at that time one of the secretaries of that mission, stating the results of our experience on this point on the New Hebrides, and making some suggestions as to the construction of their houses. He forwarded my letter to Dr. Stewart, who thanked me very kindly for my suggestions. How far they considered it necessary to adopt our plans, or how far they had the means of carrying out these principles, I do not know. At Lovedale and in South Africa, where the soil is dry and there is no malaria, men may live as they list, and that with impunity, as far as houses are concerned, but it is totally different in Central Africa; witness Mrs. Livingstone, Bishop M'Kenzie and his party, and even the history of Livingstonia. Traders and settlers come down to our islands, and think that they may camp out with impunity, as they do in Australia; but fever and ague, sickness and mortality, quickly arouse them to a sense of the altered conditions of existence; and they soon adopt our principles of house-building. Some missions have suffered severely by neglecting those principles of sanitation that we have adopted. The sixth commandment dominates the success or non-success of missions in unhealthy climates far more than most people think, and as much so as any of the other nine. The sixth commandment requires all lawful endeavours to preserve our own life and the life of others. But it is a commandment which good men, and even good missionaries, too often overlook, as if it were merely a sort of bye-law, and not one of the ten, written on tables of stone. They seem to think that their bodies are their own, and they may treat them as they please, that the soul is everything, and the body nothing, at least comparatively. But God is wiser than man, and the arrangements of His Providence are such that in those climates the penalty speedily follows the transgression, and the punishment inflicted for disobedience is swift as well as sure.

CHAPTER VII.

THE SABBATH ON ANEITYUM.

THERE was no Sabbath on Aneityum up till March or April 1841. There was not even the slightest tradition that such a day had ever existed. For untold centuries, year after year, and generation after generation, there had been nothing but long unbroken weeks of toil, extending from the 1st ot January till the 31st of December, but with no Sabbath either at the commencement or the close. But from the first Sabbath of April 1841—the first Sabbath after the first teachers were landed—up to the present time, the Sabbath has been observed on Aneityum, and has marked the first day of every week. It was not a Popish or prelatic Sunday, it was a Christian Sabbath. Dr. Andrew Thomson of Edinburgh says that some people speak of the Scottish Sabbath as if it were some institution peculiar to Scotland. It would be just as correct to speak of the Scottish sun as something peculiar to the country; for the sun and the Sabbath were both alike made for man, not for Scotchmen only. On Aneityum we had no Sunday—a day, the one half for devotion, and the other half for diversion. It was a Sabbath—a day, as the word signifies, of rest,—a day of rest for the body, and a day of worship for the soul. The Sabbath and the sun were both recognised, not as burdens, but as blessings.

We invariably found that the Sabbath was the first part of Christianity embraced by the heathen. If at war, they gave up fighting on that day. They gave up fishing; they gave up digging, &c. They adopted the Sabbatic part of the day; it became simply and entirely a day of rest, before it became a day of worship. The Christian natives would come and tell us of some heathen tribe, and say, "The people of such and such a land will soon become Christian now; they are begun to sit idle on the Sabbath." And it invariably turned out to be the case. They first rested, and by-and-by they came to us to attend worship.

Our teaching with respect to the Sabbath was not that usually put forth by the secular press of the present day; it was that of the school of such men as Dr. Andrew Symington of Paisley, Rev. John Angell James of Birmingham, Dr. James Hamilton of London, Sir Andrew Agnew of Lochnaw, Mr. John Henderson of Park, &c., viz., that the Sabbath is a day of Divine appointment, and of perpetual moral obligation; a holy day, not a holiday; a happy day, but not a day of frivolity; a day for the refreshment of the physical powers, for the strengthening of the intellectual faculties, for the quickening of the spiritual graces, and for the elevating of the whole man. With us too Saturday was to some extent a day of preparation for the Sabbath. On Sabbath all servile work was suspended. No work was done except works of necessity or mercy. No cooking was done on Sabbath. Some may think that this was terribly puritanical, oppressively rigid, Sabbatarianism run mad, worse than the strictest and sternest of Scottish Sabbaths, worse than anything enjoined by the straitest sect of the Pharisees. To such I would say, *Audi alteram partem*, "Hear the other side; or like Themistocles to his judges, "Hear first, and then strike." On one occasion a young missionary came out from Scotland to the New Hebrides, and was staying with us for a few weeks. On the second or third Sabbath after his arrival, while we were sitting at dinner, he said, "I did not expect to get any dinner here on Sabbath." We said to him, "What made you think that you would get no dinner here on Sabbath?" "Oh," said he, "I was told that there was no cooking on Aneityum on Sabbath, and I thought that if there was no cooking there would be no eating." "Your statement of facts," we said, "is quite correct, but your inferences from these facts are quite wrong. Both the natives and the mission families do all their cooking on Saturday; but the Sabbath, instead of being a day of fasting, is more nearly allied to a day of feasting; with respect to food it is the best day of all the seven. All our baking, boiling, and roasting are done on the Saturday; but with our American stove, the kettle can be boiled on Sabbath, the frying-pan utilised, and the oven heated to warm a roast, in the shortest possible time, and with the least possible labour to servants; so that for a hot joint and a warm dinner an Aneityum Sabbath can equal if not surpass any English Sunday. But in a climate where the thermometer always ranges from 62° to 90° in the shade, to sit down to a cold collation could never be much of a penance even on a Sabbath-day.

The natives never cook an oven more than once a day, and that is for supper; but if they should cook no oven during half the days of the week, they never miss to have one on Saturday; and it is sure to be the largest and the best in the whole week, and supplies them with abundance of food for two days; so that they are in no danger of being hungry on

Sabbath. Their cooking is a tedious and laborious process, which I shall describe elsewhere. Our object was to present to them Christ's yoke as easy and His burden as light. To a people who had never enjoyed a statutory day of rest, the weekly Sabbath was felt to be a Heaven-sent blessing; to a people whose religion had at times imposed weeks, and even months, of fasting, to secure food for some great feast, when they ate no pleasant food, and often very little of any kind, a weekly day of rest and of abundance of food was looked upon as the reverse of a gloomy day. They could say with Graham, the author of "The Sabbath"—

"Hail, Sabbath! thee I hail, the poor man's day!"

When every member of every family, young and old, weak and strong, had a good breakfast on Sabbath morning, they could join in family and public worship with joyful hearts and gladsome minds; they could enter into the spirit of the 92d Psalm, which is entitled, "A Psalm or Song for the Sabbath-day," and which says, "It is a good thing to give thanks unto the LORD, and to sing praises unto Thy name, O Most High: to show forth Thy loving-kindness in the morning" (when mercies are promised), "and Thy faithfulness every night" (when promises are fulfilled). Formerly the natives lived in a state not simply of fear, but of terror, for the *Natmasses* and the sacred men. From this state of constant dread they were all but completely delivered by Christianity. Hence in their circumstances, in the full deliverance from superstitious fears, the Sabbath was not to them a day of gloom, and dread, and sadness, but a day of joy, gladness, and rejoicing; the happiest day of all the seven.

So far as I am aware, in none of the South Sea missions

THE SABBATH ON ANEITYUM.   67

was the word Sunday ever introduced as a name for the day. On some of the islands Sabbath was adopted in the form of Sabate, or whatever the idiom of the language might require. But generally native words were found to express the idea. We had two forms on Aneityum. It was the *Nathiat alumop*, the resting day, a literal translation of the Sabbath. It was also the *Nathiat itap*, the sacred or the holy day. They called Saturday the *Nathiat auaret-ha*, the cooking day, owing to the special cooking for the Sabbath. In New Zealand the Maories called the Sabbath the *Ra tapu*, the sacred or holy day. Saturday was the *Ra horoi*, the washing day. In the beginning of the mission the natives washed their clothes on that day, to be clean for the Sabbath. Friday they called the *Ra oka*, the sticking or killing day. Tradition says that in the early days of the New Zealand mission, when the missionaries had a pig to kill, they always killed it on the Friday, that it might be roasted on the Saturday for their dinner on Sabbath.

Our Sabbath services were conducted very much as they are at home, with two exceptions : we met much earlier, and we employed much more lay agency. In this country, in many places public worship does not begin till twelve o'clock, and in no place does it commence earlier than half-past ten. Our two services were always over before twelve o'clock. In summer we commenced between eight and nine, and in winter between nine and ten. We had always two services, with an interval of fifteen or twenty minutes; each service was about an hour and a quarter. When the second service was over, the people went all direct home, and met again about three o'clock for the Sabbath-school in their respective localities. We had public worship in four places every

Sabbath: the central one, which was larger than all the other three, at Aname, and three out-stations—one at Anauunjai, a second at Ananumse, and the third at Inwaijipthav, a deep inland valley. I officiated for three Sabbaths in succession at the central station, and once a month, in rotation, at each of the out-stations. To these I went on the Saturday afternoon, and returned on the Monday forenoon, that I might devote the whole Sabbath for the benefit of these remote districts. The next point of difference was the extent to which native agency was employed. Every Sabbath I employed four natives—elders, or deacons, or teachers—two at each service; one read a chapter, and the other led in prayer. At each of the three out-stations four natives conducted the whole services. I thus employed sixteen natives each Sabbath. They also assisted in the same proportion at the weekday prayer-meeting. I had about forty on my officiating list, and I employed them in rotation. I brought them all in turn from the out-stations to Aname, and I sent them from the central district to the out-stations. In this way all the office-bearers were brought always into regular and continuous contact with the people of every district, and the state of the work at every station was always well known. Dinner was always provided by some family in the district for the men who came from a distance to officiate. I drew up a plan of service for a month, and intimated every Sabbath and Wednesday who were to officiate, and at what places, for the following week. This was the main theological training which the native agents received. But the most remote of my teachers in this way heard, at the least, one of my expositions and sermons once every month, and it was wonderful how they remembered them. On one occasion I heard one of my expositions on the anointing of David by Samuel reproduced at the end of three years, and, on the whole, it was very correctly given. We had several objects in view in bringing forward the natives in this way. It lessened, and, at the same time, largely supplemented the labours of the missionary; it gave greater variety to the services; it developed the abilities of the natives; it gave us an opportunity of observing the progress they were making in religious knowledge, in the gift of prayer, in effective reading, and in public speaking, so that we could correct them when necessary. It gave us also opportunities of hearing the native idioms employed on religious subjects, which greatly increased our knowledge of the language, and of the forms of expression best suited for communicating Bible knowledge. Their theology might be wrong, but we were sure that their language was right. Before Thomas Boston published his "Fourfold State," he read portions of Addison's "Spectator" that his English might be formed on the best model; and for the same purpose he read some parts of Cicero before he published his treatise in Latin on "Sacred Stigmatology, or the Doctrine of the Hebrew Points." But as we had no classical writers on which to form our style, we took for our models the best native speakers on the island.

As the mission advanced we had now and again to change our plans. In the beginning of the mission, almost every Sabbath afternoon we sent out small parties, headed by one or two of our wisest, most intelligent, and most influential natives, to visit the heathen, and talk with them in their own homes. These came back to us in the evening, and told us what they had said to the natives, and what objections the heathen had made to receive the Gospel. This gave us an opportunity of learning the opinions of the heathen, and of instructing the Christian natives how to meet the objections of the heathen, and in this way we had not to draw our bow at a venture; we came to know, through these conversations, where the joints of the harness lay, and where the arrows would pierce with the greatest effect. As the heathen diminished in numbers, these irregular visits gave place to regular services all over the island.

We had also a prayer-meeting once a week, both at the central and at the out-stations—at first on the Friday, and subsequently on the Wednesday afternoon. But I was always careful to draw very sharp lines and make very marked distinctions between the divine and the human, between the Sabbath and its Divinely-instituted services, and days and services of human appointment. I was very pronounced in my teaching and practice about the Christian Sabbath; its Divine authority, its perpetual moral obligation, and the promises and blessings connected with the faithful observance of that day: "The Lord blessed the Sabbath-day and hallowed it." I never recognised *Sunday* even by name. Its heathen origin, its Popish and prelatic history, and its recent culmination in the secular Sunday Society, have all strengthened my aversion to Sunday. I never attached much importance even to our week-day prayer-meetings, though they were well attended, and in our circumstances they served several important objects. I always met with my candidates' class before our prayer-meeting; all our marriages were solemnised in the church at the close of the prayer-meetings; our meetings of session, and of our deacons' court, were held at the same time, and the prayer-meeting was a fitting close to such meetings. There are some Christians who entertain such spiritual views that they think every day should be a Sabbath. But if every day were a Sabbath, it would practically end in there being no Sabbath at all. God draws a sharp distinction about days in the fourth commandment: "Six days shalt thou labour and do all thy work," &c., "but the seventh day is the Sabbath." In proportion as holidays and week-day religious services are multiplied, there is a danger that the sanctity of the Sabbath will be diminished. I used often to say to the natives, "It is a good thing to come to the week-day prayer-meeting, if you have time and opportunity; but if you have not, there is no sin in staying away; because it is a meeting simply of man's appointment, not of God's. It is altogether different with the Sabbath; it is a day of God's appointment, and is to be wholly observed as a day of rest and worship. In the beginning of the mission we could have had a semi-Sabbath every week. At first we held our prayer-meeting on Friday afternoon. This institution had travelled west from Samoa. It had served a good purpose there, and the native teachers had brought it with them to the New Hebrides, and the missionaries continued its observance. We went on the principle of disturbing no arrangements that had grown up with Christianity that were not contrary to Scripture. But one Friday, when I was from home, my wife, as usual, was at the meeting, and one of our leading natives gave the address, part of which was to this effect: "We have two holy days," he said, "two days for worship every week; we have the Friday and the Sabbath. We have worship on Friday because Christ was put to death on a Friday, and we have worship on Sabbath because on that day Christ rose from the dead. Let us therefore be strong, my friends," he said, "to worship God on these two days."

When I came home my wife told me what the speaker had said, and added, "You had better look sharp; for if the natives take up these notions about Friday, and if the French priests should return to the island, the natives will be quite prepared to adopt the Popish views about Friday—the unlawfulness of eating flesh on that day, and so forth. Mr. Geddie and I took counsel together on the subject, and on inquiry found that these views were pretty generally entertained among the natives. We had meetings with our respective sessions, and first privately, and afterwards publicly, we explained the Scriptural doctrine of the Sabbath, and testified against their erroneous inferences. "It is quite true," I said, "that Christ was crucified on a Friday, but the Scriptures say nothing about Friday being set apart in any way to commemorate that event. God appointed the Lord's Supper to keep in remembrance the death of Christ. Our Lord rose from the dead on the first day of the week; and to commemorate His resurrection God appointed the first day of the week to be the Lord's Day and the Sabbath. From the creation of the world till the resurrection of Christ, God appointed the seventh day of the week to be the Sabbath, the day of rest; to commemorate His resting on that day from the work of creation, which He had just finished; and from the resurrection of Christ till the end of the world, He has appointed the first day of the week to commemorate the resurrection of Christ, His finishing the work of redemption, and His resting therefrom, and called it the Lord's Day. The first day of the week commemorates two rests—the rest of creation and the rest of redemption. It is, therefore, at once the Lord's Day and the Christian Sabbath. Hence we do not need two Sabbaths—the one day commemorates two events;

the completion of creation and the completion of redemption; and serves two purposes—that of rest and that of worship. From that time forward we changed the week-day prayer-meeting from the Friday to the Wednesday, which otherwise was, in many respects, more suitable than the Friday. Thereafter the Sabbatic character of the Friday disappeared.

But the Sabbath question was not yet quite ended. Some years afterwards I was at Anauunse examining the schools. The teachers, I may remark, were in general more zealous about the week-day prayer-meeting than ever I was. My zeal was concerned chiefly about the Sabbath. On this occasion, when I entered the school-house, I observed a sentence written in large distinct letters on the black-board, and the writing was, not *Imiehva nathiat atumop*, "Remember the Sabbath-day," but *Imiehva nathiat wenste*, "Remember the Wednesday." After the meeting I took the teacher and explained to him what I have said above, as to the difference between the Sabbath and a week-day prayer-meeting; and ever after, this addition to the fourth commandment ceased to appear on the black-board.

I have no doubt but that the steady and rapid progress of the Gospel on Aneityum was due, in no small degree, to the manner in which we emphasised the Scripture doctrine of the Sabbath, and established its observance. We thus secured time for religious instruction, quietness for devotional exercises, and the largest possible amount of social sympathy in the public services of the sanctuary; and, above all, brought down upon us the influences of the Holy Spirit, in accordance with the Divine promise. The exile of Patmos, too, was in the Spirit on the Lord's Day.

CHAPTER VIII.

THE SCHOOL ON ANEITYUM.

I MAY here state, once for all, that, while I am describing what occurred on my own side of the island, I am virtually describing Mr. Geddie's also; for the work on the two sides of the island was conducted on the same principles, and the results accomplished were much the same; save that, when we arrived on Aneityum the mission was a good deal farther advanced on Mr. Geddie's side of the island than on the other, as a mission family had always been residing there, and for a considerable time too; whereas there had been no resident mission family on the other side except for a short time. Hence, owing to that, and to Mr. and Mrs. Geddie's longer experience and better acquaintance with the language, for a number of years their side naturally took the lead in the general progress of the mission.

On our arrival at Aneityum, comparing small things with great, we found what might be called a system of National Education hopefully inaugurated. Mr. Geddie had brought with him a small second-hand printing-press, and a small font of half-worn type. He had prepared a primer, a small Catechism, six hymns, and a small selection of Scripture extracts. A school was in operation at Aname, our station; it was conducted by Amosa, a Samoan teacher, his wife, and their daughter. At the end of six months they were removed to Ahaij, and took charge of the district of Anauunjai, where they remained for six years, till they were removed to Niwe, or Savage Island. We had three districts that attended our school at Aname, viz., Ipeke, Aname, and Isav, containing a population of 120. They were nearly all professedly Christian, but only a minority of them attended school. A small number could read a little, and might with difficulty have passed the examination in the reading classes in the Second Standard of the Scottish Educational Code. At first I made no changes; I allowed Amosa and his wife to carry on the school as they had been doing. We met every morning except Saturday and Sabbath for an hour at sunrise, which in summer was from 5.20 to 6.20, and in winter from 6.40 till 7.40. The school was opened with singing and prayer; subsequently I added the reading of a chapter at the opening service. At the close a section of a small first Catechism was read or repeated simultaneously. The rest of the time was spent in teaching them to read. The system followed was the monitorial. As my wife and I were wholly unacquainted with the language, that we might lose no time, I took up a class of fourteen boys in the alphabet, and she took up a class of twelve girls of the same standing. By the time they had mastered the alphabet, we had acquired as much of the language as enabled us to conduct them through the primer. When we arrived at Aneityum Mr. Geddie had completed a translation of Matthew. He next proceeded to translate Mark. At the end of a twelvemonth we resolved to get a gospel printed, and to appeal to our friends to assist us in paying for the same. It was too far to send the manuscript to London; but it was expected that the *John Williams* would be calling on us as she went up to Sydney; and as the second gospel was much shorter than the first, we resolved to have a translation of Mark prepared for the press, and to get it printed in Sydney. This was done. The translation was carried through the press by the Rev. J. P. Sunderland of the Samoan mission; and, considering the circumstances under which it was executed, it was, though not a perfect, yet a highly creditable production, and it gave an immense stimulus to education all over the island.

My plan was this, to make the school at my station as much of a model school as possible, and to aim at education being national, scriptural, free as far as fees were concerned, but compulsory as to attendance, that is to say, so far as moral suasion could compel—and when vigorously applied it can go a long way—very much as we do at home in keeping up the attendance at Sabbath-schools.

When Amosa went to Ahaij the full charge of the school fell into my hands. I then reorganised it; I enrolled the entire population as scholars, and supplied books to all who had none. I divided them into classes. The men sat in the one end of the school and the women in the other. I appointed a monitor to each class of eight or ten scholars. To make the work as light as possible, I had two sets of monitors; these taught week about; and I taught the monitors myself the week they were not teaching, so that they might always keep fully abreast of their scholars. Mrs. Inglis did the same with the women. We also extended education over the whole of my district as fast as possible. Every Sabbath at the close of public worship some of the leading natives came to me, and told me the name or names of any who had come to church that day for the first time. These

THE SCHOOL ON ANEITYUM.

I inserted in my list of names; I also gave them a book, and directed them to attend the nearest school. It was always understood that whenever any one came to church, he had given up heathenism, professed Christianity, and placed himself under missionary instruction. The progress of the work was steady, but not rapid. On one Sabbath there would be two or three new names to be added to the roll; the next there would perhaps be only one; on the third there might be five or six, but scarcely ever more on one Sabbath. But there was hardly ever a Sabbath but there was one or more, till the whole island was Christian. On this point there was a marked difference between the Malays and the Papuans. In Eastern Polynesia, among the Malays, when a chief became Christian, every one belonging to the tribe felt that he must adopt the religion of his chief, and so become Christian. After Mr. Buzacott went to Rarotonga, he was surprised to see such remarkably good attendances at public worship; but his satisfaction was greatly diminished when he found out that it was not their love to the Word of God that brought such crowds to the chapels, but their fear for the commands and threatenings of the chief. But among the Papuans the chiefs have no such power; democracy rules. Hence religion is a personal rather than a tribal affair; every man acts on his own personal responsibility.

As soon as in any land we had six or eight scholars, we got these and their friends to erect a school-house—at first a small grass hut—and I appointed a teacher to them, generally a husband and his wife. Another grass hut was erected for the teacher and his family, and thus another district school was called into existence. The teacher and his wife met with their scholars every morning, except Saturday and Sabbath, for about an hour. On Sabbath they brought them to church, and held a Sabbath-school in the afternoon; and on Wednesday afternoon they brought them to the weekly prayer-meeting. When the morning school was dismissed, the natives went all off to their work; they were not a lazy or indolent people, even in their heathen state, and Christianity, as it was embraced, greatly stimulated their industry.

At first our teachers were often persons of very slender attainments in scholarship; the ground had to build the dyke; but we chose, as far as possible, men of character and influence, to whom the people would look up. Sometimes we sent a young lad of more than average ability and attainments to assist the teacher in his tutorial labours. By-and-by I opened an afternoon class for the teachers, their wives, and assistants, so that the whole teaching staff might be kept fairly abreast of their scholars. This was the germ of our Teachers' Institution, which bore good fruit in after days. At first we confined our instruction solely to teaching the natives to read. And during the whole of my missionary life I applied my chief strength, as far as education was concerned, to make the natives good readers. The ability to read, and that easily and correctly, lies at the foundation of all good scholarship. A man can learn nothing from books till he is able to read; and he will never read much till he can read without difficulty. Our primary object was to teach them to read, that they might be able to read the Bible, and learn the will of God and the way of salvation for themselves—the great aim and object of all missionary work. Our first books, owing to the small and worn-out types that we had to employ, were very indistinctly printed; hence the progress of the natives in learning to read was comparatively slow.

The gospel of Mark, printed in Sydney, though in small type, was very clear and distinct, and was thus a great advance on our former books. Subsequently I applied to Mrs. Dr. Symington of Glasgow and other friends at home, and they sent us out a new press and a font of new English type—one of the largest sizes. With this Mr. Geddie printed the gospel of Matthew. When the natives got the gospel printed in this type, their progress was one-half more rapid than it had formerly been. It was quite gratifying to see how fast they learned to read Matthew.

Our first year was educationally one of great success. I opened eight new schools, and had on my list 550 scholars above six years of age. I calculated that there might be about fifty more nominally Christian, but attending no school, and of children under six, belonging to Christian families, probably 100, giving us thus 700 of the population more or less under missionary instruction. But, as we afterwards found that the population on my side of the island at that time was 1900, we had still 1200 natives in all the darkness and degradation of savage heathenism.

Our public worship was held in the Sabbath morning and forenoon, and both services were over before twelve o'clock. Our Sabbath-schools met in the afternoon about three or four o'clock. In the early part of the mission, every Sabbath afternoon I sent deputations of two or three of the most intelligent of the natives to visit each of the schools, to assist the teachers, and encourage the people, and hold a short prayer-meeting at the close. I always accompanied one of these deputations myself, and in this way I visited all the schools in rotation. After we returned home we held the Sabbath-school at our own station, and with that terminated the public services of the Lord's Day. Every night we had worship in our own house with the natives living on our premises, and all those living round about us who chose to come in. We sang a hymn, then read verse about all round, and closed with prayer, thus giving an educational as well as devotional value to the exercise.

We also commenced at this time a Female Industrial School, with the view of elevating the women. Mrs. Inglis, in addition to superintending the female department of the morning and Sabbath-school, held an afternoon class certain days of the week for the female teachers, and subsequently commenced this other school. She took in seven young women to live on the premises. Their parents and friends provided them with food, and she supplied them with clothing, and, in addition to attending all my classes in the Teachers' Institution, she instructed them in sewing, washing and dressing of clothes, and general household work. Two of them were daughters of principal chiefs, and the rest were daughters or relatives of influential families. We had a neatly plastered lime house erected for them, and appointed a man and his wife—one of our best couples—to live with them, and be responsible for their behaviour. The average number accommodated was from ten to sixteen. This Institution was kept up all the twenty-five years that we lived on the island. Almost every young woman on our side of the island was for a longer or shorter period in this school, and the results were most beneficial. In after years the most of our teachers' wives were drawn out of these young women's classes. In learning to read, men and women, boys and girls, were about equally expert; in writing and arithmetic, the men and boys excelled, but in committing to memory, the women and girls were by far the best. For the first twelve years after we joined the mission we had the four Gospels, the Acts, and the Epistles, from Galatians to Philemon inclusive; also Genesis, Exodus, Jonah, and the historical portion of Daniel, each bound up as a separate book as they were successively printed. We had thus a new book on an average once a year; and the more advanced scholars had fully mastered the one book before the other appeared. One of the exercises in the Sabbath-school was to repeat the portions of Scripture they had committed to memory during the week. In this exercise the women and girls greatly excelled. A number of the younger women and girls in Mrs. Inglis's class not only learned to read one book before another was printed, but also to commit each of them to memory. On one occasion a lady in Paisley sent out a piece of cloth to be made into a dress, and given as a prize to the woman who excelled in committing Scripture to memory. Mrs. Inglis prescribed as the task for competition the first six chapters of the Acts. But instead of one she had six who repeated these chapters, every one of them without missing a word; and she had to provide six dresses instead of one.

We went on, year by year, covering the island with schools, till I had twenty-eight on my side of the island, all fully equipped. At first the school-houses were merely grass huts; but by-and-by these were all superseded by beautiful lime houses, plastered and whitewashed; also a teachers' house and a house containing two small rooms, for the missionary when he visited the place, and in which he might either stay all night or take a meal, as he might require. Every native was within a mile of a school, and was supplied with all the necessary books. For the first fifteen years of the mission they were supplied with books gratis, till the New Testament was all printed, and came out in one volume strongly bound in calf. After that they paid for all their books;—they paid in all £1400 for books, and all by arrowroot, prepared and contributed by themselves, but disposed of for them by the missionaries. But while we gave them their books for nothing, we did not give them away indiscriminately. We instituted a thorough system of something like competitive examination. We never gave a scholar a new book till he had thoroughly mastered the old one. In the early part of the mission I visited all my schools once a quarter, on weekdays. When the schools increased I was able to visit them only once in the half-year, and finally only once in the year. I examined every scholar, and gave a new book to every one who could read the old one, but to no one else. To be able to read the old book was the one and sole condition of obtaining a new one; and as I examined every scholar myself, there was no chance of favouritism, and no danger of injustice. The system wrought well. At first, when a large proportion of our scholars were advanced in years and could not see well, and hence were not able to distinguish the letters, they learned to repeat the words by rote, and when I would ask them at the examinations for new books, if they could read, one and another would say, "I can read the words, but I cannot read the letters!" They came to know the words from their appearance, or their length, or their position on the line or on the page. In short, they learned in this way to repeat the sentence. And as our primers were for the most part made up of choice texts of Scripture—doctrinal and practical—they thus committed to memory important portions of the Bible, even although they did not know the letters; and they learned them all the easier, that they could see the words in the book. It was like the Egyptians reading hieroglyphics, or Belzoni deciphering the Rosetta stone.

There was another peculiarity in reading that sprang up at the beginning of the mission. Amosa, the Samoan teacher, and his wife were diligent and conscientious in their efforts to teach the natives to read, but although they could read their own language well, the Aneityumese was so different from the Samoan that they had very considerable difficulty in learning to read it. Hence, when they were teaching the alphabet and the primer to the natives, they kept the right end of the book to themselves, and held the side of the book to the scholars. In this way all the natives whom they taught to read kept always the side of the book to them when reading, and read, not as we do, across the page and along the line, but from what was to them the top of the line to the bottom; and so inveterate had the practice become, that some of them continued to read in this way as long as they lived.

The teaching of writing we began on slates. But after we got our Teachers' Institution, which was fully fitted up with desks and furnished with all necessary appliances, we introduced writing with paper and ink. Arithmetic was a more serious undertaking; we had not only to teach them how to form figures—for they were without figures as well as without letters—but we had to teach them the English names of the numerals. They counted by fives, not by tens, as we do. They counted their fingers up to five, then said *nikmak*, or *my hand*, for five. They then said "my hand and one" for six, "my hand and two" for seven, and so on till they came to ten, and then they held up their ten digits, and said, "my two hands." They repeated the same process on their ten toes, and then said "my two hands and my two feet" for twenty. All beyond was "many, many," or "a great many," &c. To teach arithmetic with this vocabulary was impossible. Our first practical want was to express the names of the chapters and verses in the Gospels. The twenty-sixth chapter and the seventieth verse of Matthew would have run thus—"My two hands and my two feet, and my hand and one chapter, and my two hands and my two feet, also my two hands and my two feet, and again my two hands and my two feet, and my two hands verse of Matthew." We saw that we could teach arithmetic only by adopting the English names of the numerals, and hence, as far as arithmetic was concerned, we taught them to speak English. One way of teaching them was this. Every morning after the school was opened I stood up and counted the scholars, and made the whole school count them simultaneously after me, thus: I pointed to the first scholar and called out *one*, and the whole school shouted out *one* after me. I then pointed to the next and called out *two*, and the whole school shouted out *two* after me; I did the same with *three*, and so on till every scholar was counted, and the whole school followed me till I had finished. This process I repeated morning by morning for years in all our schools, till these English numbers were as familiar to every native as their mother-tongue. For a considerable time we gave special attention to instructing them in notation and numeration, till they were somewhat familiar with the names and forms of the figures and their combinations; afterwards we proceeded to the four simple rules. When we got the whole New Testament in one volume, to repeat the books in their order, and find out book, chapter, and verse, was at first a formidable task. But by daily teaching and constant

THE SCHOOL ON ANEITYUM.   85

practice, by-and-by a good many of the younger scholars became very expert in finding out the places, when book, chapter, and verse were named. At first we used only the cardinal numbers. They had only three ordinal numbers, viz., first, middle, and last. These always reminded me of Isaac Ambrose's famous treatise entitled, "First, Middle, and Last Things." When they were tolerably well grounded in the cardinal numbers, I tried to initiate them into the use of the ordinal; but, simple as it appears to us, it was very difficult for them to understand the difference between one, two, three, and first, second, and third, between ten men and the tenth man, between the twelfth chapter and the fifteenth verse and twelve chapters and fifteen verses. Our object in the Teachers' Institution was to give secondary or middle, rather than what might be called higher, education; to secure the greatest amount of education possible for the greatest available number. We wished to raise up a large number of native agents moderately qualified, to act as teachers to their fellow-countrymen, who should instruct them in the art of reading, so as to make them able to read the Bible; and not a select number to be specially educated to act as pastors, or for teaching the higher departments of an educational curriculum. The education that we required for our teachers was a totally different education from that required in India, in South Africa, or even in Samoa. Dr. Duff's Institution in Calcutta was eminently suited for the requirements of India. Dr. Stewart's at Lovedale for South Africa, and Dr. Turner's at Malua for Samoa. But we could not have had on Aneityum an institution such as those. You cannot establish a national university in an isolated country village. It cannot be supported by the village, and it is not required by the wants of the villagers. For their own mental, moral, and spiritual improvement, the natives cannot be too well educated; but for professional objects their education cannot be raised above a certain point. The means of acquiring a high education cannot be obtained; and even should such an education be acquired, there is no scope for the exercise of such attainments. The language of Aneityum is spoken only on one island, and hence they are shut up "within a single reef," as John Williams would have said. Besides providing a permanent staff of fifty teachers and their wives for our own island, at one time or another, and for longer or shorter periods, we sent away as many to the other islands, to assist the missionaries, or prepare the way for them. But it was not chiefly as evangelists or teachers that they were valuable; but as house-builders, boatmen, cooks, nurses, household servants, goatherds, and general helps all round; but the better their Christian character, the greater their Scriptural knowledge, and the more advanced their general civilisation, the more helpful did they prove to the missionaries in introducing the Gospel among the other islands. At first Mr. Geddie and I arranged that he should take charge of the printing-press, and that I should carry on the Teachers' Institution; but by-and-by, owing to various circumstances, we could not carry out this plan as we intended. Among other reasons, the supply was not equal to the demand, and Mr. and Mrs. Geddie had to undertake the higher education as well, and supply a native agency both for their own side of the island and also for other mission stations. I conducted this institution for two hours every afternoon, four days in the week, for two sessions of four months each annually. The institution was always popular and well attended. It was as well attended, if not better, the last year I was on the island than it had ever been. Including a junior division of promising boys and girls, the number on the list was nearly ninety. But what could that do to raise up a high scholarship from the very lowest strata of an ignorant and degraded section of humanity?

Biologists tell us that there are two things necessary to the development of life: there must be the organism and the environment. The growth of the organism depends upon the environment. In nature these invariably correspond with the result contemplated, or the effect intended to be produced. In his famous Elegy Written in a Country Churchyard, Gray brings out the same idea. Among the "rude forefathers of the hamlet" there slept what had been the organisms, the embryoes, of patriots, poets, statesmen, and warriors; at least, perhaps, there was a "village Hampden," a "mute, inglorious Milton," a "Cromwell guiltless of his country's blood." But they were all undeveloped, the organism was there, but the environment was awanting. Their lot forbade, and hence their destiny was obscure. We too on Aneityum had men who, had circumstances been favourable, would doubtless have been equal to Narayan Sheshadra for their powerful platform oratory or their fervid, persuasive pulpit eloquence. But we had not the educational appliances necessary for developing such talents, where they might have existed; and we had not the needful arena for exercising such acquirements when they might have been developed. Hence, had Gray been our poet laureate, he might have found on our little island representatives of all the classes immortalised in his world-renowned Elegy; and our Teachers' Institution, like his country village, must remain content with producing scholars equal to the requirements of the place and the times,—with sending forth men whose utmost attainments in literature is the knowledge of the three R's, and to teach the same to their fellow islanders, or to act as hewers of wood and drawers of water to missionaries on other parts of the group; and who, having served God in their day and generation, by such humble ministration, will be accepted of the Lord for their labours, and will receive the commendation of their Master, for doing what they could, and maintaining the "noiseless tenor of their way."

CHAPTER IX.

THE BIBLE ON ANEITYUM.

The Sabbath being a recognised institution on Aneityum, the next great work was to give them the Bible in their own language. The work of translation was like the mustard-seed in the parable. From a very small beginning it grew, grew steadily, and at last rapidly, till the people read the whole Bible in their own tongue in which they were born. When finished—printed, bound, and placed in their hands—it was the fifty-eighth complete printed translation of the Bible to be found in the whole world—the second complete translation of the Bible executed by a mission wholly Presbyterian; the first having been made by the missionaries of the United Presbyterian Church in Old Calabar.

Our translations at first were confined to single verses, then to single parables, then to single chapters, then to single gospels, and other single books; then to the New Testament, and finally to the whole Bible. But it may be interesting to give some details of the progress of the work. It was executed under the auspices, and at the expense, of the British and Foreign Bible Society. They laid down the conditions, and bore all the expenses of printing and binding it, and also made a liberal allowance for translating it. When the New Testament was finished, the Society gave to the Presbyterian

Church of Nova Scotia and to the Reformed Presbyterian Church of Scotland £250 each, with the express desire that the services of the translators should be handsomely recognised. This was done; Mr. Geddie and I were allowed £100 each, Mrs. Geddie and Mrs. Inglis received £20 each, and £10 were given to Williamu. When the Old Testament was finished, the Society allowed £600 to the Free Church of Scotland, with which the Reformed Presbyterian Church was now united. £100 of this was given to me as a honorarium for translation and editorial work. They also allowed £100 to the Presbyterian Church of Nova Scotia for the first half of the Pentateuch, edited by Mr. (at that time Dr.) Geddie, and printed in Melbourne. After these payments the copyright belonged to the Society.

The principles on which translations are conducted by the Bible Society are these. They must be satisfied that the translators are orthodox, and that they will translate honestly, and that they possess sufficient scholarship for doing the work in a satisfactory manner. They also maintain an editorial superintendent—one of the best linguists they can secure—who carefully examines every translation, and who, by every available test, satisfies himself that the version is correct. The translations of the New Testament must be all made from the *Textus Receptus*—the Received Text—or the Authorised English Version, or the Marginal Readings of the Authorised Version. The translations of the Old Testament must be from Van Der Hooght's Hebrew Text, or the Authorised Version, or the Marginal Readings of the Authorised Version. The translator may choose from any one of these readings, where they differ, but he must follow no other readings. He may consult as many other versions as he

THE BIBLE ON ANEITYUM. 91

pleases, and express himself in whatever words he may think proper, provided his meaning is fully borne out by one or other of these three authorities respectively. We found it often of great advantage to consult other versions, especially English and South Sea ones. Our difficulties with respect to idiom and modes of expression were often very much the same as those felt by our brethren in other missions, and we thus saw how they had overcome the same difficulties. Other versions, too, often suggested easier and more idiomatic forms of expression than these authorised readings supplied. Twenty-five years ago I had an opportunity of reading a correspondence which had passed between a South Sea missionary and the Foreign Secretary of the Bible Society some fifty years ago now. The missionary was complaining about the restricted and confined conditions prescribed by the Bible Society to their translators, and pleaded hard that they should be allowed to exercise a discretionary power, to select readings from a wider range, as they might see fit; that in the New Testament they might select, say from Griesbach, Scholz, the Latin Vulgate, Boothroyd, and others. The answer from the Bible-House was rather curt and cavalier-like. The Secretary wrote to the effect that they had adopted these rules for security's sake; they knew those readings, and all that could be said for and against them; but they were not always quite sure if their translators had the ability, the scholarship, and the skill necessary for selecting other and better readings, and they thought it was safer to retain the present version till a new recension was made by scholars in whom the Churches had the fullest confidence; and that those versions of the Greek and English New Testament which, for nearly two hundred and fifty years, had satisfied the whole of the English-speaking people on both sides of the Atlantic, and on both sides of the globe, if carefully and accurately translated into their respective languages, might, he thought, be quite sufficient for the untutored savages of Polynesia, whose Christianity was but of yesterday and their Biblical knowledge in its very infancy. The translator prudently made no reply.

The first gospel that we printed was Mark. It was printed in Sydney. We selected Mark because it was the shortest, and we were eager to give the natives a complete gospel. Mr. Geddie had translated Matthew before our arrival on the island. But after we had finished Mark, he was so satisfied that the translation of Matthew could be greatly improved that he translated it anew, and I assisted in the revision of it. We had now got a new press and a new font of English type, and Mr. Geddie, who had learned to print before he left Nova Scotia, printed it on the island. This large type facilitated the acquisition of the art of reading amazingly among the natives. Our next gospel was Luke, the manuscript of which we sent home, and the translation was printed by the Bible Society in London, also in English type. When I speak of English type I do not mean Roman letters in which all English books are printed, but the large type known among printers by that name, as distinct from longprimer and other sizes. It is one of the largest types used for printing the Society's Bibles, the largest used by them being double pica. We next had John's Gospel, which was printed on the island. Next came the Acts of the Apostles, and then the Epistles of Paul from Galatians to Philemon inclusive. Each of these portions was bound up as a separate book, making six in all. We now began preparations for the print-

THE BIBLE ON ANEITYUM. 93

ing of the entire New Testament. The *John Williams* was to leave the island on her return to London in the end of 1859, to take home the missionaries' children and undergo repairs. It was agreed at first that Mr. and Mrs. Geddie should go home on furlough with their family, and take the translation of the New Testament with them, and get it printed by the British and Foreign Bible Society. Afterwards family considerations prevented this arrangement from being carried out. Their infant child was considered too young to be exposed to the perils of such a long and tedious voyage; and it was finally arranged that my wife and I should accompany the *John Williams*, and carry the New Testament through the press. The New Testament was all translated; but we considered that it would take Mr. Geddie and myself all our spare time for a twelvemonth to revise and correct the translation, so as to have it fit for the press. But the sailing of the *John Williams* belonged to the same category as Time and Tide that will wait for no one. To meet this difficulty, however, we took a native—Williamu—home with us. We were seven months on the voyage; we spent three and a half months between Aneityum and Tahiti, visiting all the stations of the London Missionary Society, and three and a half months more between Tahiti and London. Williamu and I read over and corrected about the half of the MS. during the voyage. On our arrival in London I was placed under the direction of the Editorial Superintendent of the Bible Society's translations, the late Rev. T. W. Meller, M.A., Rector of Woodbridge, in Suffolk. He had previously carried the gospel of Luke through the press, and had so analysed that gospel as to form a lexicon and grammar of the Aneityumese language, as far as Luke supplied the vocables; and he felt no difficulty in making out the sense of the translation, so as to satisfy himself that the meaning of the original was faithfully given. He was a man of remarkable linguistic gifts, an able and accurate scholar, perfectly familiar with every textual difficulty, fully abreast of the most advanced Biblical scholarship of the day, and a very hard-working, painstaking man. In addition to superintending the Aneityumese New Testament, he was editing a version of the Bible in modern Greek, and superintending a version of the Fiji Bible, and also one in the language of Madagascar. He was a thoroughly orthodox theologian, and very pronounced in his views of inspiration. He held strictly by what is usually called verbal inspiration— not only the words, but the very letters were to be conserved. He quoted Paul's words in support of his view, Gal. 3. 16: "He saith not, And to *seeds*, as of many; but as of one, And to thy *seed*, which is Christ." Here the sense is fixed not by the use of one word, but by the use of one letter. Holding these views of inspiration, he was extremely particular in seeing that in every translation there should be brought out the original, the whole of the original, and nothing but the original; which had its dangers as well as its advantages; it was apt to lead to an over-literal version. Mr. Meller was so impressed with high views of inspiration, and the importance of bringing out in the translation the very mind of God's Holy Spirit, that he was in danger of overlaying the idiom of the Aneityumese with the idiom of the Original; just as Mr. Spurgeon is reported to have said of the revisers of the New Testament, that they have spoiled their English with their Greek. But I had no difficulty in holding my own with him. While he was an exact scholar, he was a very sensible man, a thoroughly Christian gentleman, kind and considerate; he had no crotchets, and could always see the force of an argument. He often said to me, "My only wish is to help, I have no wish to dictate; and in every doubtful case, in connection with the Aneityumese language, the decision lies with yourself." But our version was very much improved by his supervision. He had superintended so many versions, especially South Sea versions, that he knew all the difficulties and all the difficult passages that met the translators, also the true principles by which translations ought to be carried through; so that he was a safe guide and a wise counsellor. I was greatly helped by his valuable suggestions, and acquired from him much important knowledge on the principles of translation, which was of great use to me in translating and editing the Old Testament, as well as the New. I was always certain that if my renderings were satisfactory to Mr. Meller they would stand the test of all other criticism. Of this I had a satisfactory proof at the meeting of the Free Church General Assembly in Glasgow in 1878. The then Lord Provost of Glasgow, Sir William Collins, held a *Conversazione*, at which he gave a semi-official reception to the members of Assembly and their friends. As part of the entertainment he had borrowed from the British and Foreign Bible Society, and brought down from London, a copy of every known version of the Scriptures. In that list was a copy of our Aneityumese New Testament, to which, during the evening, I called the attention of the Rev. Dr. Brown, Principal of the Free Church College in Aberdeen, and one of the company of the New Testament revisers. The printing and binding were all that could be desired; and then, with the ease of an expert, he selected some half a dozen of testing texts, and began by saying, "How have you rendered this one? What is the meaning you have given to that one? And what is the translation you have made of this other one?" Happily in every case we found that he accepted our rendering, as in accordance with the latest utterances of the highest sacred criticism.

There are two ways of translating out of one language into another, viz., the literal and the idiomatic, the rendering of word for word or idiom for idiom. Dr. Robert Young of Edinburgh, in his translation of the Bible into English, carried out the principle of literal translation more fully than any translator I have seen. Moses and the Prophets are made to speak in English words, but their idioms are all Hebrew; his readers are taken over to the ancient seers, and allowed to hear them speaking to the Jews in the idiom of the Hebrew language—an interesting and profitable exercise to the select few; but it sounds barbarous, harsh, and to a great extent unintelligible, to those whom the Apostle calls the unlearned. Boothroyd's English translation is on the opposite principle, and is, perhaps, the most idomatic translation that we possess. The Authorised Version is between the two. In our Aneityumese translation we have followed the idiomatic rather than the literal, and rendered idiom by idiom, rather than word by word; although, like the Authorised, we have often retained the Hebrew idiom when it did not obscure the sense, as seeing with the eyes, hearing with the ears, and walking with the feet, &c.; although the natives, like ourselves, speak only of seeing, hearing, and walking, without any reference to the organs by which these actions are performed. This fuller form of expression gives a greater freshness to the style, without obscuring the sense. Instead of saying, with the Authorised Version and Dr. Young, "Thou shalt not uncover," &c., we have followed Boothroyd, and say, "Thou shalt not marry so and so," which is the true meaning of the expression. Again, blood, the shedding of blood, the pouring out of blood, the sprinkling of blood, &c., are ever-recurring words in connection with the sacrificial system of the Israelites, and they pass over from the old economy to the new, and supply vocables for expressing the nature and efficacy of the atoning death of Christ. His blood becomes equivalent to His atonement. Blood has no such meaning in the language of Aneityum. It never means life. But death, the death of Christ, and His being killed or slain as a sacrifice for the sins of men, are expressions quite plain and intelligible to the Aneityumese. In our translation we have endeavoured to make the Hebrew writers speak as they would have done had they been Aneityumese speaking to natives of Aneityum. For example, the figurative has almost always to be changed into the literal, and the abstract into the concrete. The Hebrew writers address, or speak of, the inhabitants of a land, or of a city, by the title of daughter, as daughter of Sion, daughter of Jerusalem, daughter of Tyre, daughter of Babylon, &c.; or they use simply the name of the city, or the country, for the people, as O Jerusalem, O Judah, O Israel. We have to drop the poetry of such expressions, and translate them into plain prose, and speak of the people, or the inhabitants, of Judah, of Sion, and of Jerusalem. Again, "They shall fall by the *sword.*" As the Aneityumese have no swords, this sentence would be meaningless if translated literally. But when we say, "They shall be killed in war," the expression is both intelligible and forcible. "To your tents, O Israel," we render, "To your homes, O men of Israel." The Hebrew writers speak of a righteous man, a wicked man, a rich man, and a poor man, when they mean the class as a whole, not a single individual. The Aneityumese never speak in this way. If we rendered these passages in the singular, they would understand them as referring to an individual, not to a class. In the Scriptures, especially in the laws of Moses, and in the prophetical books, there is a frequent interchange both of the number and of the person, the singular for the plural, and the third personal pronouns for the first. The Aneityumese have no such transitions; hence, in order to prevent misapprehension, we have often to render the singular by the plural, and the plural by the singular, when such is the evident meaning. The singular would, no doubt, be more forcible to a Hebrew, but it would be bewildering to a native of Aneityum. A Hebrew would perfectly understand the singular for the plural, a native of Aneityum would not. For instance, in the Lamentations of Jeremiah, the prophet, to give a more vivid description of the misery and wretchedness of the nation, concentrates, to a large extent, the sufferings of the people upon himself, and uses the first person singular; whereas, in our translation, to prevent mistake, we have used the first person plural. Jeremiah says, "*I am the man* that hath seen affliction;" in the Aneityumese translation it is rendered, "*We are the people* who have seen affliction." Paul often uses the plural when he is speaking simply of himself, as in 1 Thess. iii. 1, "*We* thought it good to be left at Athens alone." Conybeare and Howson, in their Life of the Apostle, when translating his Epistles, have rendered the idiomatic Greek into equally idiomatic English, and made uch plurals all singulars, and says, "*I* thought it good," &c. We have done the same, because the Aneityumese have no royal, or editorial, ·or oratorical *we* for the first person singular. *I* means *I*, and *we* means *we*, and neither more nor less, and *you* never means *thou*. The first point in connection with the use of the pronouns is to ascertain distinctly the meaning of the passage, and then select the proper pronoun. There are four numbers in the personal pronouns, the singular, the dual, the trial, and the plural; as *I*, *we two*, *we three*, and *we all*. It requires four at least to form the plural, and wherever a plural has to be translated, the context must be carefully examined to see how many persons are being spoken of. Hence in the very first chapter of Genesis we have to assume the doctrine of the Trinity to be true, and to say not, "Let *us* make man in *our* image, after *our* likeness," but "Let *us three* make man in the image of *us three*, after the likeness of *us three*;" and in Genesis xi. 7, not, "Go to, let *us* go down," but "Go to, let *us three* go down." If we had used the plural, as in English, and not the trial number, it would have implied that there were at least four persons here taking counsel, and hence that there were at least four persons in the Godhead. In the first person, dual, trial, or plural there is both an inclusive and an exclusive form, both in the pronoun and in the verb *to be*. *We two* has two forms, viz., *akaijau*, "you and I," the inclusive, including the person spoken to; and *aijumrau*, "he or she and I," the exclusive, excluding the person spoken to. Hence the translator and the preacher have to be very careful in the use of the inclusive and exclusive plural. If, in addressing God in prayer, the speaker says, "We are all sinners," if he uses the inclusive pronoun, *akaija*, "we all," he includes God among the number, which would be blasphemy. If in preaching he says *aijama*, " we all," exclusive, he would mean, " we missionaries are sinners, but not including you natives." To be correct he must reverse the order. He will then be understood, and his words will be appreciated.

Some people are apt to think that low, degraded savages like the Papuans can have no right language at all; their speech must be merely a kind of gibberish, having neither correct sense, sound, nor grammar. Quite recently the Anglican Bishop of Western Australia issued an appeal for funds, to assist in educating the blacks in his diocese through the medium of the English language, on the ground that their language was not adapted for conveying to their minds religious instruction. The editor of the *Sydney Presbyterian*, himself a missionary for twenty-three years, and an expert in native languages, very pertinently asked, " Has the Bishop tried the experiment fully? Is there a white man in the colony who really knows the language of these blacks? Let them set to and acquire a knowledge of the language or languages spoken by the natives, and they will doubtless find that it is a vehicle capable of conveying to the native mind a clear conception of the truths of the Bible." Such, at least, has been our experience on Aneityum and other islands of the New Hebrides. When the missionaries went first to Aneityum, in 1848, they found a language having no affinity whatever to the Malay, or to any language known to them, floating indistinctly, as they thought, on the lips of the natives. There was no literature; not a word of it had ever been written or made visible to the eye; but they began at once to reduce it to writing. They formed an alphabet; they found out the meaning of the words; they discovered their true pronunciation; and they ascertained the grammatical structure of the language; and the result is, that we have a language at our command both copious and exact, capable of giving utterance to every thought and every idea, every want and every wish, known to those to whom it is their mother-tongue. The words are all as precise in their meaning as if they had been defined by Johnson or Jamieson. The grammar is as regular and uniform as if it had been formed by Murray, Lennie, or M'Culloch; while the pronunciation is as exact as if it had been settled and phonographed by Walker, Webster, or Worcester. We have felt no special difficulty in finding words to express every idea contained in the Bible, in both the Old and the New Testaments, also in the Pilgrim's Progress and the Shorter Catechism. We have had now and again to use circumlocutions, but we have had to introduce very few new words. It is matter for thankfulness to know that in the Aneityumese language God had provided a vehicle by means of which His whole inspired Word can be fully, clearly, intelligibly, and exactly communicated to the inhabitants of that remote and obscure island, although the idiom and form of their language are in many points different from that of Hebrew, or Greek, or Latin, or English. This is clearly seen from the fact that the natives value the Bible. They pay for it; they read it daily; they have an intelligent understanding of its meaning; they accept it as God's own Word, and believe it as such; and it has become largely the guiding principle of their lives.

When we say that there are twenty languages spoken in the New Hebrides, and a hundred languages in the whole of Melanesia, that the one will require twenty Bibles, and the whole will require five times that number before every individual among them can hear or read the wonderful works of God in his own tongue—when we say this, people hold up their hands in amazement, and say, "Why, that is equal to a fourth or a fifth of all the languages of the world. Is there no one language that you can discover that would be understood by them all?" When we assure them that no such language can be found, they then say, "But can you not teach them all to speak English?" And when we assert this to be impossible, they look upon the case as hopeless. But I meet the difficulty in this way, and say to them, "We have hitherto had so few translations of the Bible, that the labour of producing one is no doubt greatly exaggerated. It has been only men of gigantic intellect, like Wickliffe, or Tyndale, or Luther, that were deemed capable of undertaking such a task." But if Dr. Geddie and myself, assisted to some extent in the Old Testament by Mr. Copeland—if two average missionaries, during the length of an average missionary lifetime, after discharging an average amount of other missionary duties, have given to the natives of one island a complete translation of the Bible, and given to the world a dictionary of 5000 words and a grammar of the language; have not only given the natives the Bible, but have taught them to read it; and, what is perhaps more difficult, have succeeded in teaching, or rather training them to pay for it,—if we have done this, surely any other two average missionaries may do the same thing for the people speaking another language; and surely, in these times of enterprise and activity, the same effort may be nineteen times repeated; and then, as far as the New Hebrides is concerned, the work is completed. But the work is going on; eight different translations are in progress just now, and eight more grammars and dictionaries are being prepared. Moreover, four other missions are at present engaged in the evangelisation of the Papuan race, viz., the American Board of Foreign Missions, the London Missionary Society, the Wesleyan Missionary Society, and the Church of England Melanesian Mission; if each of these, as they are well able to do, supplies twenty translations of the Bible, as well as our own Presbyterian Mission, the work would be finished. It is therefore not only possible, but it is probable, yea, highly probable, all but morally certain, that at no distant day a complete translation of the Bible will exist in every language spoken in Western Polynesia. Let the Churches arise in their strength, and the work is done.

The process by which we produced the Aneityumese Bible was this. Saturday was the day which I generally appropriated to translating, and if I could not say, *Nulla dies sine versu*, "No day without a verse," I could say, to a large extent, "No week without a chapter." After I had been six months on the island I began to translate Genesis. At first I got only a few verses done, and in a very imperfect manner. But week by week, and month by month, the work became easier. After I had finished Genesis I translated Luke. Our mode of proceeding was this. The first duty of a translator is to ascertain and fix upon the meaning of the author. For this end I read the original text, versions, and commentaries, and all helps that I could lay my hands on. Then I translated the original into the Aneityumese as I best could. Then I brought into my study one or two of the most intelligent of the natives, and read the passage to them, verse by verse, asking them if this word or that sentence was correct Aneityumese; and such-and-such being the meaning, was that the best word, or the most suitable expression? or what changes would they suggest? and making every correction that could be thought of.

On the Sabbath morning before church-time, when the people began to assemble, I brought in ten or a dozen of the most intelligent of the natives, and read the portion translated over to them verse by verse, and embodied whatever corrections they might suggest. This was to the natives a kind of Bible lesson, as they necessarily heard a good deal of exposition under circumstances very favourable for being remembered. Subsequently I read it in the church to the whole congregation, following it up with a running commentary—a kind of lecture, after the manner of a Scotch forenoon service in the olden time. I had previously instructed the congregation that, if any of them observed any words incorrectly used, they were to come to me and tell me after the service. And though they were anything but forward to display their critical acumen, yet now and again one and another would come to me, and say, "Misi, would you read over that verse," near the beginning, or the middle, or the end, as the case might be, where such-and-such a word occurs, "I was not sure about it." The verse was read, and the remark would be made, "Oh, it is quite correct; I had not heard it right;" or, "I think such-and-such a word would be better there." When I had embodied the results of all available criticism, I wrote out a clean copy of the translation, and when the book was finished I sent it over to Mr. Geddie, and he went over it all carefully with his pundits, bringing a fresh eye and a new critical apparatus to eliminate remaining errors and secure further improvements. If there were any doubtful passages left, these were marked, and we examined them together when we met. Mr. Geddie did the same with his translations, and finally we read them over together in the hearing of two or three of our best pundits before we said *Imprimatur*. In the case of the New Testament Mr. Meller read over the translation book by book, and sent them back to me. He wrote no fewer than nine hundred pages of note-paper filled with criticisms, which I stitched up into a volume. Williamu and I examined all his suggestions, and approved or rejected as the case required. Finally, besides daily consultations during the whole time, Mrs. Inglis and I went over the entire translation verse by verse, as it was printed. She read the English, and marked every stop. I followed her in the translation, and watched most carefully that nothing was omitted, and that nothing was added. We then reversed the process. I read the translation, and she checked me with the English. To make so many corrections, to revise and revise again, to read the Greek or the Hebrew, the English, and then the Aneityumese, may appear like a work of supererogation. But those who know anything of the work either of translating or editing the Bible will feel no surprise. I once heard the late Dr. Mitchell, Professor of Biblical Criticism in the United Secession Church, say to his class in the Hall, that not one person in a thousand who reads the English Bible has the slightest conception of the labour that has been bestowed upon that book, which they can now buy for a shilling. When I came home in 1860 to carry the New Testament through the press, Mr. Meller gave me a copy of the Greek New Testament, of the Received Text, published by the Bible Society, that I might have an authorised standard to guide me. This Greek Testament had been printed at Cologne, in Germany, and the proof-sheets had been read over in succession by four German professors, so that perfection might be secured. And yet, when Mr. Meller read the book, after it was printed, he found that half a verse had been omitted, viz., the first half of 1 Cor. x. 23. Instead of "All things are lawful for me, but all things are not expedient; all things are lawful for me, but all things edify not," the first half was left out. In the Aneityumese New Testament there are about a quarter of a million of words, and in the whole Bible more than a million. To read over a million of words in a foreign language, and see that not one of them is misspelled, that not a capital is misplaced, and that not a point is omitted, is no easy task. To revise, correct, and edit the whole Bible, under the very exact conditions imposed by the Bible Society, is a very laborious work. Dr. Chalmers, however, says that the most imperfect translation of the Bible that ever was made, if honestly done, will not fail to convey to the reader a knowledge of the way of salvation. We can safely say of ours, that it was honestly made, and executed to the very best of our ability, and that we called to our aid every available help, whether the works of Biblical critics or the living voices of intelligent natives.

The translation of the New Testament was prepared wholly by Mr. Geddie and myself. I translated Luke, 1st and 2nd Corinthians, Hebrews, and the Revelation; Mr. Geddie translated all the rest. I revised, corrected, and edited the whole, with the assistance of Williamu. Of the Old Testament Mr. Geddie translated the last four books of the Pentateuch, Joshua, Judges, 1st and 2nd Kings, 1st and 2nd Chronicles, Ezra, Nehemiah, the Psalms, the historical portion of Daniel, and Jonah. Mr. Copeland translated Ruth, Esther, the prophetical chapters of Daniel, and all the twelve minor prophets except Jonah. I translated Genesis, 1st and 2nd Samuel,

Job, Proverbs, Ecclesiastes, Song of Solomon, Isaiah, Jeremiah, Lamentations, and Ezekiel. Mr. Geddie by mistake translated Job after I had finished it, and I by a mistake also translated Judges; and as the latter half of Mr. Geddie's translation of Leviticus was lost after his death in some printing office in Melbourne, I had also to translate that. But in revising I compared both these translations, and they were improved thereby. Mr. Geddie hastily revised the first half of the Old Testament. Mr. Copeland revised the whole. I had to revise, correct, and edit the whole of the Old Testament as well as the New. Mr. Geddie brought out an edition of the Book of Psalms printed in Nova Scotia. This edition was used up before the Old Testament was printed. He also edited the first half of the Pentateuch in Melbourne before his death, which was put in circulation some years before the Old Testament was published.

After the Old Testament was finished, the Religious Tract Society published a volume for us, which I edited, and which consisted of the first part of the Pilgrim's Progress (abridged), a Selection of Psalms and Hymns, a First Catechism, and the Westminster Shorter Catechism. The "Pilgrim" was translated by Mrs. Geddie, and revised and printed by Mr. Geddie at the Mission Press. This was a second edition that I revised and edited. Mrs. Geddie had a great command of the colloquial. The natives used to say, "She spoke just like an Aneityum woman," which was the highest praise they could bestow upon her. Hence she rendered Bunyan's idiomatic Saxon into scarcely less idiomatic Aneityumese. The "Pilgrim" was a favourite book with the natives. The First Catechism was prepared by Mr. Geddie, and passed through a good many editions on the island. The most of the Psalms and Hymns were prepared by Mr. Geddie and myself, a few by Mr. Powell, Mr. Copeland, and Mr. Annand respectively. I was the sole translator of the Shorter Catechism, but it was all revised by Mr. Copeland. Both the Bible and the volume published by the Tract Society were clearly and beautifully printed in large type, so as to be easily read, and they were all strongly and tastefully bound in calf, so as to wear well. One volume would last as long as three bound in the usual way. The New Testament in one volume cost four shillings. The Old Testament was bound in two volumes. The price was five shillings each. The other book cost three shillings each copy.

When I came home in 1877 to carry the Old Testament through the press, Mr. Meller had gone to his rest and his reward, after eighteen years of valuable labours for the Society. Another Editorial Superintendent was occupying his place, viz., the Rev. W. Wright, A.M. (now also D.D.), who had been for ten years a missionary to the Jews in Damascus, from the Presbyterian Church of Ireland. Dr. Wright is an eminent Hebrew scholar, and has greatly distinguished himself by his researches and discoveries in connection with the Hittite Inscriptions. My relations with him were in every way as satisfactory as they had been with Mr. Meller. Dr. Wright also rendered very important service both to the Bible Society and to our mission, by keeping the expenses of the printing down to the lowest point. The printing for the Society was all done by contract, and the competition kept the prices down; but the correction of the proof-sheets was charged by time. The temptation to the printers was this—to give in low estimates for the printing, so as to secure the work, and to make up the loss by charging high for the corrections. Dr. Wright and one of the Foreign Secretaries saw the danger to the finances from this arrangement, and they took every necessary precaution to prevent either carelessness or overcharging on the part of the printers. Printing in a foreign language is so much more difficult than in English, that the price paid is about double. In English the sense and the words guide the printer, so as to prevent mistakes; but in a foreign language the printer knows nothing about the spelling of the words; he must follow the MS.; he has nothing to guide him but the words; and however carefully written, it is difficult to avoid mistakes; c, e, i, l, t, m, iu, ni, n, u, w, &c., are all frequently interchanged in the printing. The best way is to keep two or three of the most skilful printers at one work, whose eyes soon acquire the quickness of experts. This is what is generally done. Instead of this, however, our printers set on a party of unskilled ordinary compositors, and the consequence was, that the number of the errors was legion; and the corrections were costing more than the original printing, and the proof-sheets had to be corrected not once, twice, or thrice, but six, seven, or eight times, before they could pass.

On seeing this Dr. Wright caused me to make out a list of the errors on every page, and after the first proof was corrected, to keep a distinct list of the changes made by myself, and another of the errors made by the printers. The rigid supervision exercised by Dr. Wright soon reduced the printers' errors to a minimum, the workmen became so much more careful. The result was that, comparing the price paid for the printing of the Old Testament with that paid for the New, there was a saving effected in the printing of the Old Testament of nearly £100.

It may not be out of place here to add a word about the Bible-House. It is one of the wonders of London. It was the first place of interest to which we took our visitors while we lived in the metropolis.

In that house there resided a quiet, unostentatious power, not surpassed by anything in London; a moral power, silent as the falling dew, and gentle as the still, small voice at Horeb. You enter, but there is nothing to be seen save half a dozen highly respectable looking gentlemen, all sitting at their desks in their respective rooms. But in the depots, in the lower flats, there is an orderly, well-arranged, ceaseless activity going on. Every day in the week, and every week in the year, Sabbath and holidays excepted, ten thousand copies of the whole Bible, or the New Testament, or portions of the Holy Scriptures, were coming into that house, and the same numbers were being sent out, or, in the case of versions printed abroad, were accounted for as passing through that depository; while £700 were daily passing through the treasurer's books. Those ten thousand copies daily, in three hundred and fifty of the principal languages of the world, must exert an influence on the human race, that cannot be calculated, and extending from the mightiest empires in Asia to the tiniest islets in the Southern Ocean.

The next great work in connection with the Bible on Aneityum was the teaching of the natives to read it. But to this I have fully referred when speaking of education; and the third question was, how to get the natives to pay for it. But this I will explain in another chapter, when I treat of the arrowroot. The natives of Aneityum paid to the Bible Society £1200 for the Scriptures, and to the Tract Society £200 for the volume containing the

"Pilgrim," the Selection of Psalms and Hymns, and the Catechisms. They were supplied with all their books gratis at first — with Primers, Catechisms, Hymnals, Scripture Extracts, Gospels, &c.—but they paid in full for the Book of Psalms, the first half of the Pentateuch, and the entire Bible.

In connection with Mr. Meller, I may add a sentence or two about Rev. Aaron Buzacot of Rarotonga, who carried the Rarotongan Bible through the press, under Mr. Meller's superintendence. Mr. Buzacot was an excellent translator, and very highly esteemed by Mr. Meller; and though he was one of the most earnest and conscientious of our South Sea missionaries, yet he was ready-witted and full of quiet, genial humour. Mr. Meller was strong for the uniform rendering of Greek words, and he would say to Mr. Buzacot, "How is it that you use such-and-such a word, or such-and-such an expression, in such a parable in Matthew, but in the corresponding passage in the other Gospels you use a different word, or a different mode of expression? I am quite willing that you take any one of them you think best; but having made your choice, then abide by it." Mr. Buzacot would answer, "Oh, the rendering in Matthew belongs, as we say, to a former dispensation. That was the word we first used, but we found a synonym, and we afterwards used them both. You know that we Dissenters are not like you Churchmen, we are not bound by the Act of Uniformity. We are like King James's Translators, who preferred variety to unvarying sameness." Mr. Meller, like the recent revisers of the New Testament, insisted on the rendering of the same Greek word being always the same, except where the sense was evidently different. On one occasion Mr. Buzacot went to visit one of the English bishops, and see through his palace; but when he arrived, he found that the bishop was from home, and the palace shut up. After a few questions had been asked and answered, the servant said to him, "Who shall I say was calling for his Lordship?" Mr. Buzacot at once answered, "Oh, please say it was the Bishop of Rarotonga." To save his conscience he was using the word bishop in its ancient, not in its modern acceptation; in its Scriptural, not in its Ecclesiastical meaning. When the official heard that the visitor was a bishop, although *in partibus infidelibus*, although in the most distant see, not simply in Christendom, but in Heathendom, his feelings of reverence were so aroused, that he made a bow to the Oriental prelate, as profound as Dr. Samuel Johnson would have made to the Archbishop of Canterbury, and promised the most dutiful obedience to his commands.

I have extended my remarks on this subject to an unusual length, but the translation of the Scriptures is one of the most important parts of a missionary's work. I never felt that the work was secure till the natives had the whole Bible in their hands. The natives felt this to some extent themselves; at least they highly appreciated the printed Word of God. On one occasion one of our elders was addressing the week-day prayer-meeting, when he said, "It is all very well to hear the missionary explain the Word of God to us, but here," he said, holding up the New Testament, "if we forget it, we can read it for ourselves and bring it all back again."

We printed the last volume of the Old Testament first, and sent it out to Aneityum, because they had less knowledge of the prophetical books than of the historical. They got the second volume in 1879, and the first volume in 1881. I was not on the island when the Old Testament was received, nor have I been there since, but I know that its reception must have been much the same as that accorded to the New Testament in 1863 and afterwards. And Mr. Laurie, my successor, bore emphatic testimony in his letters to the delight which the natives evinced when they got the entire Bible. Perhaps I cannot close this chapter better than by making two brief extracts from my reports to the Bible Society for 1865 and 1868. In 1865 I wrote:—" The natives are for the most part reading the New Testament with great diligence, and are advancing steadily both in Scriptural knowledge and Christian character. One-fourth of the entire population have been admitted into church-fellowship, and I have at present on my side of the island a candidate's class of 127. Some may think that our admissions must be very loose when we receive so many; but this is not the case. We rarely admit any one till after a year's instruction and probation. It must also be remembered that every person on the island, above childhood, is reading the Scriptures daily, and hearing them expounded every Sabbath. The Bible is their only book, and Scripture truth is thus kept more constantly before their minds than it can ordinarily be before the minds of most communities. The field is limited in extent, and hence manageable, so that the ordinary appliances for the instruction and evangelisation of the population may be expected, by the blessing of God, to be productive of favourable results. There are two missionaries on the island. We have nearly sixty native teachers; every native is within fifteen minutes' walk of a school, and within about an hour's walk of a place of public worship on the Sabbath. The population, by measles and other causes, has been reduced to about 2100. We visit all the schools twice a year, and hear every examinable person read. As soon as they know the letters, they commence reading some portion of the Scriptures: our education, therefore, is thoroughly Scriptural; and the results may be seen in the striking contrast between this and the adjoining islands, which are still in heathen darkness. All here is peace and quietness; life and property are secure. We may say that we have no crime."

In 1868 I wrote thus:—"It is in a polyglot mission like this that the value of your Society is specially felt. The Word of God, the sword of the Spirit, is our grand weapon of attack for carrying on the war against ignorance, sin, and Satan. The Word of God is the channel through which the Spirit of God operates on the souls of the heathen, and it is only when opened to them in their own tongue that the Word reaches their understanding and conscience, and becomes the instrument of the Spirit's operations. All our missionaries here feel that their first object, whatever labour it may cost them, is to acquire a knowledge of the language of the people among whom they are labouring, and the next is to give them the Word of God in their own tongue. As soon as this is done, but not until then, does the work of evangelisation begin.

"On Aneityum, where almost every person above infancy has the New Testament and the Psalms of David in his hands, the effect of God's Word is strikingly visible. The diligence of the natives in reading the Scriptures privately has been repeatedly noticed by strangers who have visited the islands. There are a few waifs and strays here, as elsewhere, but the population as a whole are being largely influenced by the Word of God. The Sabbath is particularly well observed.

Churches and schools are well attended. One-third of the entire population are fully accredited church members; while peace, quietness, and contentment pervade the whole island. The same process is going on, and the same results are being brought about, in all the other islands occupied by the mission. The leaven of God's Word is beginning—it may be slowly, but still steadily and surely—to leaven the whole mass of heathenism."

CHAPTER X.

THE PULPIT ON ANEITYUM.

BESIDES giving the natives the school, the Sabbath, and the Scriptures, we also, from the beginning, set up public worship among them on Sabbath, giving an outstanding prominence to the preaching of the Gospel. I had four places for public worship on Sabbath on my side of the island—one at the central station, and three at the out-stations. Mr. Geddie had the same on his side of the island. We had two services every Sabbath, with an interval of twenty minutes between them, and a week-day afternoon prayer-meeting. We had no evening service, either on Sabbath or week-days. Evening meetings were not suitable for native arrangements. In summer Sabbath services commenced between eight and nine in the morning, and in winter between nine and ten. Both our services were over before twelve at noon. The Sabbath-school began between three and four in the afternoon. Our public worship was conducted very much in the same way as in Scotland—a lecture at the first diet, and a sermon at the second. Following out the principle enunciated by Mr. David Dickson, minister of Irvine, afterwards professor of theology in Edinburgh University, who used to say, "It is always a good thing to give God's bairns guid blauds of their Father's bread." We always read two chapters of the Bible at each diet of worship—one out of the Old Testament and the other out of the New. For my lecture I generally took the chapter which I had translated during the previous week, or one of the last that Mr. Geddie had translated. This secured a new subject for every Sabbath, and maintained continuous freshness for all our services. At our second diet there was a sermon on some important text. Thus the lecture was the exposition of a chapter, and the sermon was the expounding and enforcing of some Scriptural doctrine or of some Christian duty. Twice in succession I preached through the Shorter Catechism at the rate of a question for each Sabbath. This, with occasional sermons on other subjects, occupied nearly three years for each course. This of itself was a whole body of divinity, containing what Bishop Jeremy Taylor calls the *credenda*, the *agenda*, and the *postulanda*, all that is to be believed, to be done, and to be prayed for, "for the institution of young persons in the Christian religion." When I have spoken in public about my preaching through the Shorter Catechism to the natives, some of my hearers seemed to think that I was not feeding babes in Christ with milk, but with very strong meat. But such seemed, at the same time, to forget that the object of preaching was to make deep and dark things clear and plain. But the question still arises, Is it true that the Shorter Catechism is so deep and mysterious? Is there any exposition of Christian truth extant that is plainer, clearer, or more intelligible? Archbishop Usher said, "It requires all our learning to make things plain." There is a large consensus of opinion to the effect that the Westminster Assembly, for ability and learning, was the greatest of all the Christian councils that had ever been called together, and was therefore, on Usher's principle, the best qualified for preparing a Catechism to fulfil what was their avowed intention in drawing it up, "to be a Directory for catechising such as are of *weaker* capacity." The first draft of the Catechism is now generally understood to have been prepared by the Rev. Herbert Palmer, B.D., Master of Queen's College in Cambridge, and recognised as the best catechiser of his day in England. In these circumstances, one might safely infer *a priori*, what every one who has examined the Shorter Catechism carefully and candidly has found to be true, that it is the plainest, simplest, clearest, easiest, and in every way the best compendium of theology that exists in the English or in any other language, and therefore the very best text-book that any missionary could employ for instructing the young and the ignorant in the knowledge of Divine truth. The other year Mr. Froude, the historian, in one of his addresses, told his audience, that while he was a student at Oxford he had heard scores, perhaps hundreds, of sermons on the power of the Church and the efficacy of the Sacraments, but that he had never heard one on the eighth commandment; and hence, as he thought, true religion was degenerating into forms and ritual, and commercial morality into shams and shoddy. When I read this speech in the islands, I said, "What poor preaching these Universities must supply! How much better off are our poor natives on Aneityum! It is true, they hear nothing about the power of the Church, the sacerdotal character of the clergy, or the mystic efficacy of the Sacraments, yet within four or five short years they heard four sermons on the eighth commandment, and more than forty on the whole decalogue." But the teaching of the Shorter Catechism to native converts is not, as some sections of the secular press would make the world believe, a species of well-meant but sadly misdirected effort; a thing, to say the least of it, to be quietly laughed at. It is happily no innovation in missionary instruction. The agents of the London Missionary Society in the South Seas have translated the Shorter Catechism into two or three of the languages spoken by their converts. The Wesleyans embody the most of the Shorter Catechism into their denominational Catechism, which they have translated into at least three of the languages of the South Seas, for the benefit of their adherents. But a more interesting case than any of these is to be found in the missionary history of the sainted Eliot. In the admirable biographical notice of that distinguished missionary by the Rev. Professor Graham of London, he says, " But Eliot not only exhorted, he catechised, and lodged the Shorter Catechism in the minds of those wild Mohawks and Iroquois. He knew that, in the swampy ground of those Indian minds, solid massive piles of doctrine must be fixed, if any great and lasting building was to rise." Have any of our philosophical *litterateurs* any results to show equal to those of the devoted Eliot? I trow not.

Neither Mr. Geddie nor I were philosophical, or emotional, or impassioned, or sensational preachers. If anything could be said to our advantage, it would be to the effect that our preaching was plain, simple, clear, practical, earnest, and orthodox; it was devoid of speculation and all advanced thinking. We were wedded to the old Scotch theology, and accepted *ex animo* the teaching of the Westminster Standards. Whatever effects were produced, it was the matter and not the manner of the preaching, the Divine and not the human element in the service, that produced the result. Our services were about an hour and a quarter each; the lecture or sermon was about twenty or twenty-five minutes in length.

We always preached extemporaneously. After translating a chapter, the researches needful to find out the meaning had made the sense clear, and the various forms to which the words had been subjected made their utterance easy, so that very little extra study supplied me with a lecture. With respect to the sermon, I first arranged my plan as well as I could—followed Sir Walter Scott's first rule for English Composition, to get something suitable to say. The ideas being present in abundance and well arranged, the words came spontaneously and clothed them. Whatever may be said in support of read sermons to cultured congregations, extemporaneous preaching was the most acceptable and effective to these children of nature. Especially after the large portions of Scripture read to them, the more loosely compacted extemporaneous addresses laid a gentler strain upon their attention, and furnished a greater variety to the services. But I may here give a specimen of the kind of sermons preached by us to the natives, from the outlines of two discourses which I preached at the opening of a new church at Anau-unjai in 1855, and which I supplied at the time to the *R. P. Magazine*. We had strangers from all parts of the island; and within and around the church there were about 1000 natives. The doors and windows were all open. I never preached to a better-behaved audience. I preached in the morning and in the forenoon, and we held a public prayer-meeting in the afternoon. In the morning I preached from Luke iv. 16-19: "And He came to Nazareth, where He had been brought up: and, as His custom was, He went into the synagogue on the Sabbath-day, and stood up for to read," &c. On this passage I spoke somewhat as follows. I made a few introductory remarks on the occasion of our meeting in this new, large, and commodious place of worship; showed what cause we had for joy and thankfulness that God had put it into the heart of the teacher and the people of this district to build a house in which they might so conveniently and comfortably meet and worship God; and that He had given them strength to finish the house, and had preserved them from all serious accidents, —that we had met to worship and praise God for all His goodness and mercy to us and to them. I then called their attention to the *private* and *public* character of Christ as set forth in the passage.

I. His *private* character. (1). He *habitually* attended the house of God on Sabbath; it was His *custom*. (2.) He had learned to *read* the Word of God: He stood up for to *read*. (3.) He was *trained* or prepared for public teaching by assisting to conduct the services of the house of God in His youth; in the synagogue in Nazareth, where He was brought up, it was His custom to *stand up for to read*. (4.) He was *filled* with the Holy Spirit, and hence ready and forward to every good work.

II. His *public* character. (1.) He was *appointed* and *qualified* by God to be our Saviour, and was therefore able to accomplish the work of our salvation; and God was well pleased with Him in His work. (2.) He was sent to preach the Gospel to the *poor* or the *meek;* He is no respecter of persons. Men often favour the rich : Christ favours the *poor* or the *meek;* He rejects only the *proud*. (3.) He was sent and qualified to save the *miserable of all classes*—the "broken-hearted," the "captives," the "blind," and the "bruised." (4.) He was sent to overthrow Satan's kingdom, and set up a new kingdom of His own,—"to proclaim the acceptable year of the Lord."

I then proceeded to contrast the character and kingdom of Satan with the character and kingdom of Christ. Satan's object is to destroy; Christ's object is to save. "In the days of heathenism," I said, "Satan destroyed your souls, your bodies, your families, your food, your property, and everything else that you had. You feared the *natmasses* (the evil spirits), but you did not love them. Your sacred men, the servants of the *natmasses*, professed to bring diseases upon you and kill you, but not to give you health and preserve your life. When a man died, his wife, and perhaps his infant child, and some other persons, were strangled, his plantations were destroyed, his fruit-trees were cut down, and his children were left dependent on their friends. You half starved yourselves for months to make great feasts; and then the food was wasted, as it could not be eaten before it was rotten. You were continually quarrelling and making war; you were hating and destroying one another. But Christ's Kingdom is quite different from this. He came down to our world for the express purpose of saving men, and delivering them from the power of Satan. He came to save men's souls from hell and take them to heaven. And while He was on earth, that men might understand His character, as of one come to save them, He saved the bodies as well as the souls of those who came to Him. He healed the sick, He fed the hungry, He raised the dead to life, He cast out devils, He taught men to forgive their enemies, to love one another, to live in peace on earth, that they might be happy in heaven for ever." I concluded by exhorting them to follow earnestly the example set by Christ in His *private* character, in regularly attending the house of God on Sabbath, in diligently learning to read the Word of God, in being ever ready to assist in the work and worship of God, according to their respective capacities and opportunities, and in constantly seeking to be filled with the

Holy Spirit, that they might be strong for God's service; and to look upon Christ and receive Him as an authorised and appointed Saviour, as a willing Saviour, as an able Saviour, and as a present Saviour; and urged upon them to seek Him and believe in Him just now; not to put off the securing of their salvation till some other occasion; that now is the accepted time, and now is the day of salvation.

In the forenoon I preached from John i. 12, 13 : "As many as received Him, to them gave He power to become the sons of God, even to them that believe on His name; which were born, not of blood, nor of the will of the flesh, nor of the will of man, but of God." After a few introductory remarks explaining how Christ is called the Word and the Light in the beginning of the chapter—how He came to His own land, but His own professed people, the Jews, received Him not—they rejected Him, and were on that account rejected of God, and unchurched, and their privileges extended to the Gentiles all over the world—I directed their attention to the class of persons mentioned in these verses, "the sons of God." I spoke of the *privileges* and of the *birth* of God's children.

I. Their *privileges*. (1.) Their sins are pardoned, their persons and their services are accepted, and they are become friends with God. (2.) They have received new hearts, and they are being made holy and meet for heaven. (3.) They are taken under God's special care; He preserves them from Satan, from wicked men, and from all real evils. (4.) They are at last glorified in heaven, and made perfectly happy for ever.

II. The *birth* of God's children. They are born (1.) Not of *blood;* they become His children not in consequence of any outward or earthly privileges which they may enjoy, not on account of wealth, rank, parentage, or descent, not because they had Abraham for their father. (2.) Not of the *will of the flesh;* not from any power or inclination in themselves: all are dead in trespasses and sins. No man can save himself. (3.) Not of the *will of man;* not in consequence of what others can do for them; however anxious ministers, teachers, parents, or friends may be, they cannot change the heart of any one, or save his soul. (4.) But they are *born of God* only; they receive a new heart from God; it is only the Holy Spirit that can change the heart of man. I then addressed them on their duty, as they were now privileged to hear the Gospel, and took up a common objection against the thorough depravity of man. "If you cannot save yourselves," I said, "and if God only can save you, you will ask me, ' what are you to do ? ' The Word of God makes your duty plain. You must go to Him who alone can save you; you must go to Him just as you are, with all your sins upon you. You must do as Peter did in the storm, and cry, 'Lord, save us: we perish.' As many as received Christ, or believed on Him, obtained power to become the sons of God. You are to do for your souls as you do for your bodies : you cannot make the seed grow that saves or keeps alive your bodies, but because you cannot make the food grow, and God only can, do you on that account sit still and do nothing? Oh, no! you are wise as to your bodies. You dig your land, you fence it, you plant your taro, your bananas, your kumeras (sweet potatoes), and your sugar-cane; you weed them, and you water them as they require it; and you trust in God that He will make them grow, and you are not disappointed. You do all these things although ´you have no promise from God that He will cause them to grow—at least no promise so distinct as for spiritual blessings. Now, follow the same course in seeking the salvation of your souls. The Word of God is the seed : your hearts are the field in which this seed is to be sown. Prepare your hearts to seek the Lord; hear, read, and think upon His Word; lay it up in your hearts. The Holy Spirit is the water that makes this seed to grow. By earnest prayer to God, seek the Holy Spirit to come into your hearts and water this seed, and you may safely trust in God that He will cause it to grow up within you to everlasting life. God is not unwilling to save you; if you act towards your souls as you do towards your bodies, you may fully hope to be numbered among the children of God—among those who are 'born again, not of corruptible seed, but of incorruptible, by the *Word of God*, which liveth and abideth for ever.' God has promised the Holy Spirit to them that ask Him, but if you will not receive Christ and believe in Him when He is offered to you—if you act the part of the Jews and refuse Him—you must perish, and that by your own act: you refuse salvation by the only way in which God has appointed it to be obtained; you will perish, and you yourselves must bear the blame for evermore. Christ would have gathered the children of Jerusalem as a hen gathereth her chickens under her wings; but they would not hear His voice, and so they perished. You see and know how the hawk pounces down upon the helpless chickens, and bears them away if they are not under the wings of their mother. Satan, like a hawk, watches his opportunity to pounce down upon sinners who are not under the protection of Christ. Our loving Saviour is far more willing, and far more able, to save sinners than the hen can be to save her chickens. But if they refuse to come under the wings of His protection, they wilfully expose themselves to Satan, and will certainly be seized by him as his prey. But 'blessed is the man who trusteth in the Lord.'"

Our elders, deacons, and teachers, in the services which they conduct, keep up all the parts of public worship, and always give an address, more or less in the form of a sermon. The matter of their addresses may be very meagre, the teaching of these men may convey very little instruction, and their exhortations may have very little power to stimulate thought, but their addresses are all more or less original, and the number and variety of the gifts employed prevent the sameness and repetition of one speaker, though greatly more gifted than any of them; while the more common sins, the more prevailing deficiencies, and the more outstanding evils are always plainly pointed out and condemned. They all possess in a considerable degree the gift of prayer. One would naturally expect that they would pick up a few expressions used by the missionaries and confine themselves to these alone, and that it would be a great boon to them to be supplied with a small liturgy. The prayers in that case would be less diffuse, and more concise and correct in form; but they would lose in force and variety more than they would gain in elegance and propriety of expression. They have a great variety in their prayers; not individually, but collectively, as among ourselves every individual has his own trains of thought, but all more or less limited; but then no two natives follow the same process of thinking. Their prayers are largely made up of Scripture, but beyond a few outstanding texts no two men quote the same passages. Hence by drawing largely upon native agency we secure a great amount of freshness and variety. They often use plain and homely, but never vulgar or indelicate, expressions. In prayer for the Tannese, even in their own presence, I have heard an Aneityum chief use the following expression, " O Lord, pity the poor, ignorant, wicked Tannese : they know nothing, they know not Thy Word; they are all just like pigs and dogs; they are stupid, abominable, and cruel; give them new hearts, and make them good Christians." Praying for the missionaries, another would say something as follows :— " O Lord, be very gracious to Thy servants the missionaries; they left a fruitful land to come hither; they left good food and kind friends, and soft, comfortable beds, to come to this barren land of ours, to a wicked people, to poor food, and to beds hard, covered with thistles, and every disagreeable pain-causing thing; give them Thy Holy Spirit to keep their hearts strong for Thy work, and give them at last life everlasting." In their ordinary conversation there are few forbidden words. A spade is generally called a spade, but from their religious vocabulary every doubtful word is scrupulously excluded. In asking my pundits if I might use such-and-such a word, they would say, " It is not a bad word, but it is very nearly a bad word, and if you used it in the church some of the young men might laugh—you had better not use it, but take such-and-such another word."

We always preached in the vernacular, and we never employed an interpreter. At one time, in the early stages of missionary operations, missionaries often employed interpreters. They stood aghast at the idea of learning a native language, and that they might lose no time in opening up the way of salvation to the perishing heathen, they employed any stray white man or half-caste who professed to know the native language as well as the English ; but in most cases this was followed with such unsatisfactory results, that now-a-days, so far as I know, no missionary ever thinks of preaching through an interpreter. He may preach an occasional sermon in this way, but only when he has a missionary thoroughly acquainted with the language for his interpreter. But that is all that is ever attempted now. It was through an interpreter that the famous Jonathan Edwards preached to the Indians at Stockbridge. But it is through his treatise on the Freedom of the Will—which he wrote while he lived at Stockbridge—and not to his preaching through an interpreter, which gave him his world-wide and never-dying reputation. The saintly David Brainerd was almost the only missionary whose preaching through an interpreter was pre-eminently successful, but it was not till after his interpreter was converted, and his burning words were translated and repeated by lips nearly as glowing as his own, that their effects were so marvellous. However, I have no doubt but that his preaching would have been still more effective had his hearers received it at first and not at second-hand.

A *sine qua non*, an indispensable condition of success in preaching to the heathen, is a thorough knowledge of the language spoken by the natives to whom he is preaching. The late Mr. James D. Gordon of Eromanga used to say, and that truly, that next to the Spirit of God operating upon the heart of a native, is the effect produced upon his mind by hearing his own tongue correctly spoken either by a foreigner or a native. It has always been so. When the Jews heard that Paul spoke to them in the Hebrew tongue, when they evidently expected Greek, they kept the more silence; they were riveted by the sounds of their mother-tongue. Perhaps no man of his time had more influence over the natives of New Zealand than the late Sir Donald M'Lean; and, doubtless one cause of this remarkable power lay in his extraordinary command of the native language. He not only knew the Maori language thoroughly, and pronounced it accurately, but he spoke with the very tones of a native. Any one hearing him speak, and not seeing him, would have supposed that it was a native whom he heard speaking. It has been the same with all our best and most successful South Sea missionaries, such as John Williams, John Hunt, Bishop Selwyn, Bishop Patteson, and many others that could be named scarcely, if at all, inferior to these.

A trader may get along after a sort—may buy and sell, through the medium of a kind of broken, sandal-wood English, such as, "Me savy;" "Me want big fellow yam;" "This boy belong o' you?" "You too much like go Sydney;" and hold up three of his fingers, for three years, when the native understands him to mean three months—but the missionary who aims at being successful must be able to speak like a native; he must know the exact meaning of the words, the grammatical construction, and the correct pronunciation. Many people think that any sort of speaking, grammatical or ungrammatical, correctly pronounced or incorrectly, may do for savages. We can understand a Frenchman, a German, or an Italian speaking broken English. We rather relish his foreign idioms, as we can easily understand his meaning. Dr. Chalmers' strong Doric accent added an attraction, rather than otherwise, to his oratory in the ears of an English audience. But it was only a Dr. Chalmers who could produce this effect. It was in spite of his provincial tones, and not in consequence of them, that his eloquence was so overpowering. It requires a missionary to speak his very best to make himself at all intelligible to natives on a subject so new, and so foreign to all their previous ideas, as that of Christianity. When Messrs. Powell and Geddie came first to Aneityum, they thought that every day was lost till they began to preach to the natives. Mr. Powell knew Samoan very well, and having the Samoan teachers, who had been on the island for some years, to assist him in acquiring a knowledge of the language, he began in a comparatively short time to preach to the natives. Mr. Geddie, with his strongly impulsive nature, got up a sermon in a short time afterwards. The natives listened apparently very attentively to the two preachers; and the missionaries, in their inexperience, thought that they had gained the ear of their audience, and that they were now sowing the seeds of saving truth; but, alas! they were only deceiving themselves; the natives sat staring at the foreign speakers, but it was, as the author of the "Seasons" says, " with brute unconscious gaze;" and as they did not know the meaning of the voice, the hearers were, as the Apostle says, barbarians to the speakers, and the speakers were barbarians to them. Long afterwards, when Mr. Geddie and the natives could converse freely with one another, he asked some of the most intelligent of them if they understood Mr. Powell's preaching and his when they first began to preach to them. " Understand you!" said they. "Oh no! we did not understand a word that you said; we thought all the time that you were speaking to us in Samoan." Thus, speaking words that their hearers understood not, they found, as the Apostle further says, that they were speaking to the air.

When the missionaries began to acquire the language on Aneityum, it was apparently a hopeless task; there were no helps in the form either of grammar or vocabulary. Every sentence they heard was like one long undivided word; and when they asked by signs the name of this thing or that, the natives would tell them nothing without payment. In this way, as their list of words increased, the biscuits in the cask diminished, and by-and-by assumed the form of a rapidly vanishing quantity. But the end was thus gained; a nucleus of words was thus secured, which by-and-by developed into a satisfactory medium of communication. When Mr. Copeland went to Futuna, he used to sit for hours, day after day, among the idle natives, with pencil and note-book in his hand, taking down new words and new sounds, as his ear caught them up, while the natives were retailing the news of the island and discussing the gossip of the day. When a certain amount of progress has been made, one of the best modes of increasing one's knowledge of the language is to engage in translating the Scriptures. This exercise secures precision and correctness of expression, and as new words are constantly cropping up, the vocabulary continues to enlarge.

It is a dry, arduous, uphill work to acquire these unwritten and non-literary languages. But when at every stage of our progress we feel conscious that we are opening up a channel through which the living water is to flow, that gives spiritual life to immortal souls, these uncultured tongues become invested with more than classical beauty, and acquire a higher practical value than the writing on the Moabite Stone, or the characters on the Hittite inscriptions.

Some missionaries baptize all converts, and their children, as soon as they give up heathenism and place themselves under Christian instruction, and then keep them for a time, longer or shorter according to circumstances, on probation and under instruction, before they admit them to the Lord's

Supper. Our mode of procedure was in accordance with the principles enunciated in the Shorter Catechism. We did not administer baptism to any till they professed their faith in Christ, and obedience to Him; but the infant children of such as were, both or only one, members of the visible Church, we baptized. Immediately after baptism we admitted all adults to the Lord's Table. Our mode of procedure was this. We administered the Lord's Supper only at the central stations. All the church members met there. We had public worship on the Friday afternoon. After sermon we baptized all the candidates who had been previously admitted by the session; and also all the children eligible for baptism, and distributed tokens of admission to all the members. On the Sabbath morning all the intending communicants took their seats in the places allotted for them; and all arrangements for the seating both of the church members and the general congregation were carried out by the elders and deacons, who were active and conscientious in seeing that everything was done decently and in order. After the sermon, the sacrament was dispensed in the manner usually observed in Presbyterian congregations. In the afternoon the congregation again met for public worship, and a sermon was preached. On the Monday morning we held a public prayer-meeting, in which the elders and deacons largely took part, and at which addresses were delivered. When this meeting was brought to a close the people dispersed, and returned to their respective homes.

Calvin tells us in his "Christian Institutes," that Pope Zephyrinus was the author of the decree which appointed one particular day every year, that on it the whole of Christendom might give a confession of their faith by partaking of the

Lord's Supper. But the ordinance of Zephyrinus, which was otherwise good, posterity perverted when they made a fixed law of one Communion in the year. Even in Scotland, since the Revolution till about fifty years ago, one Communion in the year in each parish or congregation, in country parishes at least, was the general rule; then it became twice a year, and now four times obtains extensively. The "Directory for the Public Worship of God" says—"The Communion, or Supper of the Lord, is frequently to be celebrated; but how often, may be considered and determined by the ministers and other church governors of each congregation, as they shall find most convenient for the comfort and edification of the people committed to their charge." Acting on this principle, Mr. Geddie and I arranged to have the Communion twice a year on each side of the island, but alternately at each station, with the understanding that the church members, as often as convenient, should go from the one side to the other; thus making it for the most of the members a celebration of four times in the year. For a number of years this arrangement wrought exceedingly well. In the days of heathenism there was no social intercourse; the population of one portion of the island knew nothing of the people of any other, beyond a few principal chiefs. But at these gatherings the people were brought together from every part of the island, under circumstances extremely favourable for developing everything good in their character. These meetings encouraged the Christian party. It revealed to them their own numbers and strength. When the Christian chiefs and people over all the island came together to one point four times in the year, they for the first time realised their own power, and they were encouraged thereby. It had an equally depressing effect upon the heathen, who, never meeting, had no idea of their own numbers; on the other hand, when the Christians returned home, and published in every district the names of the chiefs and the number of the people who were assembled, the accounts all magnified with a tinge of Oriental exaggeration, the heathen felt like the spies in presence of the sons of Anak—that they were like grasshoppers in their own sight, and they were afraid to molest the Christian party. These meetings had a Christianising, a civilising, and a socialising influence upon the whole community. Year by year the gatherings increased in numbers, till they became like the great sacramental congregations at Ettrick and elsewhere in the days of Thomas Boston, when the hospitality of the parish was strained to its utmost capacity to supply food and shelter to the pious worshippers who assembled from parishes far and near. To compare small things with great, these meetings in some respects resembled the three great annual festivals among the Israelites when they met to worship the Lord, first at Shiloh and latterly at Jerusalem. They knit the people together as one man over the whole island. They went far to suppress war, murder, and revenge, and to diffuse a spirit of forgiveness, of forbearance, of mutual confidence and goodwill, which resulted in the establishment of a general and permanent peace—a firm peace over the whole island, which has remained unbroken for the third of a century. These meetings were akin to the Feast of Tabernacles. There was no lack of food. It was supplied in abundance to the strangers, but sleeping accommodation could be secured only with difficulty. It became very much like the time when the Israelites made booths of branches of palm-trees, of myrtle-trees, and willows of the brooks, and in such shelters passed the night while they worshipped before the Lord. But these gatherings, however advantageous in the earlier stages of the mission, became inconveniently large when the whole population had embraced the Gospel; and evils of various kinds began to crop up; not exactly of the "Holy Fair" type—for there was no drinking —evils which, by the way, arose from good arrangements being continued after they were not required, and were thus perverted to evil purposes. With us the friendly hospitalities increased into a species of feasting, and the secular began to overlay the spiritual; from the difficulties, too, of providing sleeping accommodation, some of the people were invariably catching colds, and occasionally with fatal results. In these circumstances we found it necessary to alter our arrangements; and after careful consideration we agreed that, instead of having the communion twice a year on each side of the island, as formerly, we should dispense it four times on each side, but on both sides on the same day, and thus discontinue the united meetings. We explained our reasons fully, first to the sessions, and then to the whole people. The natives cordially acquiesced, and the change was effected without any difficulty, and has been carried out with great advantage up to the present time. During the early and transition period of the mission, the first arrangements were the most suitable; but when that period was passed, and when Christianity was fully established, then the ordinary and normal arrangements which obtain in Christian communities were found to be the best adapted for securing permanently the benefit of this ordinance.

CHAPTER XI.

THE SERVICE OF SONG ON ANEITYUM.

FROM the very beginning of the mission "the service of song" occupied an important place in both public and private worship. When I joined the mission in 1852, there had been prepared and printed six *Ohranitai* (things of the voice), as the natives call all compositions that are to be sung. When I left the mission fifty had been printed, and a few have been added since. Among these are translations or paraphrases, more or less free, of several of the psalms, or portions of psalms, as 51, 67, 72, 84, 90, 100, 121, 133. The following of the Scripture paraphrases, in whole or in part, have been translated—37, 58, 66; also several hymns, such as "The happy land," "We all shall meet in Heaven at last," &c. A considerable number are original, based on Scripture texts, or composed on important Scripture subjects, such as the grace and mercy of God, the sufferings and death of Christ, the work of the Spirit, the Sabbath, the Lord's Supper, Missions, &c. Dr. Geddie and I were the chief composers. Mr. Copeland contributed a small number, and a few have been added since by Mr. Annand and Mr. Laurie. Whatever may be said with regard to the literary and poetical character of our *Ohranitai*, it may, I think, be very safely affirmed of our sacred songs, that, as to matter, they contain nothing but what is in accordance with the analogy of faith; that the sentiments they express are all Scriptural.

They are all composed in English metres, and sung to English tunes. We have not attempted rhyme, except in a very limited degree. It is exceedingly difficult to compose anything in the Aneityumese language in the form of English metres. The words are long; it requires about two verses in Aneityumese to convey the sense that is expressed in one verse in English. And with such a small band of workmen, and with such intractable vocables on which to operate, our psalter, hymnal, book of sacred song, or whatever name our *Ohranitai* may receive, is still very small, and is not more than a tithe of what is to be found in many of the hymn-books prepared by some of the other missions in those seas. As the languages are all different, we have no means of knowing their difficulties and how far they have mastered them; no means of knowing the real or comparative excellences of those productions respectively. Their vocables may be shorter and more tractable than ours, or they may have other advantages that we do not possess. But if it be true, as Dr. Ryle, the Bishop of Liverpool, says,—and he, from his familiarity with this department of literature, should be a competent judge,—that there are not more than about two hundred good hymns, thoroughly adapted to public worship, in the English language—only a fourth more than the inspired psalms; as Cowper says—

"How slow the growth of what is excellent!"—

it may therefore be reasonably supposed, that of the hundreds of hymns found in the various Polynesian hymn-books, the number of really good ones is not great. We were forced to do just what we could—sometimes a psalm, sometimes a hymn, sometimes a text of Scripture, sometimes a Scripture sentiment, was taken as the basis of a few verses, that, with a considerable effort, were rendered as like poetry as we could make them; glad, as we were, to get anything that could be sung. We were animated by no spirit of innovation, by no wish to make the world believe that we had found out some more excellent way; that we were wiser or better than people at home or elsewhere; and certainly with no expectation that we should ever be quoted as authorities—aiming simply at doing the best we could in our circumstances—giving something to the people that they would understand, and that would do them good.

The tunes we adopted were such as are used at home, such as our musical friends out there happened themselves to know, and such as were likely to be most easily learned by the natives, such as "Old Hundred," "French," "Irish," "Martyrdom," "Tallis," "Caroline," "Mear," "New Cambridge," "Devizes," "St. Asaph's," &c., and several hymn tunes, such as those usually sung to the hymns, "Just as I am without one plea," "Oh that will be joyful," "There is a happy land," &c. We have only two secular tunes, viz., "Auld Langsyne" and "Bonnie Charlie;" but as the natives have no Bacchanalian and no Jacobite associations with those tunes, they are, in their ears, as pure and sacred as "Old Hundred" itself, or any of the twelve tunes in John Knox's Psalter; and when we adopt these tunes, it is only restoring to the worship of God what was unjustly taken away and applied to the service of Satan and the world. As a general rule each psalm or hymn has its own tune. We never read the line.

In the first years of the mission Mrs. Geddie was our sole

THE SERVICE OF SONG ON ANEITYUM. 139

instructor in sacred music, and important were the services she rendered. But for the last fifteen years or so of our stay on the island, when the mission began to increase in numbers, every new arrival possessed of musical powers was pressed in to help us forward in this department of instruction; especially on my side of the island was this done. Not being able to teach music myself, I invariably took advantage of all the musical talent within my reach, to make up for my own lack of service. I took credit simply for drilling them well into what they had learned; making them practise it thoroughly, so that they might not forget what they had got.

In 1869, as far as my side of the island was concerned, our singing received a great impulse by the visit of two lady friends of ours from New Zealand. My wife and I had accompanied the *Dayspring* to New Zealand that year, and as the vessel was expected to go back to Auckland in two months to bring the Rev. P. Milne and his wife on to the mission, when we returned from New Zealand we were accompanied by Mrs. Logan and a young niece of hers and Miss Clark. Mrs. Logan was the widow of Dr. Logan, R.N., of Wellington. Her husband and she were two of our first and best friends in New Zealand. What Lydia was to Paul and his party, Mrs. Logan has been to the missionaries of the New Hebrides and the ministers of New Zealand. In her youth she sat at the feet of Drs. Paxton and M'Crie, and imbibed much of their spirit, and she is passionately fond of music. Miss Clark, now Mrs. C. C. Macmillan, was the youngest daughter of the late Mr. Archibald Clark, the first Mayor of Auckland—a gentleman well known, especially in religious circles, both in Scotland and New Zealand. Mr. Clark and his family were among our first and most attached friends in Auckland, and have all along taken a deep interest in the New Hebrides Mission. Miss Clark, both as a singer and a player, took a first place in the *amateur* musical circles in Auckland. As the *Dayspring* was going direct from Auckland to Aneityum—only a seven days' voyage—and was going direct back in so short a time, those two friends took advantage of this unusual opportunity to pay us a visit and to see the islands and the working of the mission. The visit was pleasant to all, and, in addition, profitable to us and to the mission, and was a month longer than was expected. The two ladies endeavoured to make themselves as useful, in every way, as they could; they kept a class with the natives for singing almost every day, the whole of the three months that they were on Aneityum, which was attended by from thirty to forty; and they left a deep impress of their presence among the natives in this department of instruction. As a memento of old friendships, a lady in Auckland had made my wife a present of a small but excellent harmonium, which, under Miss Clark's skilful fingers, gave a trueness to the teaching such as it never had before. But here we were nearly brought to a stand-still, as far as this help was concerned. When John Williams was building his ship on Rarotonga, after killing his only two goats to make a pair of bellows, he found them wholly eaten by the rats in the morning; and as he had no more goats, he had to exercise his mechanical skill and construct a box for a bellows. We had the same enemies to contend with there. First they cut the rope of the footboard nearly through, so that it broke; but we did not suspect the cause till afterwards. In a few nights, however, they cut large holes in the leather of the bellows, and in the morning it was found that the voice of the charmer was gone. Fortunately, we had some chamois leather in the house, and a bottle of liquid gum; by means of these we patched up all the holes, and for practical purposes the instrument was as good as ever; and by a little ingenuity we shut up all the openings, and excluded these pests ever after.

A beginning had been made in bass by one of our former instructors, but it was only a beginning; but Miss Clark fully instructed a class of young men to sing this part in several tunes; she also taught the natives to sing two chants, so that we chanted metrical versions of the 67th and 121st Psalms in the church. I had no liking for chants myself, but the class learned them fast, and even the congregation came to join in them with wonderful readiness. I had been long anxious to have "Coleshill" introduced into the church; but all our musical friends, for one cause or another, had failed to make the attempt. Some of them did not know it. I pressed Miss Clark; she was rather reluctant, alleging that in a minor tune like "Coleshill" the native voice would be sure to fail at some particular notes. However, in deference to my wishes, she agreed to make a trial. The harmonium was taxed to its utmost capabilities. Mrs. Logan and she sang as sure and true as if their musical reputation had been suspended on the effort, and the natives followed. The teaching there was all by the ear; we had no music-books, either in the old notation or the new. To my great satisfaction, the natives made good their claim to be considered a part of our common humanity; their voices mastered the difficulties of the minor key as well as of the major; they learned "Coleshill" faster than any tune they had tried, and after it was introduced into the church, the congregation sang it perhaps better than any other tune they had ever attempted. There was one young married woman, *Paparua*, but now dead, who had, for some years, been one of Mrs. Inglis's girls, who sang it remarkably well, and whom I always employed to lead the singing when I gave out the psalm, the 90th, to which it was sung. Every time I heard them sing it, it thrilled through my heart, as if I had been at a Communion in Scotland. My old friend, Mr. Steel of Penpont, and the other singing-masters of that district of Dumfriesshire of fifty or sixty years ago, showed their knowledge both of music and of human nature when, after exercising the voices of the youngsters for a very brief period on the gamut, they plunged boldly *in medias res*, and began with "Coleshill," a tune which, in my humble opinion, with all due deference to the judgment passed by our national bard on "noble Elgin," is—

"The sweetest far of Scotia's holy lays,"

and which in thousands and tens of thousands of instances, at sacraments and deathbeds, has raised believing worshippers as near to the songs of the upper sanctuary as is attainable on this side the grave.

The result of this visit was highly satisfactory; not only were a good many new tunes learned, but a better taste in singing was created. One of our missionaries, the late Mr. Morrison, was with us one or two Sabbaths, on his way to New Zealand, and just as our friends were about to leave us, he remarked to me that he observed a much better development of the native voices than he had ever heard in our congregation before.

Among the translations which I made was one in imitation of Montgomery's version of the 72d Psalm, beginning—

"Hail to the Lord's anointed, great David's greater Son,"

THE SERVICE OF SONG ON ANEITYUM. 143

It is done in the same metre, and sung to one of the tunes usually set to that version. The natives learned it very soon. Another of my translations was the "Rock of Ages." According to Sir Roundell Palmer, now Lord Selborne, while Watts is the best hymn writer in the English language, Toplady, in his "Rock of Ages," has produced the one best hymn. Bishop Ryle's estimate of it is much the same; and I flatter myself that my translation of it is the best that I have made—perhaps the best hymn is the most easily translated. It is in the same metre as the original, and it is made to rhyme. The "Rock of Ages" has been translated into many languages. Mr. Gladstone has translated it into mellifluous mediæval Latin. To compare small works with great, my translation can make no claims to be as literal, as elegant, and as scholar-like as that of the learned Premier; but then one's vanity is flattered, or at least one's humiliation is modified, by what Lord Stanley told the world of letters a few years ago, in his rectorial address at Glasgow. "I doubt," he said, "if any human being was ever the better or the wiser for being set to spin verses in a foreign and dead language." If this applies to students, will it not apply *a fortiori* to Prime Ministers? If such exercises are of no benefit to the writers, are they not likely to be still less so to the readers? Who will sing Mr. Gladstone's translation? It is too evangelical for the Church of Rome, the only Church that uses Latin hymns in its services. But mine is a translation, if into a foreign, it is at least into a living language; it may strengthen a living faith, quicken a living devotion, and supply fuel to "beet the heavenward flame" in living bosoms.

I insert this translation that the daughters of song may, if they think proper, transcribe it into their albums, and sing it to the piano or harmonium, when they wish to call attention to the claims of our mission. Let them pronounce the vowels as in Latin, and they will produce correctly the Aneityumese sounds.

ROCK OF AGES.	ROCK OF AGES.
	Translated into the language of Aneityum.
Rock of Ages, cleft for me,	Nij amelith um itu,
Let me hide myself in Thee !	Natimarith asitu,
Let the water and the blood,	Ek apol iram ainyak ;
From Thy riven side that flowed,	Imiatamairg nesnyak ;
Be of sin the double cure,	Imyialep nyak aiek,
Cleanse me from its guilt and power.	Iesu, tak eriss irak.
Not the labours of my hands	Netho unyak takitai,
Can fulfil Thy law's demands ;	Nemtha unyak nevitai?
Could my zeal no respite know,	Nimtau unyak yek etha,
Could my tears for ever flow,	Vai netho has asenga?
All for sin could not atone ;	Imyigoho nyak aiek,
Thou must save, and Thou alone.	Iesu, asitu irak.
Nothing in my hand I bring,	Et itap inja iram ;
Simply to Thy cross I cling ;	Er ati inmas unyum,
Naked, come to Thee for dress—	Par adahpoi alupas
Helpless, look to Thee for grace :	Netho o atimi has.
Foul, I to the Fountain fly ;	Imyiaras nyak aiek,
Wash me, Saviour, or I die !	Iesu, jim aru irak.
While I draw this fleeting breath,	Ek wit emehe ainyak,
When my eyestrings break in death,	Tup atenghe nyak aiek.
When I soar through tracts unknown,	An naopan apitag,
See Thee on Thy judgment throne—	An naopan mas unyak,
Rock of Ages, cleft for me,	Imyiehva nyak aiek,
Let me hide myself in Thee.	Iesu, jim ahnang irak.

Burns was the best lyric poet—the best writer of songs—that Scotland, or perhaps any other country, ever produced. It is said that the way he wrote his songs was this : he hummed over the tune to himself till he got the spirit of it into his mind, and then proceeded to write such words as would give full and fitting expression to the music. Sir Walter Scott never did this; he made his words without any reference to music. In many cases, however, other hands made fitting music to his words. It would have been a vain expectation for any of us to think that we could produce words in the Aneityum language that any one would ever set to music; nor, if possible, could we afford to wait till such was done. But it was not necessary; there were plenty of excellent tunes already made, and our only question was how we could get suitable words for them. But latterly I endeavoured to carry out Burns's principle in my own way. A tune was fixed upon, I looked at the notes in the book,—I heard it sung in English words,—I tried to enter into the spirit of the tune; and wherever there were long, or strong, or what might be called emphatic notes, I endeavoured to have emphatic or strongly accented syllables in that part of the line, and to have feeble words, or unaccented syllables, where the notes were short. In this way the sense and the sound were made to run hand in hand. When these principles were attended to, mechanical as the process may seem, though not more so than the rules of prosody, I found that the natives learned the tune much more quickly. I was led to adopt this plan when I was preparing a hymn for the tune "Mothers," or "Daughters of Salem," an American tune, in peculiar metre, sung to the words, "The Sabbath bells are ringing," the repeating words being, "Come, come away." The tune was taught by Mr. Robertson, the Cotton Company's agent, who, being an excellent singer, taught the natives a good many tunes—and it soon became a remarkable favourite.

For a while they never gave over singing it. When, at the end of five years, the company was dissolved, Mr. Robertson returned to Nova Scotia, and completed his education for the ministry, under the direction of the Mission Board. He was ordained, sent out, and appointed to Eromanga, where he has proved one of our most successful missionaries.

Besides proceeding in this way, I always got them to sing over those translations before I finished them, to see if there were any words that could not be easily sung: some words can be sung so much more easily than others. Sometimes two syllables have a tendency to run into one, and then the singers go out of the time. In one of the last translations that I made, I found that we had misspelled and mispronounced one of our most common words from the beginning of the mission till then. We had pronounced and spelled the word in four syllables, while in reality it contained only three. I had inserted it in one of the lines to be sung in four syllables. I was trying one of our best singers—one of our most intelligent natives—to sing the verse in which this word stood, but when she came to the word she always made it three syllables instead of four, and hence had a note over at the end of the line. I tried her again and again, pronouncing the word distinctly myself in four syllables, but always with the same result. I finally changed the line by substituting another word. Had I got the translation printed before it was tested in this way, this limping line would have marred the whole verse. I afterwards carefully watched how the natives pronounced the word when reading or speaking, and found that they uniformly pronounced it in three syllables. The mistake had arisen from this: the first syllable of the word ends with a consonant, and the second syllable begins with a consonant. In pronouncing the word there is a slight break or pause between the two syllables, which, unless carefully observed, may easily be mistaken for the short sound of *i*, which letter we had inserted, but which totally disappears when the word is sung. When every sound has to be caught as it floats rapidly and indistinctly on the lips of the natives, it is extremely difficult to avoid mistakes; it is long before every nicety like this can be discovered and mastered; they are often discovered by the merest accident.

The natives possess a fair amount of musical talent; they are capable of attaining an average degree of proficiency, wherever the requisite amount of instruction is bestowed. They learn music fully as fast as anything else. But here, as in all other things, in the case of a people sunk so low, very moderate attainments must satisfy us. One of our missionary sisters—herself a first-class musician—who handles the pen of a ready writer, when she first came to Aneityum, evidently thought that their attainments in music were very limited. Mrs. Logan and Miss Clark, however, had not been there before her. In describing a service at our station, she said they sang vigorously, but they kept a much firmer hold of their books than they did of the tunes, which I believe would be quite true. But passing on in the voyage, and seeing the genuine heathen—the pits out of which those singers had been dug, and the rocks out of which they had been hewn—her views became greatly modified; the "fair penitent," regretting her hastily-formed opinions, listened ever afterwards with a much more charitable ear to those sable children of Ethiopia lifting up their voices unto God, and showing forth His praise.

But while our psalms and hymns, and all the psalms and

hymns in Polynesia, are written in English metres, and sung to English tunes, and many of the natives in all the groups have learned to sing well, nevertheless I have long thought that a false principle runs through the whole system. But the remedy will not be easily applied; it is this, that both their sacred songs and their sacred music should be framed on the same principles as their secular songs and their secular music. I have only heard of one missionary in those seas, Rev. Mr. Pratt of Samoa, adopting something like those principles; but he, as I understood, took simply the old tunes and set them to his new hymns; and as the associations connected with the old tunes were almost all bad—saturated with the abominations of heathenism—his brethren disapproved of the plan, and his hymns, thus arranged to that music, were suppressed. I think he was thus far on the right path, but had not fully wrought out the right method; he should have had new tunes on the same principle as the old, as well as new hymns.

At the Reformation, when the emancipated souls of whole nations sought full expression in songs of joy, like the birds in early spring, mediæval Latin hymns and Gregorian chants were vehicles far too confined to afford utterance for such exuberant feelings. No doubt the old church music was far finer—of a greatly higher order—than the music adopted by the Reformers; just as the old cathedrals were a far higher order of architecture than the humble, unassuming parish kirks—far better adapted for the display of grand processions and the performance of high mass, but not for leavening the masses of the people with the knowledge of God's Word and the felt power of a preached Gospel. Hence the minstrels of the Reformation—Luther and his compeers—seized and sanctified the national or popular music, and translated psalms or composed hymns in the common ballad metres. In this way both the music and the metres were such as everybody could understand and learn, and the voice of the whole people rose simultaneously, like that of one man; it was loud, like the voice of many waters, and the effects were marvellous. Wherever the Reformation spread the same course was pursued. In England, in the days of Edward VI., Sternhold, Hopkins, and Whyttingham rendered the Psalms into the common ballad metres; they never thought of throwing them into the form of Greek hexameters or Latin pentameters, and setting them to Gregorian chants, now, like cathedral architecture, coming so much into vogue, and indicating, I fear, a craving for the sensuous rather than the spiritual in Divine worship. The people sang them to the ballad tunes, or others composed on the same principles. The late Rev. J. B. Laughton of Parramatta, writing in the *Sydney Christian Herald*, said—"It is undeniable that all the standard metrical versions in use to this day in all Protestant Churches of Anglo-Saxon origin are written in the ballad metre; and it is equally undeniable that they were sung by our fathers to the old ballad tunes. The writer has repeatedly heard the ballad of 'Chevy Chase,' which Sir Philip Sydney used to say moved his heart more than the blast of a trumpet, sung on the border-land between England and Scotland, to the identical tune known in our sacred collections as 'St. George's;' and a fine stirring old tune it is, when sung, as our martial sires used to sing it, with life and fire, and not as our congregations generally sing it, as they sing everything else, with funereal slowness and coldness."

Music and language must go together—the one must affect

the other. Forty years ago, when Dr. Mainzer was lecturing on sacred music, and teaching large classes in Scotland, he was seriously accused of Popish tendencies, because in some ladies' boarding school in Edinburgh he taught the *Stabat Mater* to the Latin words. He replied that he had no wish to countenance Popery, but he was engaged to teach the music of that piece, and he could not teach his pupils to sing the music to perfection except to the Latin words.

We go to those seas with our English tunes; these can be sung only to English metres; these metres are like the bed of Procrustes, a bed admirably adapted—made to order, if you will—for our short, monosyllabic, nervous Saxon; but into this bed we try to squeeze the long, sesquipedalian, intractable vocables of those Polynesian tongues, and the result is painful and disappointing.

A good many years ago, Dr. Grant, of the American Mission to the Nestorians, said, "I have for thirty years been straining my voice to try and teach the Nestorians our English tunes, but with very indifferent success; now I have discovered that they have chants of their own in abundance, that have possibly come down to them from the days of Asaph, Heman, and Jeduthun, and which they sing with ease and spirit." The Nestorians were Christians, and had a long traditional history; and music, once embodied in the songs of a people, sacred or secular, possesses an amazing vitality. But we have no music on Aneityum such as the Nestorians had. Ours is all heathen to the core.

Although the natives, judging from their songs, possess a fair amount of poetical as well as musical talent, although they are ready and willing to make prayers and sermons, yet I could never get one of them to attempt to make a hymn, on the principle of their own songs. One must remember, however, how few uneducated men or women at home make hymns. But no doubt some one will rise up to tune the sacred lyre, and serve the Lord by embodying the best thoughts of his heart in a genuine native hymn. The Aneityumese recognise the inspiration of the poet; not the inspiration of genius, as accepted by a sceptical or a secular philosophy, but a personal inspiration, a *natmas*, a personal spirit, distinct from the man's own soul, speaking through the lips of the poet. It is really the Scriptural idea of inspiration, as expressed by David in his last words, when he said, "The *Spirit* of the Lord *spake by me*, and *His word* was in *my tongue*." This was no idea infused into their minds by the missionaries, it was their own idea of inspiration in the days of heathenism, before ever they had seen the face or heard the voice of a missionary. It was stereotyped in the language, and supplied us with the vocables for translating intelligibly such expressions as "All Scripture is given by inspiration of God." The plenary inspiration of the Scriptures was to them a doctrine involving no difficulties. The natives have a number of songs, but none of them of any great length, and none that claim any great antiquity.

The songs and the music of the Aneityumese have nothing in common with European poetry or music. Their poetry seems more akin to Hebrew than to either English, Greek, or Latin. It is measured by no feet. It is neither rhyme nor blank verse, nor does it correspond in structure to the Hebrew parallelisms. It seems little else than prose—elevated prose, it may be—but cut up into divisions like verses, and these are followed by choruses, chiefly single syllables with no meaning. One very common one is, *Lil le, lil le; lil la, lil la; lil le, lil le*. This, according to Dr. Kitto, was the kind of singing with which Laban wished to send away Jacob. The style of the poetry seems to afford facilities for improvising, of which the natives are fond. Their music is a kind of chanting. It runs along on the principle of a short note and a long alternately, within a narrow scale. It is evidently from its resemblance on this point to their own music that they sing the tune "Ortonville" with more life and spirit than almost any of our tunes, it being composed throughout of a short and a long note alternately. They are very fond of singing their native songs; they will sing away at these syllabic choruses for any length of time, apparently, as onlookers would suppose, more for the love of the noise than the love of the music. I never, till I went to Aneityum, saw the full force of those expressions in the Psalms, where men are exhorted to sing and play with a *loud noise*. We are disposed, with our ideas of music, to look upon these expressions as figurative. But if the Hebrew music and the Hebrew mind were in any way akin to the Aneityumese, such expressions must be understood quite literally; for a prominent characteristic of their singing, as regards their native songs, is the "loud noise joyfully." In lamenting for the dead, the counterpart of Jeremiah's mourning women could easily be found there; and the utterances of parental anguish are expressed in the very spirit, often in the very words, of David, "O Absalom, my son, my son!"

Missionaries have so much to do—their duties are so heavy and so multifarious—that they cannot overtake much that they wish to do. I never had time to examine the poetry of the Aneityumese to any extent, and to analyse its structure, so as to discover fully the principles on which it is composed and the laws by which it is regulated. Besides this, we all go out to those islands with strong prepossessions in favour of home excellences, hence it is a long time before we can tolerate, far less appreciate, much that is good in things purely native. A German professor, delivering a charge to a young missionary appointed to India, spoke to this effect:— "Our wish is, that you make the natives Christians; but we do not wish you to make them *German* Christians; our simple wish is that you make them *Tamil* Christians." There was great wisdom in the distinction.

My hope is that some of our younger brethren may possess the requisite poetical and musical powers, and find sufficient time to enable them to investigate this important subject, and compose sacred songs and sacred tunes so nearly akin in principle to their own songs and their own music, that the natives will learn them with ease, and sing them with the heart, the spirit, and the understanding; that, as their language has been the medium of conveying to them a knowledge of God's Word, their poetry and their music may, in like manner, be the channel through which shall ascend unto God the sweet incense of praise and thanksgiving, and all the holy emotions and devotional feelings of contrite hearts and sanctified affections.

CHAPTER XII.

NEW HEBRIDES MISSION SYNOD.

THE name *Synod* came to be applied in 1872 to the annual meeting of our missionaries in this way. For a considerable time a felt desideratum in the mission was a proper word to designate our annual assemblings. We ourselves generally called them the Annual Meeting of the Mission; but in the Colonies and elsewhere this seemed to be too vague a designation, and they began to speak of the Mission *Conference*, the Mission *Council*, the Mission this and the Mission that, and hence the question began to be raised, Could no more appropriate name be adopted? *Meeting*, we said, is rather a vague term, and is applied generally to more popular assemblages than ours is. *Conference* is a very good word, but the Wesleyans and other Methodist bodies have appropriated it to designate their highest Church Courts, and we would prefer leaving it in their ecclesiastical vocabularies. *Council* is also a good word, but at that time, owing to the General Council held at Rome, it savoured strongly of the Vatican, and as we had no Ultramontane proclivities in the New Hebrides, we felt shy of doubtful connections. On the whole, *Synod* appeared to be the least objectionable word we could adopt. It is euphonious, high-sounding Greek, and at the same time a strictly orthodox, fully naturalised Presbyterian vocable.

It has both a popular and a strictly ecclesiastical meaning. In the once famous, but now obsolete, science of Astrology, the conjunctions of the heavenly bodies were called Synods; and in his Dictionary Dr. Johnson quotes passages from Crashaw, Milton, and Boyle in which these starry synods are spoken of as exercising a benign or a baleful influence on human destinies. In referring to the mythology of Greece and Rome, Shakespeare, Milton, and Dryden, as quoted by the great lexicographer, speak of "Synods of the gods;" and M'Kenzie, in his "Life of Principal Cunningham," speaks of a "Synod of Carriers" that, in the old ante-railway days, met every Wednesday in Edinburgh in the yard of the "Harrow" Inn, which had great attractions for Cunningham while a student. On the other hand, we have the strictly ecclesiastical application of the word. The Church of England has its Synods as well as its Convocations; while among Presbyterians, we have the Synod of Dort and the Synod of Jerusalem, we have the Reformed Presbyterian Synod, the United Presbyterian Synod, the English Presbyterian Synod, the Synod of Otago and Southland, and in the Established and Free Churches we have Provincial Synods in any number. Our Synod is somewhat different from any of these. It is neither strictly a Synod *quoad sacra*, nor yet a Synod *quoad civilia*, although it is somewhat of both, and possesses at the same time the fullest amount of spiritual independence. The Church out there in the New Hebrides is non-established and unendowed, she owns and claims neither teinds nor tithes, but she is united and national, and there are no dissenters! There is the freest Voluntaryism, without the slightest manifestation of national Atheism. It is a principle with us in translating the Scriptures rather to take a native word, though it convey only a part of the idea, than use a foreign word which expresses the whole idea, but requires to be explained before it is understood. The native word, without any explanation, conveys some part of the idea to the native mind; the foreign word none. In like manner the name Synod will convey to every Presbyterian ear some idea of the character of our meetings; while, to prevent mistake, and explain ourselves as far as possible, we have added the word *Mission;* and our Annual Meetings are to be called Meetings of the New Hebrides *Mission* Synod.

No doubt our Synod is *sui generis*. At the time of the union of the Free and Reformed Presbyterian Churches, when all the principles and all the practices of these two respective Churches were carefully scrutinised, the ecclesiastical lawyers of the Free Church, from the Procurator and the two principal Clerks of Assembly downwards, were puzzled to understand exactly the constitution and character of our Synod. The New Hebrides Synod bore no resemblance either to the Synod of Glasgow and Ayr, or that of Perth and Stirling, or any other Synod either in Scotland or England. It was different from anything known either in France or Geneva. In the long *catena* of ecclesiastical history, from A.D. 52, when the apostles and elders met at the first Synod in Jerusalem, they knew of no Synod exactly like ours. In Scotland, from the days of Knox, church courts have risen in succession from kirk sessions to presbyteries, thence to provincial Synods, and thence to the General Assembly. In the Australasian Colonies most of the Presbyterian Churches have a General Assembly, but they have no Synods. The Church of Otago, which is looked upon as the most conservative at the antipodes, has a Synod, but no Assembly. Our mission, which is the most abnormal of anything known, has a Synod, but no Presbytery. Nevertheless, both in the Colonies and in the islands, we are all most orthodox and loyal Presbyterians. We adhere firmly to the spirit of Presbyterianism, although circumstances have required us to depart, in some cases, from the letter of the system.

With us we had the thing before we had the name. In the early days of the mission Mr. Geddie and I met, as occasion required, and made all the needed arrangements for carrying on the work of the mission. But after our numbers increased, and especially after we got the *Dayspring*, we found it necessary to have a meeting of all the missionaries once a year, to make arrangements for the sailing of the vessel, for selecting mission stations, for settling missionaries, for sanctioning the printing of translations, and generally for transacting all necessary business connected with the mission. It was at this time, as I have said, that we found it convenient to apply the name Synod to the annual business meetings of the mission; and it has been universally accepted as expressing the corporate existence and the corporate action of the missionaries. Every missionary is *ex officio* a member of the Mission Synod, and represents the Church by which he is supported, and protects its interests. Ministers and elders belonging to Presbyterian Churches visiting the New Hebrides, and present at the meeting of Synod, are always associated, but no native elders sit as members. The Synod elects annually a Moderator and a Clerk; the Clerk is eligible for re-election as often as the Synod may think proper; the Moderator is not, till the list of members has been gone over; so that there is no danger of a perpetual Moderatorship springing up among us—an evil once so much dreaded in the

Church of Scotland, as being the thin end of the wedge by which bishops were stealthily introduced into the Presbyterian Church. The Synod manages the mission interests in the New Hebrides of ten Presbyterian Churches, *viz.*, of one in the Dominion of Canada, one in Scotland, two in New Zealand, and six in Australia. The Synod manages the *Dayspring*, as the property of those Churches, directs her movements, appoints on behalf of those Churches a board and agents in Sydney to look after the vessel in the Colonies. The Synod is the supreme authority in the mission in all general matters; all the missionaries are under the Synod, in a general way, while each one is personally responsible to the Church by which he is supported. If any missionary feels aggrieved by any action of the Synod, he can appeal to his own Church, and from the decision of that Church, in such a case, there is no further appeal. In a few cases, I think, the Synod may have exceeded its authority. Its relations with different parties have at times been a little strained, but they have never been broken off; and, on the whole, I feel certain that the Synod has done its work well, and from its decisions no appeal has ever been made. It has a great deal of work to do. The meetings of Synod have usually occupied about a week. A copy of the minutes is always sent to each of the Churches connected with the mission. There were often long sederunts, and able, tough, spirited debates, that would have done no discredit to larger and more important Synods than ours. Burning questions, too, sometimes gained admission into our discussions. The use of unfermented wine, or rather palm wine, as it has been called, that is, the liquor of the cocoa-nut, at the Lord's Supper, was on one occasion fully discussed.

When my wife and I went to the islands, thirty-four years ago, Mr. Geddie had formed a church and dispensed the Lord's Supper, and had used the ordinary fermented wine. In due course I followed the same practice. The missionaries had no allowance from any fund for the purchase of Communion elements. The missionary's wife baked the bread, the missionary himself bought the wine. While the communicants were few the expense was not heavy; a bottle of wine served for each Communion, which was celebrated twice, thrice, or four times in the year. When the church members amounted to 300 or 400, the wine-bill would have been a more formidable item of expense to a missionary with only £100 a year. But we reasoned from the sacrament of Baptism to that of the Lord's Supper; if a few drops of water is as true an emblem, equally effective sacramentally, as a whole river, may not a small quantity of wine, diluted with water, be as true an emblem as a gallon of the same liquor? So, after the manner of the Ritualists, those pronounced sacramentarians, though not from the same motives, we diluted it largely with water, and added some dark sugar. The advanced critics of the Tubingen school say that, although the Bible is not exclusively God's Word, yet the whole of God's Word is in the Bible, whatever else may be in it; so, although our cups were not filled exclusively with wine, yet there was wine in every cup, and every communicant partook of wine, and the ordinance was therefore valid.

For nearly a century port wine has been used in this country in the Lord's Supper. From the Reformation up till near the end of last century the light white wines of France, which Mr. Gladstone is so eager to introduce, on temperance grounds, were used both for sacramental and ordinary purposes; but when, in consequence of the great French war, our trade relations with France were broken off, our wine merchants went to Portugal and brought over port wine; and as no living man has any personal remembrance of the old state of things, many people are in the belief that port wine was always used at the eucharist, and that it was employed because it was red, and in this respect was the most appropriate symbol for the blood of Christ. Things went on with us in their usual way for some twenty years; the saccharine diluted wine was used without any misgiving, and no change was contemplated; but time brought changes. Commerce had visited the island, and traders there, as everywhere else, were causing annoyance by the introduction of intoxicating liquors. Several of our young men had been killed by the use of them. But matters were brought to a crisis by a very trivial and accidental occurrence. One day Ester, our principal native woman, was telling my wife that So-and-so, a very promising young man, had been drinking till he was drunk. "And what did he drink?" said Mrs. Inglis. "Oh," said she, "it was British kava, of course; they call it wine; it is all the same as what we use at the sacrament." This was certainly, in the estimation of the natives, drinking the cup of the Lord and the cup of devils; it was filling both cups with the same liquor. What was to be done? The traders would soon fill the cup of devils, but what was to be done for the cup of the Lord? We could get no unfermented wine; Mr. Frank Wright had no agencies in these Colonies; and although Australia is one of the best vine-growing countries in the world, yet the inspissated juice of the grape, so well known to the ancients, is literally unknown there. The grapes are all fermented, and the Government experts connected with the excise certify that Australian wine, without being fortified by brandy, contains more than thirty per cent. of alcohol. A solution of the difficulty, however, seemed to be easy, by following the example of the missionaries of the London Missionary Society in the South Seas. For a long time past they have used palm wine—that is, as I have said, the liquor of the cocoa-nut, which is a species of the palm-tree—instead of the ordinary wine. I therefore introduced an overture into the Mission Synod asking that an act should be passed giving liberty to any one who might desire it to use palm wine instead of the common wine at the Lord's Supper. I allowed the overture to lie on the table of the Synod for a twelvemonth, that there might be plenty of time to consider it fully.

It was fully and freely discussed. Everything was said, both for it and against it, that could well be said; but when the vote was taken, there were, I think, eight against the overture, and only four for it. One member said that rather than use palm wine he would use pure water; another said that he had once taken cocoa-nut liquor at one of the stations of the London Missionary Society, and that afterwards he seriously doubted whether he had rightly observed the Lord's Supper or not. When our Saviour established the ordinance of the Supper He selected bread and (not wine, for that word is never used in connection with the ordinance, but) the fruit of the vine—the former the choicest food and the latter the choicest liquor known in the land of Canaan, the two substances the most pleasant and nourishing to the body—as pointing out that the blessings procured by His broken body and His shed blood were to the soul what those were to the body. Now, what the vine and its fruit are to the inhabitants of Palestine, such are the cocoa-nut and its fruit to the inhabitants of the South Seas. One writer, speaking of the cocoa-nut in Africa, says, "It is worth while going to Africa, were it for no other object than to drink cocoa-nuts, they are so delicious." Another writer, who spent some months among the South Sea Islands, uses almost the same words, and says, "It is worth any one's while to go to those islands, were it for nothing else than to drink cocoa-nuts, they are so delightfully refreshing." No substance known on the islands is calculated to convey to the mind of a native the idea of the soul-reviving influences of Christ's death so vividly as the liquor of the cocoa-nut. And to stickle even for the grape, in such circumstances, was substituting the letter of the law for its spirit, holding by the rule and overlooking the reason of the rule. Our diluted saccharine wine was perfectly innocuous. It might have been drunk by the most recently reclaimed drunkard without the slightest danger, —happily we had none such,—but then it was associated in their minds at that time with nothing but the cup of devils, the intoxicating British kava. The members of our Synod were all either pledged or practical teetotalers, but the majority was made up mostly of the younger members of the court, of new arrivals from home, strongly imbued with home and hereditary notions about sacramental wine; they were men who abhorred drunkenness, but nevertheless adhered to some extent to the common but false belief that alcoholic drinks would be good if they were not abused; that it is in the abuse rather than in the use of these liquors in which the great danger lies; who held more or less the doctrine recently promulgated to the trade by the great brewer, the Hon. George H. Allsopp, M.P., who says, "In spite of all that our teetotal friends may say, there is no sin in the drink;

it is only the excess of it which should be discouraged;" whose teetotalism rested on the grounds of Christian expediency, for the sake of others rather than themselves, and not on the scientific principles that alcohol is a poison, that it is not a food, not a heat-producing agent, and as an article of support for the system it is utterly useless and wholly pernicious; that it is injurious to both blood and brains, to body and to mind. Moreover, our young friends had not been sufficiently long in contact with the widening and liberalising influences of island and colonial life to bring them into proper touch with their new relationships, and to realise that the traditions of home life are not always in accordance with the never-failing fitness of things.

There was one thing, however, that strongly impressed me in connection with the decision of our Mission Synod on this wine question, and that was, the soundness and the far-seeing ability of the Westminster divines. In the thirty-first chapter of the Confession of Faith they say, "All Synods, since the Apostles' times, *may err*, and many *have erred;* therefore, they are not to be made the rule of faith or practice, but to be used as a help in both." Now, if those divines formulated so correctly the doctrine of Scripture concerning Synods and Councils, is there not a strong presumption that their dogmatic utterances concerning the Divine Decrees were equally correct? "God executeth His decrees in the works of Creation and Providence." God is almighty and infallible—He cannot err; but man is feeble and fallible; for, as some one says, "The best of men are only men at the best."

CHAPTER XIII.

MISSION VESSELS—THE "DAYSPRING."

WHEN we had seen something like the beginning of the end in the Christianising of Aneityum, we felt somewhat like John Williams on Huahine, or Raiatea, when he said, "I cannot be shut up within a single reef." We turned our attention to the islands beyond us, and considered as to what we could do for them. By the aid of the mission ship the *John Williams*, we got two teachers and their wives settled on Tanna, and other two couples on Futuna; but, when settled, we had no means of visiting them, except by our own whale-boats. We made known our circumstances to the Rev. Dr. Ross of Sydney, the agent of the London Missionary Society, and who was also kindly acting as our agent. He applied to some of his friends to help us, and they kindly sent us down a fine boat by the *John Williams*, which would have suited our purpose well. But, through the absence of a letter, that had been mislaid, a mistake was committed, and we were given to understand that the boat was intended for the Loyalty Island Mission, and not for ours; and hence it was passed on to the brethren in that mission, and did not come into our hands at all. In course of time, however, the error was discovered, the mistake corrected, and the price of the boat was transmitted to us, and we obtained an equally suitable boat, which we named

MISSION VESSELS—THE "DAYSPRING." 165

the *Columba*, after the apostle of Iona, as we were striving to make Aneityum the Iona of the *New* Hebrides. This boat served us for some time, till we received from our friends in Glasgow a small schooner of twelve tons, which was called the *John Knox*, after the great Scottish Reformer. This enabled us to extend our visits as far as Eromanga. Beyond this we could not go, although in subsequent years the *John Knox* was employed by the brethren of the London Missionary Society, in their first visit to open up their mission to New Guinea. The *John Knox*, however, did good service in the New Hebrides.

But the idea of a much larger vessel was still cherished by us. Accordingly, in the end of 1861, when Mr. Paton was driven from Tanna, the missionaries arranged that, partly for the sake of his health, and partly with the view of creating an interest in Australia on behalf of the mission, Mr. Paton should proceed to Sydney and New South Wales, which he did, and afterwards went on also to Melbourne and Victoria. He was very successful in both places, but especially in Victoria. The Presbyterians there had just completed a union of all the denominations, and the idea of a new vessel for the Presbyterian mission in the New Hebrides was caught up with enthusiasm as their first united missionary effort. Chiefly through the Sabbath-school children, Mr. Paton raised £3000 with which to purchase a mission vessel, £1000 with which to bring out new missionaries, and £200 for the support of native teachers. Having completed these arrangements, Mr. Paton went back to Scotland, and visited all the congregations of the Reformed Presbyterian Church. Meanwhile it was agreed that the vessel should be built in Nova Scotia, under the direction of the Foreign Mission Board of the Presbyterian Church in that province, by whose agents the New Hebrides Mission had been commenced, and whose members also raised £1600 to the Ship Fund. This was accordingly done. The *Dayspring*, a vessel of 120 tons, was built in New Glasgow, and sailed from Halifax in the autumn of 1863—Mr. William A. Fraser, master. She had a remarkably fine passage out to Australia. She brought out three missionaries with her, viz., Revs. Messrs. Morrison, M'Cullagh, and Gordon. The first two were married. In Melbourne, under the sanction of the Ship Committee, a deck-house was added to the *Dayspring*, which made her equal to a vessel of 150 tons. In June of 1864 the *Dayspring* arrived at Aneityum, and visited among the Loyalty and New Hebrides Islands till the beginning of December, when she returned to Sydney. Here Mr. Paton, having returned from Scotland, met her, and spent three months visiting the Australian Colonies. In April Mr. Paton accompanied the vessel to the islands, visited round the group, and attended the Annual Missionary Meeting. It was found that in some respects it was easier to purchase a mission ship than to keep her afloat: the one was a special single effort, the other was to be a permanent annual struggle. It was, therefore, at once agreed that Mr. Paton should go up to the Colonies, consult with friends, and make arrangements for raising such a sum annually as would meet the current expenses of the vessel. Mr. Paton went immediately up to Australia, and by his untiring energy and marvellous organising capacity, he arranged that the Sabbath-school children who had chiefly purchased the vessel should raise about £1800 a year to support her. Of this sum the children connected with the Presbyterian Church of Nova Scotia should raise £250; the children of the Reformed Presbyterian Church in Scotland, the same; the children of the Presbyterian Church of Victoria, £500; the children of the Presbyterian Church of New South Wales, £200; and the remaining £600 to be raised by the children of the Presbyterian Churches of New Zealand, South Australia, Tasmania, and Queensland. So excellent were the arrangements that were made, and so loyal to the engagement have been the successive generations of the Sabbath-school children, that, during all the twenty-five years that the *Dayspring* has been afloat, she has never incurred a penny of debt, she has never been crippled for want of funds, and she has always had a good working balance on hand. This shows also, I think, that the public have had the fullest confidence in the management of the *Dayspring* funds; they felt satisfied that they are judiciously and economically spent—a point of vital importance in all public trusts, especially for those raised by annual contributions. The *Dayspring* being intended exclusively for the use of the New Hebrides Mission, the management of the vessel has all along been left in the hands of the Mission Synod. The Synod has appointed a Board in Sydney, consisting of three ministers and three laymen, to attend to the management of the vessel when in the Colonies. These laymen especially are well acquainted with the requirements of shipping. At first the headquarters of the *Dayspring* were, for the most part, in Melbourne, as a large proportion of the funds for the support of the vessel were, through the energetic efforts of the Rev. Dr. Macdonald, at that time agent for the vessel, supplied from Victoria. But when it was found necessary that the *Dayspring* should make two voyages from the islands to the Colonies each year, to save time and minimise expenses, the headquarters of the vessel had to be removed to Sydney; occasionally, however, she visited New Zealand, Melbourne, and other places for special purposes.

The history of the *Dayspring* was one of uninterrupted success, till the 3d of January 1872, when she was completely wrecked in Aneityum harbour, in one of the most terrific hurricanes that ever passed over those islands, the full particulars of which I have given elsewhere in this volume. For the ensuing season we chartered the *Paragon* of Sydney, a new vessel of 160 tons burden. In the meantime we recovered the insurance of the vessel—£2000. Mr Paton and Mr. Copeland were deputed to raise funds to purchase another vessel, the former in New Zealand, the latter in New South Wales. They raised other £2000. With this £4000 we bought the *Paragon*, and fitted her up for the work of the mission, and had her name changed to that of the *Dayspring*. She has served us now satisfactorily for fourteen years. But great changes have been going on during the last quarter of a century. Steamships are everywhere displacing sailing vessels; the very kidnappers, in the labour traffic in Western Polynesia, are employing steamers to carry on more effectually their nefarious practices; and unless our mission had consented, which it had no thought of doing, to be left completely behind in the march of modern progress, it was found necessary that we must go in for at least auxiliary steam-power.

On this account the Presbyterian Church of Victoria agreed to place at the disposal of the mission the services of Mr. Paton, who is supported by that Church, and is always at its disposal, that he might come to this country and plead for funds with which to buy a new ship. Accordingly he arrived in London in April 1884, duly authorised for his mission, by the General Assembly of the Presbyterian Church of Victoria, to all the General Assemblies and General Synods of the Presbyterian Churches in the three kingdoms. He addressed the two Scotch and the one Irish General Assembly, and the Synod of the United Presbyterian Church in Scotland and the Synod of the Presbyterian Church in England. He was cordially thanked by these Supreme Courts for his addresses, and recommended to the liberality of their congregations respectively. He also attended and addressed the Pan-Presbyterian Council that met in Belfast that year. He visited congregations and addressed meetings in most of the principal cities in the three kingdoms—in London, Manchester, and Liverpool; in Edinburgh and Glasgow, Aberdeen and Dundee; in Dublin, Belfast, and Derry. He displayed all his accustomed tact, he spoke with all his wonted energy, and pleaded with all his well-known fervid and pathetic eloquence; he solicited only in public, he made no private personal appeals; but, in addition to his public collections, he received many private contributions, and that from all classes of persons and members of all denominations, from the widow's mite to the offerings of the wealthy; his donors ranged from the titled nobility to the poorest and obscurest of servant girls. I am not aware of the name of any member of the royal family being found on his lists, but then a paragraph has been going the round of the religious newspapers affirming that neither the Queen nor any of her family contribute to any of the missionary societies; but one thing is certain, that the Lord-Lieutenant of Ireland and his distinguished and liberal-minded lady—that the Earl and Countess of Aberdeen and all their children were warm and generous supporters of

Mr. Paton's *Dayspring* fund. There is a story told which is quite in keeping with similar well-authenticated anecdotes connected with Mr. Paton's labours. One morning Lady Aberdeen went into the nursery, and found one of her little boys crying. She asked him what was the matter. "Oh," said he, "I am afraid that Mr. Paton will have all the heathen converted before I am big and able to be a missionary, and then there will be nothing left for me to do!" It was at this very time that the Hon. Ian Keith-Falconer and his young, beautiful, and accomplished wife were accepted by the Free Church of Scotland to carry on their mission to the Mohammedans in Aden. Mr. Keith-Falconer is a younger son of the late Earl of Kintore, generally known, like Lord Shaftesbury, as the "good Earl." He undertook not only to act as a missionary, but to bear all the expenses of the mission himself. He is understood to be one of the best Arabic scholars of the present day. Hearing so much from Mr. Paton about the New Hebrides Mission, and so much from Mr. Keith-Falconer about the Aden Mission, it was quite natural for the young Gordons to catch up enthusiastically the missionary spirit, so fully in accordance with the traditions of that ancient, noble, and religious family. A young Gordon, who would himself have been an Earl of Aberdeen had he lived, had it in his heart to go out as a missionary to Africa.

Notwithstanding the very depressed state of the country, at the end of eighteen months, Mr. Paton had succeeded in raising £9000, with which he returned to Victoria. The New Hebrides Mission Synod, the *Dayspring* Board, and the New Hebrides Mission Committees of the different Australasian Presbyterian Churches have been collecting information, and are consulting as to the size and shape of the vessel, and examining into the details, so as to see how the money can be disbursed to the best advantage, so as to secure the greatest benefits to the mission, with the most economical expenditure of the funds; and as there are among them many able, practical men, well acquainted with seafaring matters, there is no doubt whatever but that these objects will be carefully attended to and largely secured.

It is not to secure speed when sailing on the open sea that we wish to employ steam in our mission vessel, but chiefly to avoid danger and difficulties in going into or out of harbours, and to keep her from drifting into peril when caught in calms. While among the islands she is continually either entering or leaving harbours, and she is often becalmed in circumstances where a few hours' steaming would save a day's, or, it might be, a week's, detention, or where a current might drift her into serious danger. Both the first and second *John Williams* were lost in calms—the first at Danger Island, and the second at Savage Island. On one occasion my wife and I, and some other missionaries, were on board the *Dayspring*, on the coast of Eromanga, when the current all but carried her against the rocks in a calm; both boats were down, and it was pulling for life. Providentially a light breeze sprang up, which carried us out of danger.

CHAPTER XIV.

ASTRONOMY ON ANEITYUM—ECLIPSES.

ASTRONOMY, as every one knows, had its origin in the East. Under the clear mild skies of Mesopotamia, the sage, thoughtful shepherds, keeping watch over their flocks by night, had their attention constantly drawn to the wonders of the starry heavens. They recorded their observations; they divided the visible heavens into sections; and, following the example of the Most High, they counted the number of the visible stars, and called them by names. Hence the Lord, when He spoke to Job out of the whirlwind, recognised the astronomical vocabulary, and said, as rendered in our Revised Version, "Canst thou bind the cluster of the Pleiades, or loose the bands of Orion? Canst thou lead forth the Mazzaroth" (the twelve signs of the zodiac) "in their season? Or canst thou guide the Bear with her train?"

In the South Seas they have not the long-continued, clear, cloudless Oriental sky, but they have advantages in this respect of which we know nothing in this country. Their knowledge of astronomy, however, was very limited, as much so as of any of the other sciences. They had given names to a few of the constellations, and to a few of the more prominent stars, and to certain celestial phenomena. They had given the names of *Katgapohoth* to Venus, when a morning star, and *Inwang*, when an evening star. They call the Southern Cross *Nohoaing Wai*, the Duck, from the resemblance which its four principal stars bear to that fowl. They call the Milky Way *Inwau an nathiat*, that which binds the Way. The reason of the name is not very obvious. They call Orion the *Nelgau*, or Canoe, and the Girdle of Orion *Nehev*, the Paddle for propelling the Canoe.

With us Orion stands upright on his feet—quite a martial hero. At the antipodes he stands upon his head—by no means a dignified attitude. But within the tropics, and, consequently on Aneityum, he seems to lie on his side, and, canoe-like, continually sails along the centre of the sky; and thus he is degraded by these maritime people, from being a conquering hero, to be a quiet, slow-sailing ship—the grand and the noble are exchanged for the merely utilitarian. They call the Pleiades, or the Seven Stars, the *Children of Kumnyumoi*. But whether they were men or women, the natives cannot say; whether they were women, like the Greek Pleiades, the seven daughters of Atlas and Oceania, or men, like the seven Greek poets who bore that name, the Aneityumese cannot determine; but since they speak of them as cooking taro, we may safely infer that they were female deities, in the island mythology, as that was a female occupation. They had names for several other stars, but what seems strange to us, they had no name for *Ursa Major*, or the Great Bear. It may have been because it is invisible for six months in the year, and is never seen on the south side of Aneityum, although on the north side, for six months every year, it hovers over Tanna every night, and is a noticeable constellation. They knew nothing about *Mazzaroth*, or the twelve signs of the zodiac. They had never mapped out the heavens into equal divisions, like the ancient astronomers.

Like the Jews, they divided the day and night into eight watches. They had the four principal divisions, of sunrise, sunset, noon, and midnight. They had a word for the other four subdivisions, viz., nine o'clock in the forenoon and three o'clock in the afternoon, when the sun was half up the sky, and again when half down, and another word for nine at night, and another for the morning watch, the cock-crowing—the *true* and also the *false* crowing, which I have described fully elsewhere. They had no weeks; the week has followed the Jewish and the Christian Sabbath. Where there have been no Sabbaths there have been no weeks. The Romans had *Nundinæ*, their *nine*-day periods, but seven days have followed the Sabbath. The week is a positive, not a natural, division of time, like the day, the month, and the year. They counted by moons, but they had no names for the different months; they simply counted the number of moons. They counted by years, but they had no eras, no epochs from which they began to count their years. They had no Olympiads, like the Greeks; no year of the building of the city, like the Romans; no A.M. or A.D., like us. They had no word for the whole year; but they had three seasons, the summer, the winter, and the hungry time; that was the time when the old crop was eaten up, and before any of the annual crops were ripe, corresponding to the spring. They never spoke of so many years, but of so many winters. They marked the beginning of the year by the blossoming of the reeds, an annual plant. The expression for everlasting was *irai iji ieng*, while the reeds blossom; or *irai iji mesese*, while winters remain. They have at least twenty-five names for the winds, but they are not divided equally, like the thirty-two points in the mariner's compass. The winds blow mostly from south round by the east, and on to the north, but very little from north round by the west on to the south. The prevailing wind is the south-east trade-wind, but this does not blow from one point only, but all along from the south to the east. On Aneityum we have the words of Solomon almost literally fulfilled : " The wind goeth toward the south, and turneth about unto the north ; it whirleth about continually, and the wind returneth again according to his circuits." The wind maketh the circuit of the horizon about once a fortnight. The process is this. There is a calm day. On the following a light wind springs up, a little to the west of south ; day by day it draws, little by little, towards the east, and increases daily in strength till it reaches its maximum ; but that is not always the same. In summer especially it passes the east on to the north ; when blowing north of east the atmosphere is often laden with humidity ; you cannot move but you perspire, and then you feel very uncomfortable. At the north-east it often dies away, takes a leap to the west, where it remains from one to, sometimes, five or six days ; but it is not reliable. Then it dies away, and is calm for a day or so, and then springs up as before at south by west, and proceeds on its circuit, going in the opposite direction to the hands of a watch ; but it never returns in the other direction. They have not four cardinal points in the horizon, as we have ; the east is called the rising of the sun, and the west is the setting of the sun. They have no word for south or north, but round the island everywhere it is seaward and landward. On both sides of the island it is called up towards the rising of the sun, and down towards where it sets. They have names for all kinds of hurricanes ; they have a name for the rainbow, for a halo round the sun or moon, for a comet, a meteor, a falling or shooting star, the Aurora

Australis or Southern Lights or Streamers, Magellan's Clouds, &c. But they never distinguished between the fixed stars and the planets. I occasionally called the attention of the more intelligent to the planets. They had often observed eclipses both of the sun and of the moon. Owing to the great clearness of the atmosphere these phenomena are remarkably well seen. I never fully realised the Scriptural description of eclipses till I saw them on Aneityum, when I saw the sun become black as sackcloth of hair, and the moon become as blood. We had a good view of four eclipses—two of the sun and two of the moon.

On the 25th October 1855 we had a total eclipse of the moon. We observed the eclipse first about half-past seven in the evening. It was then total, and continued so for about an hour; the lower limb of the moon then began to emerge from the shadow of the earth, and by nine o'clock the moon was again "walking in brightness." As we had no almanacs there at that time, except one we had made ourselves, for the use of the natives, merely to teach them the months and the days, and one that our Samoan brethren had prepared for the use of their mission, which, although it marked the changes of the moon, gave no intelligence about eclipses, we were not at all on the outlook for such a phenomenon, and but for the natives we might not have observed it. I was busy writing in my study, and Mrs. Inglis was doing the same in another room, when one of her girls came running in and called out to her, "*Ak Misi, et mun mas inmahog, et alupas yang; apam aiek um almoi*"—"O Mistress, the moon is dead, she is so yellow; do come out and see her." We went out immediately; and if yellowness, or rather a dull blood-like redness, had been a sure sign of death, the moon had been dead to a certainty.

This furnished me with a good opportunity to give the natives, both then and afterwards, some lessons on the elements of astronomy, and on the causes of eclipses, both of the sun and moon, with which they appeared to be much gratified. Formerly they had no idea of the causes of eclipses. Like some of the heathen nations of antiquity, they looked upon them as prognosticating evil, as indicating the death of some great chief, or some similar calamity, and they used to blow on conches, beat wooden drums, cut down trees, howl, and make hideous noises, either through fear, or to avert the dreaded calamity.

Although eclipses of the sun and moon were occurring every year, it was not often that we observed them. In 1871, however, we were singularly favoured in that respect. Within two weeks there were two eclipses, the one of the sun and the other of the moon, both predicted to be visible, and both actually observed on our side of the globe; and we had a fine view of both. I was at Futuna during the eclipse of the sun, which took place on Sabbath the 18th of June. The morning was cloudy and threatened rain, and no traces of the sun were to be seen; but about mid-day the clouds broke up, and the sun shone out among them. At about half-past one the first contact was visible, and the eclipse continued till about half-past four. Regarding the sun as a map, hung up on a wall, with the north at the top, the south at the bottom, the east on the right hand, and the west on the left, the appearance of the eclipse may be thus described. It began on the south-west of the sun's disc, crept gradually round to the east side, and finally went off at the north-east. At the middle of the eclipse the shadow of the moon extended to about the middle of the sun's disc; about a fifth part of the disc was obscured; the light around was sensibly diminished.

178   ASTRONOMY ON ANEITYUM—ECLIPSES.

The eclipse of the moon took place a fortnight after that of the sun, on Sabbath the 2d of July, or rather, on the morning of Monday the 3d; it began about half-past twelve, and ended about half-past two. The missionaries for the Annual Meeting had all landed on Aniwa, from the *Dayspring*, on the Saturday before. When the services of the Sabbath, public and private, were over, I volunteered to sit up and awaken the others when the eclipse began;—we always went early to bed on the islands. I did so; but some of the brethren were so eager for the sight that they kept peeping out now and again, evidently afraid lest I should fall asleep during my watch. Up till midnight the sky was remarkably clear, not a cloud passed over the face of the moon; but about twelve o'clock large masses of clouds rose up, and it appeared for a time as if the moon would be entirely hid; but the wind carried them along, breaks occurred, and every now and then we had some clear glimpses, which enabled us to observe the progress of the eclipse during its whole course. This eclipse proceeded in an opposite direction to that of the sun the fortnight before. It began on the north-east quarter of the moon's disc, the place where it ended on the sun; it then crept down along the east side, and finally went off on the south-west side, where that of the sun began. When the eclipse was at the greatest, about a sixth part of the moon's disc was obscured. There was one very striking difference between the two eclipses. In the eclipse of the sun, one-half of the moon's shadow was seen on the sun's disc; a half-circle was distinctly marked, reaching to the centre of the sun's disc. But in the eclipse of the moon it was only a small part of the earth's shadow that was seen on the moon's disc; it was a segment of a large circle, and extended only about half-way to the centre of the moon's disc, but covering a much larger portion of her perimeter.

On both occasions we tried to improve the phenomena, for the benefit of the natives, both in conversation and in our public services; not by spiritualising them—which some can do very pertinently—but in a way which seemed to us more suitable for our auditors, viz., by explaining the causes of the eclipses, and calling in God's works as the witnesses for the truth of His Word. "You see," we said to the natives, "that large, deep, dark hollow place on the sun's face, as smooth and round on the edge as if it had been cut out with a knife;—what is the cause of that? That is the moon, the half of which is come in between us and the sun." Their eyes opened wider, and they watched with newly awakened interest the progress of the eclipse, as they understood something of the cause of this strange phenomenon. A similar explanation was given when the moon was eclipsed. They were shown how the earth was at that time exactly between the sun and the moon, and how the shadow of the earth was falling on the face of the moon.

The natives were told beforehand what was to be expected. At Futuna the afternoon service took place during the eclipse of the sun. Mr. Copeland met with the Futunese in the church, and I held a short service in the schoolroom with the Aneityumese teachers and some other Aneityumese who were there at that time, and the drift of our remarks was somewhat as follows:—"Your wise men formerly professed, and the wise men among the heathen in all these islands still profess, to make rain and wind, good weather and bad weather, health and sickness, to kill and to cure, at their pleasure. Our wise men never profess to do any such things; because they know that God only can make rain and wind, send sickness and death, give life and health, make food plentiful or cause famine; but they can do what the wise men among the heathen never attempted to do; they tell long beforehand when the sun and moon will die (the native word for an eclipse, as we have seen), and why? How do they know this? They know it because they study the works of God, and they find that all the works of God are true. Everything that God does, and everything that God says, is true. He has spoken a law to the sun and to the moon, and they hear His word and obey His law. He has made the paths of the sun and the moon so true and exact, and He has made the rate of their travelling along these paths so true and exact, that our wise men, who search out these things, can, by counting—for they have made themselves very expert in counting figures—tell long beforehand the very month, and day, and hour when we may see them pass one another, as we have seen them do to-day. Everything that God does is true; there is nothing deceitful in it; and everything that God says is true; His word is as true as His works. In the Bible He says that every one that believes in Christ, and repents of his sins, shall be saved, and go to heaven; but that every one who refuses to believe in Christ, and to repent of his sins, shall be condemned and go to hell. And as certainly as the predicted eclipse has been seen to-day, so certainly will God's word about our souls be found true at the day of death and at the day of judgment."

During our stay at Futuna the natives of that island had another lecture read to them on the evidences of Christianity, more convincing to their minds than the whole of Butler's "Analogy," with the volumes of Paley and Chalmers on the evidences superadded. "Ye men of Athens," said Paul, "I perceive that in all things ye are too superstitious," or, as most critics now render it, "ye are very religious." The Futunese, like the Athenians, are "very religious" in their own way. Till certain religious ceremonies and observances have been attended to, they will not plant a single yam; otherwise, it is believed, the yams would not grow, or some calamity, such as sickness or death, would befall the man who planted them. The year before that Mr. Copeland had had some yams planted in his garden before any of these ceremonies had been performed by the sacred men, and they were now ripe. A day was appointed for their being dug, and a number of natives, heathen and Christian, were invited, and came to see the produce taken up. The mounds were opened by the Aneityumese teachers, and out came such yams as had scarcely ever been seen on Futuna, to the great delight of the Aneityumese and the Christian natives of Futuna, but to the manifest surprise and confusion of the heathen. But, alas! it was there as it is elsewhere—

"Convince a man against his will,
He's of the same opinion still."

The following Sabbath came, but there was no accession to the number of worshippers. Many an infidel has read Butler, or Paley, or Campbell, or Chalmers, and remained as much an infidel as before. The Pharisees saw our Saviour's miracles, and yet rejected His message of mercy. No doubt the heathen on Futuna would say, as other heathen have repeatedly said, that it might do very well for Mr. Copeland or the Aneityumese to plant their yams without propitiating the gods of Futuna, because they were foreigners, but it would be perilous for them to do so. The gods would certainly be angry, and punish them. No one who has not grappled with the superstitions of heathenism can have any idea of the darkness, and hardness, and obstinacy of the heathen heart. They really think that what they believe is true. They have been born into this belief; it has "grown with their growth and strengthened with their strength," and with them their religion is no make-believe. However erroneous, it is a part of their very nature. Nothing can effect a change in their beliefs but Divine power. Still, the more suitable the means, and the more diligently these are employed, the more confidently may we expect the Spirit's influence from on high. Exhibitions such as these serve very much the same purposes among the heathen that lectures and essays on the evidences do among ourselves; and where they do not convince the sceptic, they often confirm the faith and fortify the mind of the true but weak believer.

CHAPTER XV.

EARTHQUAKES AND TIDAL WAVE ON ANEITYUM.

On the 28th of March 1875 we were startled by a very severe earthquake, followed immediately by a tidal wave, which raised the sea ten or eleven feet above its ordinary level at spring-tides. At our station the sea rose about four feet higher than during the hurricane of 1873, when the *Dayspring* was lost. It was not merely the height to which it rose, but the force with which it rolled in, that rendered it so formidable. It covered all the low land of Aname, the district on which our houses stood. It broke open every door, and rushed into every house. It made large breaches in the walls of the church, and broke completely down one-half of the outer walls of the Teachers' Institution, a building seventy feet long, and its walls ten feet high. It broke open the front-door of our dwelling-house, and rushed in, two feet deep, through the lobby, although the floor was raised two feet above the ground. The sea rose round the whole island, and did serious damage at every exposed situation. In all the low-lying districts the taro—the staff of life on the island—was more or less injured. There had not been such an earthquake, or such a rise of the sea, within the memory of living man. Tradition had to be called in to supply a parallel case. The natives said that their fathers had told them that there was an earthquake in their days which loosened the rocks on the mountains, and sent the stones rolling down into the valleys, and that the sea rose and covered the low lands; but no one now living saw that earthquake—this was the heaviest and most disastrous that any living man had seen.

On our side of the island there were several narrow escapes from the sea, both of adults and of children, but no lives were lost. On the other side of the island one boy was drowned and two men were severely hurt, and several also had narrow escapes from the sea. As the other station (Mr. Murray's) stood high, it sustained no injury from the sea; but the large stone church was considerably damaged by the earthquake, the front wall being considerably rent. Several schoolhouses on the shore, on both sides of the island, were destroyed. At Mr. Cronstedt's whaling-station at Anau-unse, on the west, or lee, end of the island, considerable damage was done to the premises by the earthquake; and the wave, as it retired, carried off two whale-boats; but on the return of the wave—for it returned, but in a very modified form, doing no injury—the boats were brought back towards the shore, and the natives recovered them, without their having sustained any injury. But at the other whaling-station on the island of Inyeug the scene was appalling, and the ruin was all but complete. The small island of Inyeug forms one side of the Aneityum harbour. It was a lovely and a healthy spot, and had been occupied for nearly thirty years as a whaling and trading station, and been exposed to all the hurricanes that had passed over the island, without sustaining any very serious damage; even the great tidal-wave of August 1868, which came rolling up along the whole eastern coast of New Zealand, and was observed in Port Resolution, in the island of Tanna—as the *Dayspring* was lying there at the time— was not noticed on Inyeug. On this occasion, however, the sea rose on both sides of the island, and nearly covered the whole of it. Mr. Underwood, with one of his sons and a few natives, were on the station at the time. He heard the sea coming, and called on the rest to run to a little eminence at the end of the island. He himself ran, but was either met or overtaken by the sea, which carried him off his feet; providentially he caught hold of some firm object, and held on by it till the sea receded, and in this way he escaped with only a few bruises. One whale-boat was carried out to sea, and nearly every house on the island was destroyed. Mr. Underwood's dwelling-house, a large, strong, weather-boarded building, was lifted up, and carried to the very edge of the sea, and there left a ruin. The whole island was a scene of desolation.

Having given this brief general account of the earthquake and the wave, I shall now proceed to describe more fully how they affected ourselves.

On Sabbath evening the 28th of March we had retired to rest at our usual time, between nine and ten o'clock. About a quarter past eleven we were awakened by an earthquake. It was heavy for earthquakes there; it would have been considered a very moderate one in New Zealand—at least in Wellington; it was, however, unusually long. I thought, and others thought the same, that it must have been more than a minute, and it had a peculiarly alarming motion. After it was over I rose and went through the house, but, so far as I could observe, nothing was injured. I went out; the natives were all aroused, and out of doors too. It was a beautiful, clear, calm night; not a breath of wind was blowing; nothing was heard but the usual sound of the reef; while the sea seemed quiet and still as a sleeping infant. The moon was within two nights of entering her last quarter, and was about an hour up; below her, and near her, hung a drapery of sable clouds, with a bright silver lining. Orion, the most conspicuous object at that time during the evenings in the western sky, had just set. The Great Northern Bear, stretched out at his full length, was keeping his nightly watch over the island of Tanna. The Southern Cross had just attained its highest elevation, and was standing perpendicular. Centaurus, Argo Navis, and other constellations were shining with their usual brilliancy from "the chambers of the South." A lovelier night could not have been witnessed. I returned to the house and went to bed, hoping that the disturbance for the night was over; but in about fifteen minutes after the earthquake we heard a sound in the distance. My wife said, "What sound is that?" I said, "I think it is a gust of wind coming through the trees "—no uncommon thing on calm nights. "It is not wind, that," she said; and springing out of bed, she looked out at the eastern window, in the direction whence the sound was coming. "There is not a leaf moving," she said.

The sound was increasing, and she hurried to the door. I sprang up after her. As she opened the back-door she saw one of our natives coming out of their house, just opposite to ours; and she called out, "Yamin, what sound is that?" "It is the sea, Misi," he said; "run, run, Misi, run." She called out to me to make haste. He took her by the hand, just as she was, in her night-dress, with a sheet which she had accidentally wrapped around her. Fear added wings to her feet, and, under the young man's guidance, in a few moments she had cleared both the back-yard and the back-garden, broken down the reed fence, and gained a slight elevation beyond.

EARTHQUAKES AND TIDAL WAVE. 187

They saved their distance and no more; the sea just touched their feet before they got out of its reach. They were there joined by others, mostly women and children, and thence threaded their way through the bush to our cottage on Lolannapjis, nearly half a mile distant, at least by the path along which they went, and where they were fairly beyond the reach of the sea.

In the meantime I had turned back, but only for a few seconds, to draw on a pair of trousers, and experienced a very striking illustration of the value of our Saviour's admonition (Mark xiii. 16), "Let him that is in the field not turn back again to take up his garment." These few moments proved a dangerous, and might have been a fatal, delay; the sea was in the bedroom before I got out of it, and I had to pass through something like the waters seen in the prophet's vision. At the threshold the waters were to the ankles; when I had gone, not a thousand, but only thirty paces, the waters were to the knees; and when I had gone only thirty more, the waters were nearly to the loins, and running in a strong current. In the middle of the back-yard I met our principal native man, carrying his step-daughter on his shoulder; he took hold of my arm, and we waded together till we reached the back part of the yard, and got hold of a native house, in which was lying an elderly woman, the widow of one of our teachers, and who was nearly blind. Mrs. Inglis had called out and aroused her as she passed the house; but, poor woman! she could do nothing. In a moment the sea was at her door, which was shut, and to open it would have been to let in the enemy faster than he was coming; but she wisely sat up in her bed, and left herself in the hands of God. We stood still, and held on by her house, as we could do nothing better. In a short time the worst was over; the waters rapidly abated, and in five minutes the sea had returned to its wonted channels. Immediately thereafter all the men near us came into the premises to ascertain our condition, and render whatever assistance might be needful. I learned from them that my wife, under safe guidance, was on her way to Lolan-napjis. I therefore sent on clothes, blankets, &c.; and after seeing that there was no returning waves of any consequence, I followed with the other natives to Lolan-napjis myself, where we spent a safe but rather anxious night.

About half-past three o'clock on the Monday morning we had another shock of earthquake, much heavier, though greatly shorter, than the first, and which brought down the stone chimney in our cook-house, and which, I presume, was the shock that damaged the stone church at Anelgauhat. About five o'clock, a little before daylight, there was a third, not so heavy as either of the other two; and about eight o'clock there was a fourth, which some thought to be heavier than any of the former three; but as all the damage had been done by the second that could be done, without a considerable additional force, this fourth shock left no special traces of its presence. From that time for more than three weeks there was not a day in which there was not one or more shocks. During the first ten days they amounted to upwards of a hundred; a good many of them were rather sharp shocks, but none of them doing any damage. So far as my experience and information go, the law of earthquakes seems to be this:—All the damage is done by the first shock or shocks; these, again, are succeeded by a number of lighter shocks, which inflict no serious injury. After the severe earthquake in Wellington in 1848, while we were living there, there was not a day for three months without one or more shocks, but they did no damage; and we then learned that some old whalers had had a similar experience at Dusky Bay many years before.

On Monday morning, when daylight revealed the effects of the earthquakes and the wave, the scene on the premises was one of great desolation; every house was more or less a ruin, and every place was covered more or less with rubbish and debris. I have already referred to the condition of the church and the Teachers' Institution, but nearly every building had sustained some damage. There being no wind, our roofs—the thatch of which was rather a fragile preparation, being made of sugar-cane leaf—were all uninjured, a circumstance which greatly mitigated our calamity; but the walls had been frightfully battered by the action of the sea. The extent of the damage done to our walls may be judged of when I mention that, as near as I could calculate, we had to put up anew four thousand feet of wattle and plaster. The sea had entered every house on our premises on Aname, and every room in every house, with the exception of our bathroom; the wave had spent its force just before it reached it. All the matting on our floors was saturated with mud and soaked with sea water; the amount of washing and cleaning that had to be performed was almost fabulous. Chests and boxes had been knocked about in all directions, and the most of their contents had been injured by salt water. My boat had been carried out to sea, and brought back again towards the shore, but it was so much injured that I had to break it up. It was an old boat, however, and not of much value. Nearly all our reed fences were laid prostrate, and one-half of them carried completely away;

while our bananas, which nearly half fed our natives, did not yield more than a third of their usual produce for more than nine months afterwards.

But that which rendered the calamity more vexatious to us than it otherwise would have been was this: our summer nominally, but our winter really—that is, the time when we expected heavy rains, storms, and hurricanes—was over, and our premises had undergone all those renovating processes which were considered necessary to make them look decent and respectable for another year. All the whitewashing, painting, cleaning, fencing, repairing of coral walks, &c., required by our houses, our gardens, and our glebe, for the ensuing season, had been finished a few weeks before. We fancied that we were now secure from all labours of this kind for a twelvemonth to come. In a week or ten days we were expecting the *Dayspring*, with whatever visitors she might bring us; when, lo! in less than ten short minutes all our fond hopes were blasted, all our fair prospects were blighted, all our sanguine expectations were signally disappointed; an overwhelming amount of difficult and discouraging labour was thrown upon our hands. But all is not lost that is imperilled —the gloomiest prospects do not always prove the most disastrous. We were signally favoured by a gracious Providence; in little more than three weeks all our damages were repaired; our ruins, so far as houses were concerned, had disappeared, and *cosmos* had again emerged from *chaos*. The premises were as good as they were before; some parts of them were even better, as they were now quite new. But it caused some twenty days hard work to the natives; and all that and more very hard and harassing labour to Mrs. Inglis and myself.

The natives on that occasion, however, behaved uncommonly

well; I never saw their sympathies flow out towards us so fully or so spontaneously. They came out and wrought with a will, unsolicited and unpaid. Our principal chief, Nowanpakau, who generally took the management and direction of native labour in connection with the mission, was absent on mission business on Tanna; but so willing were the natives themselves, that his absence was not felt. It was almost worth all the losses we had sustained, and all the labour we had performed, to see the reality of their Christianity so unmistakably brought out, in the readiness and heartiness with which they wrought, without pay and without food, to repair the damages done by the sea and the earthquake. From the morning after the calamity we had on an average fifty natives a day working for us. They came in rotation; we had a new party every day, with the exception of a few of the more skilled workmen, who assisted me daily in preparing the framework of the buildings, where these were broken down, or in otherwise making ready the work for the less skilled natives. On the last day but one of these repairs we had a hundred men working at the reed fences, and on the following day we had fifty women collecting and bringing coral to cover our walks—the last process in restoring our premises to their former condition.

Our garden was the only part of our station that showed the effects of the sea, without any possibility of their being speedily removed. Our large and beautiful bananas, the staple produce of our garden, on which our natives depended so largely for food, which combined so fully the *utile cum dulci*—the profitable and the beautiful—were to a great extent completely destroyed; and it required time as well as care to restore them to their former flourishing and fruitful condition. After the terrific hurricanes that swept over the north and west of Scotland in December and January 1883-4, and committed such awful havoc among our woods, it was reported that the Earl of Stair said, when he saw the destruction around Castle Kennedy, that he would rather have seen his noble mansion levelled to the ground, than the devastation produced among his trees; he could have rebuilt the castle, but he could not restore the woods. Comparing small things with great, our feelings were somewhat akin to his, supposing his castle had been left in ruins as well as his woods.

I felt a good deal the interruption to my mission labours proper. At that time I was busily occupied correcting our translation of the Old Testament. I had just finished a very careful examination and correction of Mr. Copeland's translation of the twelve minor Prophets, and was going on with a correction of my own translation of Isaiah, embodying Mr. Copeland's corrections of that translation. I had also finished the correction of Genesis and the first fifty Psalms, and was tasking myself to the utmost extent that time and strength would permit, when all these labours were suspended for a month. But the Lord alone knows what is best for us; change of employment is often as good as rest, and that month's physical toil probably did us as much good as a month's holidays might have done; it was certainly greatly to be preferred to a month's sickness. We felt thankful, after all that had happened, that we were still alive and enjoying our usual health, and were again surrounded, as fully as formerly, with means and appliances for being useful, and with the conveniences and comforts of civilised life.

I should have mentioned that on the Monday morning the natives found a considerable number of fish of various kinds left high and dry by the receding wave; also one large turtle and several young ones not half grown: these latter are very rarely seen or caught.

In these tropical islands vegetation is rapid and luxuriant, food can be raised or procured with great ease, and many advantages are held out to those who will take up their abode in those sunny isles. But Paley's great law of compensation holds good all the world over, and those islands prove no exception to its operation; floods, storms, hurricanes, earthquakes, tidal waves, and fever-producing *malaria* are some of the conditions attached to island privileges, to prevent people in other less favoured lands from "envying or grieving at the good" of those, in many ways, highly favoured islanders, and to keep them from indulging in any "inordinate motions or affections towards" any of the special privileges which they enjoy.

But some will say, "Why did you select for your station such a low and exposed locality?" In answer to this I may state, that when we fixed upon that place for our mission station, we were not aware that those powerful agencies with which, unhappily, we became so familiar were likely to become such frequent visitants to that particular spot. If we had had to commence the mission again, we would doubtless have avoided some mistakes that we had committed, and it is to be hoped that young missionaries proceeding to other islands will profit by our experience. Twelve years before that I did think of changing our station, and I carefully examined another locality with that view; but the labour involved in making the change would have been so great that I shrank from the undertaking, and, as a compromise, erected our cottage on Lolan-napjis, which, besides being a sanitorium, proved a valuable refuge when the earthquakes and the tidal wave came so suddenly upon us, and where we and all our natives stayed ten days, till our sea-soaked dwellings were again habitable. But our station was so central, so convenient, and had so many advantages, as largely counterbalanced those occasional but severe drawbacks. There had not been on Aneityum an earthquake or a tidal wave like that one for fifty or perhaps a hundred years; and, relying on the strictly mathematical principles that govern the calculation of chances, we thought we might reasonably hope that the chances were at least like fifty to one, that another such catastrophe would not occur for many years to come. Mr. Laurie has, however, removed the station wholly to Lolan-napjis, not so much from the fear of a tidal wave, as for the sake of what chiefly led me to erect the cottage at first, viz., the greater salubrity of the situation.

The earthquake and the tidal wave were severely felt on Aniwa and Eromanga, as well as on Aneityum. There were also at both islands a severe earthquake and a high tidal wave, higher than the first wave, two nights afterwards, on the 30th of March. The Robertsons and their natives on Eromanga fled to the hills, but no lives were lost. But the place where the tidal wave was most severely felt was at Lifu, on the Loyalty Islands. Three villages were swept away, and from twenty to thirty people were drowned. But the forces of nature were still in a state of activity. On the 5th of May following, at two o'clock in the morning, there was the heaviest earthquake we ever felt on Aneityum. Not only did the earth quake, but the rocks were rent. In different parts of the island large blocks of overhanging rock were rent off, and precipitated to the valleys below,

On other parts where large boulders were lying half buried on the surface, they were upheaved and shaken out of the earth, and left strewed about like the riddlings of creation, as Burns said of the stones on his farm of Ellisland. Both our chimneys were thrown down. The kitchen one was razed to its foundation; the other was brought down to a level with the side walls. The chimney in our dining-room, the lime of which was only slightly cracked by the earthquake of March 29th, was rent to the foundation, and would have shared the fate of the kitchen chimney had not the lower part of it been strongly braced by a partition and the frame of a door on the one side, and of a press on the other; but the top of the chimney, which was four feet high above the roof, was pitched over to the ground with apparently as much ease as a man's hat would have been blown off his head by a strong gust of wind. It touched the roof only in one place; the house stood nearly north and south, but the chimney was thrown diagonally, in a south-east direction. Afraid of another tidal wave, we all fled inland as fast as we could, and threaded our way through the bush to our cottage on Lolan-napjis, where we stayed till daylight; happily there was no rise of the sea at all. While we were in the bush there was another heavy shock, which made the trees quiver and move backwards and forwards all around us. For three months afterwards we were never more than a few days without earthquakes, mostly slight, but a good many rather sharp; but they did no damage. They were generally preceded by a loud hollow rumbling sound, under the ground, resembling distant thunder. We heard it coming from the north-west, and waited, expecting a severe shock; sometimes there was a sharp quiver, sometimes a slight one, and sometimes none at all; but as you never can calculate what an earthquake may be, those hollow threatening sounds produced anything but a soothing effect upon an excited nervous system. The volcano on Tanna was unusually active during those three months; though forty miles distant, almost every day we heard the eruptions like the booming of distant cannon. The mission-house at the other station was built of stone. The Murrays, who then occupied the station, awakened by the shock, sprang out of bed and made for the door, but the door was locked, and the key had been shaken out of the door, and there appeared to be nothing before them but to be buried in the ruins. Happily they found escape by another door, and spent the remainder of the night, which was cold and comfortless, in the open air, and thus escaped unhurt.

Although at our station, in addition to the two chimneys, a great deal of plaster was brought down, and lamps, bottles, glass, crockery, and kindred articles were smashed up a good deal, yet the damage was nothing compared with that of the 28th and 29th of March. I repaired the chimneys by means of piping, and by the time the vessel returned with the missionaries for the meeting of Synod, our repairs were completed and our house again habitable. But while, for all merely utilitarian purposes, the station was as good as ever, yet, as one of the missionaries observed, our church, Institution, dwelling-house, &c., were all so patched-up-like that our premises would never again have the same appearance that they once had.

But we felt thankful. While earthquakes, floods, storms, and everything terrible in the phenomena of nature had, for the year previous, been making the circuit of earth and ocean

—while it would have been difficult to say where one could have gone to be safe—and while we once and again fled, as they "fled before the earthquake in the days of Uzziah, king of Judah"—the Lord mercifully preserved us in life and health, and secured or restored to us all our comforts.

After thirty years' experience of earthquakes and kindred phenomena, I have often said that nothing reminds one so forcibly of the day of judgment as an earthquake, especially when it happens at night; it is so sudden, so unexpected, so uncertain as to the future, so striking, so irresistible in its effects, and strikes such terror into the hearts of a whole community in a single moment. When God unbars the doors that shut up the great deep, when He suspends the prohibition, "Hitherto shalt thou come and no farther, and here shall thy proud waves be staid," men and the works of men become an easy prey to the newly escaped prisoner. When the sea came upon us in all his strength, roaring like thunder along the whole coast, it furnished a striking commentary on the passage, while they all slumbered and slept, at midnight there was a cry made, "Behold, the bridegroom cometh; go ye out to meet him;" and they that were *ready* went in. But there was no time left for *getting ready*, for "the door was shut" (Matt. xxv. 1–10).

CHAPTER XVI.

THE LABOUR TRAFFIC IN THE NEW HEBRIDES.

THE labour traffic to Queensland, Fiji, and New Caledonia has been carried on in the New Hebrides for twenty-three years. It began in 1863. Its history is well known. It has been vigorously attacked as a part of that "consummation of all villanies," and it has been as stoutly defended, not only as a profitable investment to the planters, but as an institution of unspeakable advantage to the natives. Almost everything has been said both against it and for it that could well be said; and we fondly hope that its days are nearly numbered. Volumes have been written upon the subject, and it would require many volumes more to record and expose its black and bloody history. In a single chapter I can merely indicate its outstanding features. As we have pre-historic events, and Reformers before the Reformation, so we have a prehistoric as well as a historic labour traffic. There are three names that stand out prominently in the prehistoric period of this grand enterprise, viz., Mr. Benjamin Boyd, Captain Paddon, and Mr. Robert Towns. Mr. Boyd was a Scotchman, belonging to an old and highly respectable family in Wigtownshire. He was a man of great energy and enterprise, an extensive squatter in New South Wales. He founded Boyd Town at Twofold Bay, near the southern extremity of New South Wales. He presented Dr. Lang with the first bell for the Scots church in Sydney; probably it continues to toll there still. So far as I know, he was the first to deport natives from the islands to the Colonies. He sent down a vessel to the New Hebrides, and took away about eighty or a hundred natives. I met the captain of that vessel on Aneityum a year or two after our settlement there. He told me that their mode of procedure was this. The natives were quite willing to go with them, but they took only ten or a dozen from each island. In this way each party was afraid of all the others, and, speaking eight or ten languages on board, like the builders at Babel, they could take no concerted action against the captain and crew, and they were all conveyed to Boyd Town quiet as lambs to the slaughter, and were set to work on the stations. Six or eight were taken from Aneityum, three of whom returned. From their own account, they were well used; but, like all captive exiles, they longed to be home. So on some fitting occasion the Aneityum contingent ran off and took the way to Melbourne, some 200 miles distant. As soon as their flight came to be known, a party was sent after them on horseback, who by-and-by overtook them, and ordered them to return. "No," said they; "this man is our chief, and we must obey him," pointing to the eldest of the party, whose name was Kauware. The man in pursuit seems to have been a wise and humane man, for, instead of shooting one or two of them, and driving the rest back with a musket pointed to their heads, as the practice in such cases has often been since, he conducted them to Melbourne, put them on board a vessel for Sydney, whence they found their way back to Aneityum. One or two of the number engaged to remain in Melbourne; one was drowned about Sydney. If there were any more they were not accounted for. The three that returned home were among the Christian party when we arrived on the island. They were uncommonly clever men, and were all afterwards settled as teachers on Tanna. In the beginning of June 1851 Mr. Boyd left San Francisco with two vessels, the *Wanderer* and the *Ariel*, with the view of exploring the South Sea Islands, then little known, and of trying to establish a kind of Papuan Republic or Confederation; thus anticipating the plans proposed by Sir Julius Vogel and others — plans, however feasible, yet wholly impracticable. On the 15th of October following, Mr. Boyd and a single native went ashore on Guadalcanar, one of the Solomon Islands, where he was killed by the natives. His friends on board the *Wanderer* waited several days, and made every effort to find him, either dead or alive, but without success. In 1854, three years afterwards, a report reached Sydney that Mr. Boyd's name, or at least his initials, were seen cut on trees on the island where he went ashore,—that the natives said he was alive, but that he was a prisoner. Mr. Boyd must have been very popular in Sydney. For from the strength of this report, such an amount of outside pressure was brought to bear on the Government, that orders were sent to Captain Denham of H.M.S. *Herald*, who was carrying on a Government survey in Fiji, to leave the survey at once, and proceed to the Solomon group in search of Mr. Boyd. He proceeded at once, but called at Aneityum to see if we could find him interpreters, and if he could procure any provisions, as he was short of supplies. Interpreters there were none, but Dr. Geddie and I supplied him with a few casks of flour—which, of course, he either paid for or replaced—and a quantity of native food.

He proceeded to Guadalcanar, but no traces could be found of Mr. Boyd. But Mr. Boyd, however good his own conduct and intentions were, had discovered a mine of wealth for his successors in the labour traffic, but accompanied with evils of which he could have no conception.

Captain Paddon, the next outstanding representative in the traffic, was an Englishman, connected with a good family, and who had served on board a man-of-war as a midshipman, came from India in charge of a merchant vessel, and opened a large trading station on Aneityum before Mr. Geddie's arrival, and went in largely for the trade in sandalwood, which had just been discovered on the islands. Captain Paddon was an able and energetic man, popular, and well liked by sailors and the white men afloat among the islands. He was the first to work out the principle that, in order to get natives to work well, you must take them away from their own island, and leave them entirely dependent on their employer for their food. He also adopted Mr. Boyd's plan of bringing them in limited numbers from different islands, so that they could not combine against their employer. Bishop Selwyn told me that he took some hints from Captain Paddon's mode of managing his natives, in making his arrangements for conducting his Melanesian College at Auckland; he was a keen observer, and took hints from all quarters. Captain Paddon became the prime mover in the sandalwood trade. After a residence of some years on Aneityum he removed to Tanna, and subsequently to New Caledonia, where he died in 1862. With him ended what I have called the prehistoric period of the labour traffic. He employed a large number of natives for working on his own station, collecting sandalwood on Eromango and Santo, and in sailing in his vessels; but he never took them away from the islands, and he seemed desirous to treat them kindly. But he gave a great impulse to the labour traffic, although its evils were not then greatly developed.

Mr. Robert Towns was one of the leading merchants and shipowners in Sydney; he was a member of the "Upper House," and he was the connecting-link between the pre-historic and historic periods of the labour traffic; he closed the former, and initiated the latter. He brought numbers of natives to Sydney, to work on his wharf and on his plantation at Paramatta. I met with him in 1863, when he told me that the natives in his employment at Paramatta were as fat as pigs and as merry as crickets; he seemed to think that they could not be happier than they were. He was a liberal subscriber to the hospital, and had a right to a certain number of beds; and when any of his natives were ill, they were sent to the hospital. While we were staying in Sydney with our friend, Dr. Moon, one of the surgeons of the hospital called upon me, to see if I would go and interpret for him to a sick native. "Mr. Towns," said he, "has almost always some of his sick *kanakas* with us, and we are terribly annoyed with them; we do not know their language, and they do not know ours; hence we cannot find out, with any certainty, what is wrong with them, and they cannot be made to understand what they are to do." I went with him, and found out that the man came from Efate, but his language was unknown to me. I got the Rev. Mr. Buzacot, formerly of Rarotonga, to visit him. He and a native of that island, who lived with him, went to the hospital, but they could not speak intelligibly to the sick man.

It was in the sandalwood trade, however, that Mr. Towns —at first in connection with Captain Paddon, and finally himself alone—employed the greatest number of natives. The sandalwood was collected chiefly on Eromanga and Santo, and stored on Aneityum. Mr. Towns sent down a vessel once every three months to take the wood on to China. As the sandalwood was nearly exhausted on the New Hebrides when the cotton-planting began, so Mr. Towns, who was the father and founder of the labour traffic in Queensland, at once transported his capital, vessels, and employees from the one traffic to the other. The sandalwood trade inflicted a great amount of cruelty on the natives, and caused a good deal of bloodshed; but it was nothing compared with the labour traffic proper, either in the extent of its operations or in its terribly injurious consequences. The cargoes were no longer dead matter— lumps of scented wood—but human beings with immortal souls, treated largely as chattels. No doubt Mr. Towns and those who invested their capital and employed their vessels in the labour traffic were men of average justice and humanity, who had no wish to be harsh, cruel, or unjust, but their language was like this—" We have land, but land is of no use without labour; we must have labour, get it as we may." And the instructions to their agents were understood to imply something like this—" Get labour; get it honestly if you can; but get labour!" As time went on nearly all the rowdyism and all the ruffianism of the Colonies was afloat in search of labour; the character of the agency and the circumstances of the trade soon produced a state of things the very reverse of what Mr. Gladstone aims at in his legislation, for in this case it became more and more difficult to do right, but more and more easy to do wrong. Easy and rapid was the descent to Avernus. Mr. Towns explained to me in Sydney his plans for employing natives, and assured me that, if the missionaries would assist him in getting natives, he would do more to civilise them in one year than Mr. Geddie and myself would do in ten. No doubt he thought so; but we flattered ourselves that we knew better; and the experience of twenty-three years has not changed my opinions.

At that time the American war had raised the value of cotton to such fabulous prices that Queensland, Fiji, and New Caledonia became cotton-growing countries, and the demand for labour was enormous. When peace was restored, and the price of cotton fell, the planters began to cultivate sugar instead of cotton, and so the demand for labour continued. In 1863 Mr. Towns sent down his first vessel to the New Hebrides to deport natives to his cotton plantations in Queensland. At this point of its history the traffic was all meekness; its voice was that of a lamb, mild and gentle; the labourers were engaged for six months only. If they were unwilling to return home at the end of that period, they would be allowed to remain six months longer. By-and-by the term of service was extended not only from six months to twelve, but from one year to three, and subsequently from three years to five, and numbers were kept much longer. When Fiji became a Crown colony Sir Arthur Gordon, always a true friend to the native races, sent home, at the Government expense, hundreds of natives, many of whom had been detained long beyond the period of their engagement. Year after year the traffic increased; it was almost the only trade in those seas. If it was objected that the white men could not speak to the natives, and that the natives could not understand the terms of the agreement they were said to have made, every vessel was at once provided with an interpreter—a "Tanna man." Tanna was the great emporium for interpreters. One would have supposed that every Tanna man was an "Admirable Crichton," that he could speak his way to the wall of China, or that he knew every one of the twenty languages spoken on the New Hebrides. Nothing could show more clearly the fraudulent character of the system than the sham of the "Tanna man" interpreter. Force and fraud became more and more frequent, outrages on the one hand, and retaliation on the other, rapidly increased, till the one culminated in the horrible tragedy on board the *Carl*, and the other in the lamented death of Bishop Patteson.

The *Carl* case, which was tried in Melbourne, sent a thrill of horror not only through the Australasian Colonies, but far beyond. The naked facts were these. The *Carl* sailed from Melbourne to Fiji. The head of the expedition was a Dr. Murray. The captain left the vessel at Levuka; the mate, whose name was Armstrong, was appointed captain. He obtained a license from Consul March to go on a "labour cruise." Dr. Murray accompanied the vessel as surgeon. They proceeded to the New Hebrides, and then to the Solomon group. Their mode of kidnapping was this. They had heavy pieces of iron fastened to ropes, and the ropes tied to the vessel. When canoes came alongside the ship, the captain and the sailors threw these pieces of iron into the canoes, and capsized them, and as the natives were swimming about the white men picked them up, heaved them on deck, and secured them in the hold. At Malicolla they kidnapped twelve or thirteen, at Santa Anna the same number was obtained, at Isabel they got ten, and at Florida four or five; but at Bougainville, an island densely inhabited by warlike natives, they obtained eighty, whom they also secured in the hold. But in this instance they overlooked Mr. Boyd's precaution, and took too many from one place. After being forty-eight hours on board, the Bougainvilleans, impatient of restraint and conscious of their strength, began to fight; some of them attempted to set fire to the ship; others tried to prevent them; and this caused the fighting. Every attempt was made to pacify them, but no white man understood their language. In about a quarter of an hour they were fired on with guns and revolvers by the whites, who had behaved inhumanly enough before, but who now thirsted for blood like wild beasts. The firing and fighting lasted all night. In the morning the hatches were taken off, and the killed and wounded were taken out of the hold and put on deck. There were about seventy killed and wounded. The dead natives were at once thrown overboard. There were about fifty killed and twenty wounded. The twenty wounded were thrown into the sea while still alive. The white men set to and so scrubbed the vessel and whitewashed it with lime, that when a party from a man-of-war overhauled the vessel, it was pronounced to be all right. When the case was tried in Melbourne, Dr. Murray became Queen's evidence. The captain and mate were sentenced to severe punishment; but their counsel taking advantage of some legal technicalities, the sentence was evaded, and after a short imprisonment they were released.

The *Carl* case was no doubt an exceptionally bad one, but there were scores of other cases of precisely the same character, only more limited in extent. The trade was found to be so insufferably bad, that, roused by those atrocities, the Imperial Parliament passed an Act, not to *suppress* the traffic, but to *regulate* it ; for the belief was still held that the traffic, like the old slave-trade, might be satisfactorily regulated. This Act was to be quoted as the " Kidnapping Act," the title clearly indicating the character of the evil it was intended to remedy. It was not intended, of course, to regulate the kidnapping, but it was expected to transmute those kidnappers into humane, honest, and honourable emigration agents. Yet, strange to say, all this time the Queensland authorities were pronouncing the traffic to be immaculate; everything was being done according to Act of Parliament. If anything was wrong, you must look in the direction of Fiji or New Caledonia; and when a charge of this kind was hinted at in those quarters, a cry was immediately heard, loud and indignant, as that of injured innocence. From the very beginning our missionaries and our Mission Synod, year after year, proclaimed the character and the doings of the traffic to the Presbyterian Churches supporting the mission, and to the Colonial and Imperial Governments. As I have stated elsewhere, a letter from one of our missionaries, the Rev. James M'Nair of Eromanga, having fallen into the hands of Mr. P. A. Taylor, M.P., was the cause of the evil being first brought to the notice of the British Parliament. By the Act above referred to, the Government and Parliament of Great Britain stamped the Polynesian labour traffic, during the first ten years of its existence, as being largely a system of kidnapping, and that Act was passed with the view of eliminating that element from the traffic. To secure that object all the former regulations were to be rendered more stringent, and new arrangements were to be made for redressing the grievances and securing the rights of the natives, and for putting the traffic on such a footing that it would be as beneficial to the labourers as to their employers. Hence all vessels, as formerly, were to be licensed; a Government agent was to be continued on board of every vessel, to testify that all the emigrants came willingly, and that they understood fully the terms of agreement, and that every regulation was carried out as appointed by Government. In addition to this, a small man-of-war was stationed on every group, as an ocean police, to watch the doings of the traffic. We have had thirteen years of the traffic under this reformed phase, and what has been the result? The outrageous buccaneering character of the traffic has to a large extent disappeared, but there is a very wide consensus of opinion to the effect that the spirit of the Kidnapping Act has been largely evaded. In the mission field, in the Colonies, and in the public press at home a strong belief is expressed that the essence of slavery and the slave-trade is still to be found in this labour traffic; that the natives are taken away, as Lord Derby has formulated the expression, *either by force, or by representations that actually amount to fraud.*

Our mission urges, not the further regulation of the traffic, which twenty-three years' experience has shown to be thoroughly vicious in principle, but its *complete suppression.* We urge this on three grounds—(1) the injury it is doing to missions; (2) the evil results to the natives in the depopulation of the islands; and (3) the loss of life by violence, both native and European, to which it is constantly leading. We hear much in these times of vested interests, of their sacred and inalienable character, and of the right for compensation when they are invaded or affected in any way. Now if there are vested rights anywhere, our mission certainly possesses them in the New Hebrides. We have invested £150,000 to begin with. Our claims go back for nearly fifty years. But we have invested life as well as money. Let us take the history of Eromanga, an island that unhappily has a world-wide reputation. On the second day after missionary operations had been commenced on the New Hebrides, John Williams and Mr. Harris, as I have elsewhere said, laid down their lives as martyrs on that island. Twenty-two years later the Rev. G. N. Gordon and his saintly wife were martyred, and ten years afterwards his brother, the Rev. J. D. Gordon, fell beneath the tomahawk of the savage. Before this last martyrdom, the Rev. James M'Nair, a man of an eminently missionary spirit, succumbed to fever and ague—the disease of the island—and died. At this juncture the Rev. H. A. Robertson, with his beautiful, accomplished, excellent, and heroic young wife, arrived from Nova Scotia, and, of their own free choice, they were settled on blood-stained Eromanga in 1871. They took their lives in their hands. Often were they in imminent peril from the savage heathen. Often for weeks the Christian natives watched their house day and night, lest they should be murdered by the heathen; but they wrought on till Eromanga has become virtually Christian. Mr. Robertson entered fully into the spirit and aims of his martyred predecessors; he gathered up and utilised the results of their labours. He followed out their plans, and worked upon their lines; from Dillon's Bay as a centre he opened up stations and sent out native agents on both sides of the island, till these agencies met at Cook's Bay, on the other end of the island, forty miles distant. His heart was delighted when, after years of danger and difficulty, he had completed his organisation, and placed a chain of schools, stations, and native agents round the island. But what was his disappointment when, some months afterwards, he returned to Cook's Bay, one of his most important stations, and found the school closed and worship discontinued. A labour vessel had called in, and both the teacher and every young and ablebodied man had been induced to go on board, to proceed to Queensland or Fiji, or wherever else the vessel was going, to be sold for £6 sterling a head, ostensibly as passage-money for the immigrants. No doubt in this case both captain and agent would present a clean bill at the Immigration Office; the agent would testify that the immigrants had all shipped of their own freewill, and had all perfectly understood the terms of the contract, although neither captain nor agent understood a word of Eromangan. A few words of pigeon-English picked up by some one of the natives was a sufficient medium for settling all the terms of the engagement. But let us see how the matter was looked at by the missionary. Happily we have not here to draw upon our imagination; we have it expressed in his own words, in a letter published in the *Presbyterian Record for the Dominion of Canada* for April 1880:—

"To many of those young men, especially to those who were brought out of heathen darkness by means of our labours, I am deeply attached; and were it not for those wretched slavers our hearts would be greatly cheered among them. But, oh! these so-called *labour vessels* (?) are an immense curse and drawback. May this miserable traffic soon be abolished! Within the past four months these *fishers of men* have taken away more than a hundred of my promising young men and lads, including one TEACHER!!! That is, they have bought them with muskets, axes, knives, calico, &c., paid for them on the spot! Christian friends, this is a vile traffic, and I am henceforward its decided and open enemy. What use, so far as I can see, is there in my Church paying me a salary to bring this people out of heathen darkness if it is *only* for this world ?—only to make them better servants ?—for whom ?—for those who have *no* interest in them beyond what they can get out of them."

These words are the utterances of a heart, as we can see, rent with anguish. But this is not a solitary case. It is within our knowledge that similar things have been done again and again on Eromanga. Furthermore, there is not a mission station on the New Hebrides from which some, in many cases a large number, of their most promising natives have not been taken away in a similar manner. None can deny that we have invested a large amount of blood and treasure on Eromanga; we have acquired a vast amount of valuable knowledge, we have gained a great deal of important influence, and we have obtained a considerable amount of useful experience, all of which we are turning to account for the Christianising, the enlightening, and the civilising of the poor degraded natives. But we have no Act of Parliament to protect our vested interests. We cannot sell those investments, and unless we are allowed to utilise them, and work them out in our own way, they are lost to us and to the world for ever. We have provided, and are still further providing, for the natives religious and secular instruction; but when they are taken away, their seats in the churches and in the schools are left empty, and, so far as they are concerned, our agencies become a needless expenditure; the natives go where nobody can speak to them, and where they can speak to nobody, and henceforward their progress ceases. We are quietly and peacefully carrying on our work; we are molesting nobody in Queensland or elsewhere; and what moral right has the Government of Fiji or Queensland to license the rowdyism of their respective populations, to go down and prowl about and plunder our mission of its best natives, and carry into captivity the poor defenceless inhabitants of those islands, in order that their thews and sinews may be transmuted into Colonial gold, careless as to the fate of their aged parents or their young and helpless children left behind on the islands? I shall just give another example of the way in which recruiting for labourers is carried on in the islands, with the "Kidnapping Act" in full operation.

On the 5th of September 1882 the three-masted schooner, *Ceara*—Captain Satine, a Swede—a Queensland labour vessel carrying the English flag, lay to opposite the South River, as it is called, in Eromanga, about twelve miles south of Dillon's Bay, where the principal mission station on that island is located. The *Ceara* sent in two boats manned with native crews—the one of them in charge of a white man, the other in charge of a native named Nomoo belonging to the island of Tanna. These two boats proceeded up the river; the one landed on the right bank and the other on the left. When the Tanna man went ashore, he professed to be in search of water, and to be afraid to land, lest the Eromangans should kill him. They said, "Oh, do not be afraid. You see the church there; we are all Christians now, and kill nobody." He went in the direction of the water, but did not seem to take much interest in it. He came in behind where some of the women were sitting, and made an attempt to seize Utokatak, the chief's daughter, a young woman sitting among the rest. A man, probably her brother, interposed; a scuffle ensued; the Tanna man fired a revolver and wounded the Eromangan, though happily he was not killed. The young woman fled. The Tanna man pursued, seized the girl, and carried her to the boat, and placed her securely in the stern. Meanwhile Lovo, her father, ran after them, calling upon the other men to assist him in saving his daughter; but before any effective resistance could be organised, the Tanna man had not only made fast the young woman, but had turned round and seized the steer-oar, while the natives in the boat, as directed, levelled their muskets at the father, and shot him dead at the bow of the boat. They then pushed the boat into deep water and pulled down the river. At the same time the other boat left the other side of the river, taking away a young lad; but whether he went willingly or unwillingly had not been ascertained, although, from the fact that another young lad was seen running away from the boat, as if escaping from being caught, the likelihood was, that the lad was carried off against his will. The two boats met down the river, and the Tanna man placed the young woman in the white man's boat, and the white man proceeded to the vessel with the two recruits.

Nomoo, the Tanna man, remained behind with his boat, and pulled along the shore for a few miles, till he came to a small creek, where there was a boat harbour, which he entered. There were some natives on the shore at that place. As the Tanna man could speak Eromangan, he called upon the natives to come to the boat, holding up a quantity of tobacco as an indication that he wished to trade. Umo, the teacher in that place, an excellent young man, went down to the boat. He had an owl in his hand, which the Tanna man bought.

When the teacher was delivering up the bird and taking hold of the tobacco, the Tanna man seized him by the wrist and attempted to drag him into the boat; but he succeeded in wresting himself from the Tanna man's grasp, and Nomoo placed his revolver to Umo's right side and shot him. Umo fell in the water, but springing to his feet, he ran up the ravine. The Tanna man pursued him, revolver in hand, calling upon him to stop or he would shoot him. He did not stop; the Tanna man fired, and the Eromangan, after running a short time, fell down dead on the spot. The other Eromangans fled to the bush. The Tanna man returned to the boat and rejoined the vessel, which proceeded to Havannah harbour, on Efate. Mr. Robertson and the people at Dillon's Bay saw the vessel pass, but at the time were ignorant of the terrible tragedy that had just been enacted. This Tanna man was a well-known character; he had been sixteen years connected with the traffic, and that conduct was a specimen of the boasted civilising influence which that system brings to bear on savage character. He belonged to a place called Sulphur Bay or Weasisi, where that same year we had opened a new mission station, and settled on it Mr. and Mrs. Gray, the missionary and his wife of the Presbyterian Church of South Australia. Now, if such deeds are perpetrated almost within sight of a missionary's door, what do we conceive is being done among those islands where there is no missionary residing? The Imperial and the Colonial Governments have been trying to regulate this labour traffic for the last twenty-three years, and its character remains as we see it. Had the philanthropic Wilberforce or Dr. Andrew Thomson been alive to-day, they would have denounced this euphoniously-named labour traffic as strongly as they denounced the slavery and

THE LABOUR TRAFFIC. 215

the slave-trade of their own times—denounced it as a system that contained the very essence of the slave-trade and slavery, a system that must be suppressed at whatever risks, because it cannot be regulated; for it is rotten to the core; and we call upon good Christians everywhere to help us in protecting the poor and defenceless natives from the hands of bloody and deceitful men.

A common way of conducting the traffic is this. The labour vessel lies in the offing, and two boats are sent into the bay. One of them, manned chiefly by natives, it may be from Tanna or the Loyalty Islands, goes close in to the shore to engage natives. The other lies some distance off, so as to cover the first boat, and so as to be able to sweep the beach, if necessary, with rifles, or shoot down any troublesome native. The natives, knowing these arrangements, are in general on their good behaviour; but at times misunderstandings occur and collisions take place. Some old man, the chief of the tribe perhaps, interposes to prevent his son, a young lad, from going away in a labour vessel, and he is shot dead by those in charge of the boats; and this, as was to be expected, is afterwards followed by a massacre of some other boat's crew. Is this free emigration? In this country there are Government agents to see that every emigrant gets fair play, and as soon as he lands in Canada, or elsewhere, he is met by another, to see that all contracts have been fulfilled; and even this is not considered sufficient, for it is now proposed to have Government agents on board the ship, as well as at both ends of the voyage, to see that full justice is done to the emigrants during the few days or the few weeks occupied by the voyage. And all this for emigrants who know every word that is spoken to them, who know what their rights are, and, if wronged, or supposed to be wronged, know how, and where, and when to apply for redress. It is totally different with our native emigrants. In Queensland or Fiji, it is true, there is a Government agent to look after them, but he does not know a word of their language, and they do not know a word of his. On board the vessels at the islands there is another Government agent, who is equally ignorant of their language, and they of his; and as this agent is under the strongest temptation to make matters smooth for the captain and the owners, the poor natives have no security against either force or fraud.

But although the natives were ever so willing to go to Queensland and other places, we urge the complete suppression of the labour traffic, because it is fast depopulating the islands and exterminating the natives. Let the present state of things go on, and in a comparatively short period of time those lovely islands will be uninhabited wastes. In Tasmania the native race is extinct. In Victoria there are only a few hundreds left. In New South Wales they are now only a remnant. Over nearly the whole of the South Seas, especially in Western Polynesia, the native population is decreasing. But all causes put together are not so destructive of native life as the labour traffic. At the present time there is a fleet of about thirty labour vessels afloat among those islands, each one, on an average, deporting eighty emigrants each voyage. These vessels will make, on an average, four or five voyages annually. I have known them make a voyage once a month from the New Hebrides to New Caledonia. This would make 10,000 or 12,000 of a drain on the able-bodied male population annually. The engagements are never less than for three years, but often for five. This involves the constant absence from the labour-recruiting districts of say 40,000 able-bodied men. Allowing these to be a fifth of the population, we have 200,000 people deprived of their principal bread-winners. How society must be deranged by such a process! On the islands how much the birth-rate must be reduced, and how much the mortality of the young, the aged, and the helpless must be augmented, while the death-rate on the plantations is amazingly increased! In Queensland, instead of the normal mortality of 9 annually in the 1000, among men from eighteen to forty-five years of age, it ranges from 70 to 110 in the 1000, or about *ten times* as much as it ought to be. But, to show that these statements are not hypothetical nor exaggerated, I shall quote the latest and the highest authority that can be obtained on the subject. The *Sydney Illustrated News* of August 28, 1885, quoting from the special commissioner of the *Sydney Morning Herald*, says:—"The Royal Commissioners, in their report to the Government of Queensland, say that the natives were 'seduced on board on false pretences,' 'that the nature of their engagements was never fully explained to them,' 'that the method of recruiting was cruelly deceptive and altogether illegal,' 'that a system of deliberate fraud was practised in engaging all the recruits,' and 'that, while some of the natives were forcibly kidnapped, all of them were allured on board by false statements.' Those," says the writer, "are sweeping assertions, and doubtless the evidence taken before the Commission justifies them." After mentioning some extenuating circumstances in defence of the above recruiting agents, he says:—"At the same time, it may be mentioned that a knowledge of the natives on and around their own islands shows the opportunities for recruiting native labour by deception or by force to be so numerous, and to offer such temptations to those on board a labour vessel wanting recruits, that it would be altogether opposed to human nature so situated for recruiting agents not to take advantage of them."

Out of 630 natives recruited by the labour vessels concerned in the inquiry by the Royal Commission in Queensland, the mortality in little more than twelve months was 167. The average mortality in civilised countries of men at the ages of the recruits is 9 in the 1000 annually; here it amounted to the rate of 265 in the 1000, being more than a fourth of the whole. This is the highest mortality I have ever heard of. From 70 to 110 in the 1000, as I have said, is recognised as the normal mortality in Queensland, but the very lowest estimate can hardly be characterised as anything less than wholesale murder; and is such a system to be allowed to continue in any part of the British dominions?

But we have another witness at hand. The *Queensland Evangelical Standard* of October 16, 1885, says:—" Among the figures given by the Premier in answer to Mr. Black, touching the Polynesians now in the colony, there is one point deserving of special animadversion. The number at the close of last year was 11,745, and since then there have arrived 1376, making 13,121 (not counting departures); but of these there are reported as having died no fewer than 936. Out of 13,000 we have actually had close upon a thousand deaths; that is a mortality of 122 per 1000. The most unhealthy cities in the old country, such as Glasgow or Liverpool, seldom reach the 30 per 1000; and that in Queensland the mortality of these Polynesians should be more than *four* times that high figure is appalling. Either they are in bad health before coming here, or the climate is unsuitable, or the work is deadly, or they are abominably treated; and, in any alternative, we cannot but be thankful that we are soon to see the end of the traffic." The writer of the above paragraph has overlooked one very important figure in his calculation; 30 deaths per 1000 in Glasgow or Liverpool includes the entire population of all ages; 122 deaths per 1000 in Queensland includes only persons from eighteen to forty-five years of age, among whom in civilised lands the normal mortality is only 9 in the 1000; so that the mortality among the Polynesians in Queensland is not simply equal to four times, but to twelve times, the high figures in those old cities. Dr. W. M'Gregor, chief medical officer in Fiji, found the deaths on one estate as high as 750 per 1000 per annum, on another 500, and on others from 200 to 300. Well might Jenkins, the author of "Ginx's Baby" and "The Devil's Chain," direct his scathing irony against the system, and speak of the "cannibals of Polynesia as justly resentful of the undesired benevolence of a forcible binding to labour in the sugar-fields of Queensland, for civilisation and Christianity!"

This traffic has been regulated for more than twenty long years, and we see what it still is. Let us have a trial of suppression for as long a time. But when we urge the *suppression* of the traffic, immediately a meaning is imported into our words which they were never meant to convey. We are supposed to wish the natives to be forcibly prevented from leaving their own islands. Every one, of course, consents to the suppression of kidnapping and the deporting of natives under false pretences. But they cannot agree, they say, to put a stop to free voluntary emigration. We do not ask them.

Free emigration! Where is it? For the first ten years of this traffic, it is now admitted on all hands that it was nearly out and out kidnapping, and for the last thirteen years there is abundant proof to show that it is still little better. If the natives wish to emigrate, let them do so as much as they choose, and as they best can. But let us no longer have a licensed, legalised system, of which force and fraud are the outstanding characteristics. It is this that we wish to see suppressed—the system that has existed hitherto. We have no wish to see the natives cooped up as prisoners; simply let them alone. When the African slave-trade was suppressed, nobody understood that to mean the compulsory putting down of free emigration. But how many of the Africans have since that time freely emigrated to Brazil, Cuba, or the Southern States? So will it be with the natives of the New Hebrides, the Solomon Islands, and New Guinea; the number will be small indeed who will emigrate to Queensland, Fiji, or New Caledonia. And why should they? Every native is a landowner; why should he go abroad and simply sell his *labour?* Is it not much better for him to stay at home and cultivate his own paternal acres, and then sell his *labour and the produce of his land together,* which he can always do, and at the same time live at home with his family?

This labour traffic is looked upon by some as a fine outlet for the surplus population of the islands. Surplus population! Was ever ignorance so crass? Where is it to be found? Everywhere the population is scanty. There is not an island on the New Hebrides which could not maintain ten times its present population, even with their rude and primitive modes of agriculture. The problem is how to preserve, and, if possible, to increase the population, not to reduce it by emigration.

It is certainly not necessary to colonise Queensland by depopulating the New Hebrides; leave the labour on the islands for the islands. During the present century all the Malay Polynesians and a portion of the Papuans in Eastern Polynesia have been Christianised and civilised, and life and property are everywhere secure; and as soon as that was the case, skill and capital found their way to those islands, and utilised the labour lying ready to their hand. Let our missions alone for another century, and the whole of the Papuans in Western Polynesia—still savage—will be then civilised; they will be good Christians and peaceful citizens.

I can simply refer to, without being able to insist or enlarge upon, the many and murderous attacks made upon white men by natives—attacks which are of late apparently on the increase, and which led to the lamentable death of Bishop Patteson, Commodore Goodenough, and scores, if not hundreds, of others, many of them as innocent as those two distinguished men, and for which the labour traffic is mainly responsible. In the circumstances, as British subjects, we have again and again appealed to Her Majesty's Government to protect us in our philanthropic efforts, and to protect the poor, helpless natives from the cupidity of our own countrymen. And we further appeal to our fellow-Christians in all the Churches for their sympathy, and for their prayers, that the evils which we feel may be removed, and that the evils which we fear may be averted.

CHAPTER XVII.

THE FRENCH AND THE NEW HEBRIDES.

For a good many years the proposed annexation of the New Hebrides by the French has been one of the burning questions of the day in the New Hebrides and in all the Australasian Colonies. But when it was found that the French proposed to make the New Hebrides a penal settlement for 60,000 of the worst class of criminals in France, to be sent out at the rate of 6000 a year for ten years, the Australasian Colonies rose up as one man in indignant protest against such an outrageous proposal. This attitude on the part of the colonists, so unexpected by the French, staggered the abetters of this measure, and the plan was fallen from. And now the proposal is, if the French are allowed to take possession of the New Hebrides, that they will engage to send no more *recidivists* or habitual criminals to any of the South Sea Islands. There is perhaps no portion of the globe of which the British public generally are so imperfectly informed as about the South Sea Islands; hence the doings and aims of the French in those seas are greatly misunderstood, even by our leading statesmen. Our mission and the Churches supporting our mission have never ceased in appealing to the British Government, as against the aggressive policy of the French and the dangers to our mission and to the Christianity and civilisation of the natives, if the islands should be annexed by the French; but our rulers have been singularly apathetic in not watching the persistent efforts of the French to establish a footing in the South Seas, to the certain peril of British interests throughout all the Australasian Colonies. The losses to Imperial and Colonial interests which have been sustained through this policy of indifference are incalculable, with no corresponding advantage to the French, except that of occupying the post of the dog in the manger, and holding strategetical positions which in the event of war would enable them to inflict tremendous injuries upon us.

A short time ago I was sorry, but not surprised, to read a leading article in one of the most influential of the Glasgow papers pleading very strongly for the annexation of the New Hebrides by the French, on the ground of their engaging to give up their *recidivist* scheme. The writer of that article in the *Daily Mail* said—" Seeing the French are prepared to yield to our representations in regard to penal settlements, it will be difficult for this country to find any valid reason against the step, especially as the French have a far better claim to the New Hebrides than the Germans had to the northern part of New Guinea. . . . The French Government is prepared to guarantee that no *recidivists* will be sent to any of the islands in the Pacific, provided France is allowed to take possession of the New Hebrides group. This certainly places the annexation question in a new and more feasible light. Germany undertakes to do nothing to hinder France from taking possession of the group. We have no superior claim to these islands ourselves, and it is an important question whether the French proposal to take possession of them ought not to be sanctioned in consideration of the guarantee offered.

If propinquity to an existing colony has any weight in the argument, it is decidedly in favour of France."

To those who have never been in the South Seas, and who are ignorant of the history, and doings, and aims of the French in those regions for the last fifty years, such reasoning may appear very plausible. But to those who are familiar with the history of the South Sea missions, and the part that the French have played in connection with these missions for half a century and more, these arguments carry no weight whatever. One really wonders at the gross ignorance displayed by the public press, not only in this country, but in the Australasian Colonies. Only the other day it was asserted by a leading Sydney paper, that the claims of the French to the New Hebrides were as good as those of the British. To this the Sydney *Presbyterian* replied, most truthfully, that ours were as a hundred to one against them. An agreement at present exists between the British and French Governments by which the independence of those islands is recognised. This agreement is only temporary, and has never been sanctioned by Parliament. Our Government allowed itself to be overreached by this agreement. As for the Germans giving their consent to the annexation of the New Hebrides by France, the proposal is preposterous; they have no right whatever to say a word on the subject. It is very doubtful if any German ever set a foot on the New Hebrides. Of this I am very certain, that no German man of-war, no German merchant, or no German missionary was ever seen among those islands. Moreover, what are the claims of the French? In 1768 Bougainville sailed between Santo and Mallicollo, and thus proved that the Espiritu Santo of Quiros was an island, and not a continent. That is all that the navy of France has done for the group. Her commerce did nothing till some five or six years ago, when a Land Company was formed at Noumea, the capital of New Caledonia—the chairman of which, if I mistake not, was an Irishman, and the manager a Highlander from Nova Scotia —with the view of buying land on the New Hebrides, selling it again, and developing an island traffic. In order to float this company every effort was put forth to secure annexation by the French, so that they might obtain Government titles for their land; but it is reported that this, like some other South Sea Bubbles, is about to burst, and that this company, like many other similar ones, is on the rocks for want of funds. Forty years ago a French Roman Catholic mission was established on the island of Aneityum. It was carried on for three or four years; but as the missionaries suffered severely from fever and ague, they were all removed to the Isle of Pines, and they never returned. But what did they do for the natives? They erected an iron house, and placed two small cannon on the roof, to protect themselves from the savages; and they distributed among the children a few small brass medals, with the image of the Virgin Mary on one side. They never acquired the language; they printed no books; they taught nobody to read, and they left no converts behind them. The only plausible claim that the French have for annexation is that of propinquity, and there is very little even of that. Noumea, the capital of New Caledonia, is little more than a hundred miles nearer the New Hebrides than is Suva, the capital of Fiji; and what is that on the wide ocean? But how did the French secure this propinquity? When Cook discovered New Caledonia he erected the British flag, and took possession of the island, by the right of discovery, in the name of His Britannic Majesty. This right continued undisputed till about 1854, when the French surreptitiously took possession of New Caledonia, and subsequently of the Loyalty Islands. Sir George Grey, at that time Governor of New Zealand, and on that question the most far-seeing statesman of the day, urged the Government, it was said, to disallow the doings of the French, and take possession of those islands for themselves. But it was the time of the Crimean War, and our Government had not then initiated a "spirited foreign policy," and they thought that they could not afford to risk a quarrel with France over a barren island in the South Seas. France, however, saw its importance, in a strategical point of view, as a naval station, from which she might suspend the sword of Damocles over the necks of Australia and New Zealand. Our Government saw their mistake when it was too late, as, four or five years afterwards, when a rupture was apprehended between France and Great Britain, it was understood that, in the event of war, to secure the safety of our Colonies, certain war ships were told off to assemble at Noumea and recapture that town from the French, and hoist the British flag on New Caledonia. One of these vessels lay three weeks at Aneityum. Emboldened by impunity, however, the French think they may now venture on further aggression, but the Colonies are alive, and have shown their hand.

But it may be asked, What better claims have we on the New Hebrides than the Germans or the French? I have already said the Germans have no claim at all; and the French have no claim but that of propinquity, and that they secured by an unscrupulous manœuvre. Our claim is quite different. When Captain Cook came after Bougainville, he discovered all the southern islands of the group, explored and surveyed the whole of them, and laid the islands down on the chart, and that with an accuracy that has never been surpassed. Captain Cook did so much for the islands that he felt himself entitled to rename the group, to discard the name *Cyclades* given to them by Bougainville, and call them the *New Hebrides*. From that day to this they have been virtually a British possession; all that has been done for them, and that has not been little, has been done for them by the British. For forty years they have, in general, been visited once a year by a British man-of-war, to promote the security of life and property, and to advance the interests of civilisation. All the commerce on the group has been carried on by British enterprise, and with British capital. One or two houses in Sydney exported £70,000 worth of sandalwood from Eromanga to China. All the missions have been British and Protestant. First the London Missionary Society conducted operations for about twenty years; then the Church of England Melanesian Mission was carried on by Bishop Selwyn and his successors for a similar length of time. Our Presbyterian mission has been in operation on the New Hebrides for thirty eight-years; the other two societies have resigned their claims upon the islands in our favour. We have just now thirteen missionaries and their wives, and we have three more with their wives on their way to the islands at the present time. Eleven of these sixteen missionaries are being supported by the Presbyterian Churches in Australia and New Zealand. For twenty-three years we have had a mission vessel, the *Dayspring*, of 160 tons, and recently one of our missionaries, the Rev. J. G. Paton, as I have explained fully elsewhere, was home for eighteen months, and raised £9000 with which to purchase a new vessel with auxiliary steam power, and to take out more missionaries. In one form and another those three missions, all British, have expended upwards of £200,000 in Christianising and civilising the aborigines. The native population of the group is estimated at from 70,000 to 100,000. There are no fewer than twenty languages spoken on the islands; our missionaries have mastered ten of these, and have reduced them to a written form. We have printed the whole Bible and some other books in one language, for which the natives have paid £1400; and we have printed portions of the Bible in other nine languages. But we know the attitude which the French have assumed towards Protestant missions in the South Seas for the last fifty years, especially in the Loyalty Islands, the group nearest to the New Hebrides. For more than twenty years they have harassed the missionaries to an incredible extent, and they have persecuted the Protestant natives to a degree to which there is no modern parallel. The British Government interposed and made effective representations on their behalf to the late Emperor Napoleon. Now, we feel certain that if the French take possession of the New Hebrides, their attitude towards our mission will be in no degree less unfavourable than it has been towards the missions of the London Missionary Society. Our work will be all but completely arrested; all our preparatory labours will to a great extent be lost. The British Government will hold its own, British commerce will push its way; but our mission, while it could easily hold its own against Popery pure and simple, is placed at a mighty disadvantage when it has to contend with Popery backed by the civil, naval, and military power of France, as Popery is supported in the possessions of France in the South Seas, and where, as on Maré in the Loyalty Islands, all education must be conducted through the medium of the French language, which, as every one must see, is equivalent to suppressing education altogether.

But another point of consideration still remains. What do the natives say on this question of annexation? They are human; they are not like mere goods and chattels; they are freemen; their independence is recognised in the treaty at present existing between France and Great Britain; they can express distinctly their opinions and wishes; they know the character of both the French and the British. Now, to which country do they wish to be annexed? There are not two opinions on this point. They are all anxious to be connected with the British. They are all decidedly averse to the French. Twenty-seven years ago I was the bearer of a petition to our Queen, signed by every one of the chiefs of Aneityum, representing 3500 people, and all Christian, praying for either annexation or a protectorate for their island. About the same time I was told by a scientific gentleman, an F.R.S., who had been naturalist on two British men-of-war, and was well acquainted with natives both in Australia and in the South Seas, who had spent some months on New Caledonia collecting specimens for the British Museum,—he said that, from the fact that he was a Briton, as Mr. Gladstone would call him—for he was a Scotchman, and the son of a Scotch professor—he could travel in perfect safety over the whole island of New Caledonia, but that the French, although they had been three or four years in occupation of the island, could not leave their encampments but at the risk of their lives; and the natives so disliked them, that if they did kill a Frenchman, inveterate cannibals though they were, they would neither cook him nor eat him! I might also add that all the Australasian Colonies are decidedly opposed to annexation by France.

After these statements, I leave my readers to judge as to the value of the claims which the French have put forth to justify them in attempting to annex the New Hebrides. It is certainly a very doubtful ground of merit to plead that they have agreed to abandon the monstrous *recidivist* scheme, so emphatically denounced by all the Australasian Colonies —a proposal that was an insult, not only to Christianity and civilisation, but to human nature itself. Are 70,000 or 100,000 intelligent and capable natives, a considerable number of whom can read and write, to be treated like so many head of cattle? From Santo to Aneityum, from the extreme north to the extreme south of the group, you will not go ashore on an island where you may not hear spoken more or fewer English words; but over all the islands of the group you will not hear a French word spoken. At least, during my twenty-five years' residence on the group, I never heard one word of French spoken by a native, and I never met with any person whose experience in this respect was different from my own.

The French Government cannot understand the position of Protestant missionaries in the South Seas. There the Roman Catholic missionaries are the pioneers and political agents of the French Government. They are protected, patronised, and assisted in their work, that they may serve the French Government, and the French think that we Protestant missionaries all stand in the same relation to the British Government. They cannot believe that we receive nothing but the ordinary protection of loyal, peaceable, well-conducted

British subjects, that we never act as Government agents, except on rare occasions that we may act as interpreters. Because the natives are averse to the French and attached to the British, they think that this is all caused by the teaching and influence of us Protestant missionaries. They believe that in French territory we are constantly plotting and planning in the interests of the British and against the French, stirring up the natives to disloyalty and rebellion; and hence they think they are doing God service and helping the State in proportion as they impede our missions and worry the missionaries; and were the missionaries not British subjects, they would soon make short work with them, by expelling them from French territory. When they took possession of the Loyalty Islands, they caused the missionaries to remove all their Samoan and Rarotongan teachers and their wives and children, upwards of forty in number. We had to send them all home in the *Dayspring*. The natives are everywhere averse to the Germans, but still more so to the French, because they are overbearing, selfish, and tyrannical in their treatment of the natives. On the other hand, they are attached to the British, whether connected with missions, with men-of-war, or with trading establishments ;—and why ? Because, as a rule, they are just, generous, and kindly in their conduct towards the natives. It is the difference in national character which leads to the different estimate that is formed by the natives of these respective nationalities. But the French cannot recognise this fact, and they set this all down to the underhand working of the British missionaries, and think that if they could suppress the missions and get quit of the missionaries, their troubles would be at an end, and it would be all smooth sailing in the future; the musket and the *calabooshe* would do all the rest, and convert them into model French subjects and exemplary Catholic Christians.

One of the reasons assigned for the French being so eager to annex the New Hebrides is, that they may have more and better harbour accommodation than they have in New Caledonia. This cannot be the case. On the N.W. side they have the harbour of Noumea, the capital, and on the S.E. side they have Balad, where Captain Cook lay chiefly at anchor; then they have Yengen, an admirable harbour; and they have likewise Kanala, also an excellent harbour. I have been in all these four harbours, and know what they are. I have even heard it said, by those who ought to know, that along the S.E. side of New Caledonia the harbours are like stalls in a stable, they are so plentiful and so good. The want of harbours, therefore, cannot be the cause of the French casting their covetous eyes on the New Hebrides.

In July last it was stated in the papers that Lord Rosebery, having received the replies from all the Australasian Governments on the subject of the French proposals regarding the New Hebrides, officially informed M. Waddington that the Australasian Colonies, which were the parties chiefly affected, were overwhelmingly, if not unanimously, opposed to the arrangements suggested by His Excellency, in a spirit which Her Majesty's Government recognised as conciliatory and amicable. Her Majesty's Government were accordingly unable to consent to any departure from the present understanding between Great Britain and France by which the two countries were bound to respect the independence of the New Hebrides.

In June last two French war vessels were despatched from

Noumea to the New Hebrides, with troops on board, avowedly to punish the natives for outrages committed on French subjects, although no cases have been specified; they landed troops and erected the French flag at two points on the New Hebrides, at Havannah harbour and Port Sandwich. When the British Government inquired at the French Government about this, the latter denied all official knowledge of such proceedings, but said that if they had taken place they would be disallowed, the flag would be hauled down, and the troops removed; but neither have yet been done. We all have heard of *Punica fides*, Punic faith, and perfidious Albion. We may now, I think, safely add *Gallica fides*, Gallic faith, as the more certain of the three.

CHAPTER XVIII.

THE REV. JAMES M'NAIR, EROMANGA.

I KNEW nothing personally of Mr. M'Nair till he appeared as a missionary in the *Dayspring* in August 1866. For some particulars of his early life I am indebted to a statement supplied, at the time of his death, to the *Reformed Presbyterian Magazine* by D. Dickson, Esq., Edinburgh, whose friendly interest in Mr. M'Nair was often acknowledged by the missionary himself in the warmest terms. My limited acquaintance with Mr. M'Nair prevents me from doing that justice to his character which a fuller knowledge of his history would have enabled me to do.

James M'Nair was born at Loch Striven Head, in the parish of Inverchaolain, district of Cowal, Argyleshire, in October 1829. After some instruction at home he was sent to the school at Glendereul at the age of twelve. He went to live at Dunoon three years afterwards, when he was employed by the postmaster there in delivering the letters around Dunoon. Even then his natural energy, sagacity, and openness of character drew towards him the goodwill of those with whom he came in contact. Brought under the power of the truth as it is in Jesus, he diligently improved all his spare hours in increasing his education and adding to his stores of useful knowledge. A few years after found him a very useful man in the district. As a Sabbath-school teacher and office-bearer in the Free Church congregation of Dunoon he was very active and useful for several years.

On a vacancy occurring in the office of postmaster at Dunoon, the inhabitants at once expressed their desire that Mr. M'Nair should be appointed. A memorial was unanimously forwarded to Sir Rowland Hill, then Secretary of the Post-Office, who at once complied with the wish of the people. Mr. M'Nair, while grateful for this appointment, intimated, however, to Sir Rowland that he could accept the office only on the distinct condition that no Sabbath work was to be done. The high moral principle shown by this act attracted Sir Rowland's attention. Mr. M'Nair's conditions were agreed to; and it is a striking and gratifying fact, that this correspondence, followed by personal intercourse during a summer residence at Dunoon, was the means of forming a strong regard for Mr. M'Nair on the part of Sir Rowland Hill, as shown by many acts of personal kindness both by himself and his excellent lady, and continued to the very last. Only a few months before Mr. M'Nair died he showed me a very kind letter which he had just received from Sir Rowland.

Mr. M'Nair was a self-made man. He created his own patrons. While holding the office of postmaster in Dunoon, like many other postmasters, he also carried on business as a bookseller and stationer, thus conveniently supplying the public with all the requisites for letter-writing. He had good professional prospects; he had secured the confidence both of the Post-Office authorities and of all his business connections, especially that of the well-known firm of Messrs. Dickson, stationers in Edinburgh. But he had higher aims than these; he was eager to become a minister of the Gospel, or a missionary of the Cross. He was prepared to relinquish all his encouraging business prospects if he could attain this object; and the Lord, in a singular and unexpected manner, opened up his way for the successful prosecution of his studies, so that, in due time, the desire of his heart was attained.

The beginning of Mr. M'Nair's personal intercourse with Sir Rowland, which brought about this happy result, occurred in this way. It is well known that Dunoon is a much-frequented watering-place. Among other notabilities who resorted to Dunoon to spend a portion of the summer months, for one or more seasons, was his chief, the great Post-Office reformer, Sir Rowland Hill, still personally a stranger to Mr. M'Nair. One day when Sir Rowland called at the Post-Office on business, Mr. M'Nair, as his custom was, when the office was empty, was improving his spare time in the prosecution of his studies, but, as usual, the moment any one entered, he laid down his book to attend to his official duties. While thus engaged with the business on hand, Sir Rowland's eye was attracted to the well-thumbed, dumpy little volume lying on the desk, and, curious to see what the young man was reading, he stretched over his hand and lifted the book, and found that it was Bagster's Polymicrian Greek New Testament. Surprised to see an official in this department occupied in so unusual a study, he entered into conversation with Mr. M'Nair, and learned from him that he was very desirous to pursue his studies, with the view of entering the Gospel ministry; that he was most anxious to go to college, but could not afford to give up his situation and his business; and, finally, encouraged by the kindly deportment of Sir Rowland, Mr. M'Nair put the question to him, if he thought that the Post-Office authorities would allow him to retain his situation as postmaster, providing he should employ a trustworthy and properly qualified substitute during the session of college. Sir Rowland said the case was a novel one; he did not know that such an application had ever been made; but he would think about it and advise him. After satisfying himself as to Mr. M'Nair's antecedents, attainments, and character, Sir Rowland brought the matter before the Post-Office Commissioners, and although the case was unprecedented, he secured the arrangements which Mr. M'Nair wished, and, as has been said, continued till Mr. M'Nair's death his warm and steady friend. It is an interesting fact to know that Sir Rowland Hill, the author of the penny postage and other great postal reforms, a man of world-wide celebrity, should by his kind and considerate conduct have been so largely instrumental in providing the New Hebrides mission with one of its most earnest agents. Surely the hand of God is seen in arranging the most seemingly trifling incidents. Surely "the steps of a good man are ordered by the Lord," both as to his doing good and his getting good. There are far more people interested in missions than either the missionaries labouring in the mission field or the Churches supporting them are aware of; and in times of trial and discouragement this ought to be hailed as a token for good.

Mr. M'Nair went to the University of Edinburgh, and had the privilege of pursuing his literary and philosophical studies under Sir William Hamilton and his illustrious associates. He studied theology and the cognate branches, partly in the Free Church College, under Drs. Buchanan, Bannerman, Smeaton, &c., and partly in the Reformed Presbyterian Hall, under Drs. Goold and Binnie; while, to fit himself more fully for missionary labours, he entered the Medical Missionary Institution, and also attended the lectures of Sir James Y. Simpson and some others of the distinguished medical professors in the Edinburgh University.

His mind appears to have been early directed to mission work; but it was not till one of the Reformed Presbyterian students and he were lodging together at college that he became acquainted with the history of our mission. Its claims, however, approved themselves so to his mind, that he resolved to offer his services for our field, and did so. Our Foreign Mission Committee had, only a short time before, accepted the services of two of our own students, Messrs. Cosh and Neilson, and were afraid of incurring pecuniary responsibilities which they might not be able to fulfil; but they gladly entertained the offer, and corresponded with the Mission Board in Nova Scotia, and Mr. M'Nair was finally engaged by the Presbyterian Church of the Lower Provinces as their missionary. He was taken on trial, licensed, and ordained, by the Reformed Presbyterian Church.

Before leaving Scotland Mr. M'Nair was united in marriage to Miss Galloway, a young lady belonging to Edinburgh, who, by her education, her Christian character, and her missionary spirit, proved herself to be in every way a helpmeet for her husband, while by the meekness and gentleness of Christ, exemplified so fully in her daily life, she endeared herself to every member of the mission.

Mr. and Mrs. M'Nair arrived at Aneityum in August 1866. He accompanied the *Dayspring* round the islands when she went to bring the missionaries to the Annual Meeting. At the Annual Meeting in September they were appointed to Eromanga. When the *Dayspring* returned, bringing the missionaries to the meeting, the *John Williams* was in the harbour, but so much injured by an accident she had met with while entering the harbour, that we unanimously agreed to send the *Dayspring* along with her to Sydney, lest she should founder on the voyage. The missionaries, both our own and those of the London Missionary Society, had to remain on Aneityum till her return. In the meantime a small trading vessel was proceeding to Eromanga and Efate, the captain of which kindly offered a passage to as many as he could accommodate. So eager was Mr. M'Nair to be at his station, that he and Mrs. M'Nair, in company with Mr. and Mrs. Morrison of Efate and Mr. Gordon of Eromanga, set off at once, although the vessel was swarming so with cockroaches that they were like to be eaten up alive; and Mr. and Mrs. M'Nair had to sleep on deck all the eight nights of the voyage, the cabin was so intolerable.

During their first year Mrs. M'Nair was laid down with fever and ague; Mr. M'Nair suffered from it also. In consequence of this they came back to Aneityum, when the *Dayspring* went up to the Colonies in December, and remained, mostly at my station, till the vessel returned to the islands in April, when they went back to Dillon's Bay, Eromanga, where they lived ever after till his death.

He was a true-hearted, earnest missionary. He applied himself most assiduously to acquire the Eromangan language. He taught the natives to read; he preached to them the Gospel; he translated portions of the Scriptures; he administered medicine to the sick, and in every way he and his devoted wife laid themselves out for the temporal and spiritual well-being of the natives; and their labours were beginning to tell very effectively, both on the Christian natives around them and on the more distant heathen. In the last year of his life they had the satisfaction of seeing a few converts, whom they had carefully instructed, added to the fellowship of the Church ; and the heathen, in considerable numbers and from great distances, were paying them friendly visits. During the first two years that they lived on Eromanga, owing to epidemics and a great mortality among the natives, their lives were often in danger from the heathen ; but during the last two years, owing partly to the absence of these exciting causes, but chiefly, I believe, to their being better known, the heathen had become friendly to them and favourable to Christianity.

Mr. M'Nair was a large-hearted man, and was devising enlarged schemes of usefulness for Eromanga. On that island travelling is difficult by land ; the sea is the principal highway ; but then the sea can be traversed in common boats only in fine weather ; there are no reefs along the coast forming lagoons, inside of which boats may always sail safely, as there are in the eastern and many other groups. It is surrounded almost everywhere by an iron-bound coast ; even boat harbours are few and far between ; hence a specially good boat is required for sailing round the island. Mr. M'Nair had brought this matter so distinctly before some of his friends in Australia, that the Rev. Mr. Mackie of South Yarra, Melbourne—a man who was ready for every good work —and his congregation raised a sum, which, with the addition of a gift of £40 from Mrs. Grundemann of Germany, procured him an admirable lifeboat, alike adapted for sailing or rowing, and which would be safe in all seas and in all weathers, that he might be able to visit round the island, as far and as often as he might require to do so.

One prominent feature in Mr. M'Nair's character was his thorough reliable honesty. He was a Nathanael—an Israelite indeed, in whom there was no guile. His piety was sincere and unostentatious; it was best known by its fruits. He was a reliable man, a peaceable man, a lovable man. He was naturally of a quick and hasty temper; his Celtic blood boiled up at every display of hollowness, or heartlessness, or injustice in any form. His whole soul was moved within him at the kidnapping system that had been going on so long in those seas, especially when the poor Eromangans were the victims of this "consummation of all villanies;" and he wrote on this subject to the Commodore commanding on the Australian station, in language unmistakable, distinct, and strong; and which, it is believed, did good in high places. About this time a letter by Mr. M'Nair was brought under the notice of Mr. Taylor, M.P., and, containing a distinct statement of facts, induced him to submit a motion on the subject to Parliament. This was the first time that the labour traffic was brought under the notice of the Imperial Legislature, and it has never been allowed to slumber since. It was wrong and wickedness that aroused Mr. M'Nair's indignation, but under ordinary provocation his irritation was brief and evanescent, while all the benevolent emotions of his heart were strong and enduring.

The learned and pious Hervey says:—"I have always looked upon *gratitude* as the most exalted principle that can actuate the heart of man. It has in it something nobly disinterested, and, if I may be allowed the term, generously devout." When I was in New Zealand, eighteen months before Mr. M'Nair's death, I met a gentleman to whom I was the bearer of a letter from our brother, and who had been one of his securities when he was postmaster in Dunoon. After expressing his delight at receiving the letter and hearing of the welfare of his friend, he concluded by saying, "Well, I think I never in my whole life met with a more *grateful* man than Mr. M'Nair."

He was a modest, unobtrusive man, and never strove after effect; and hence first impressions of him were often less favourable than of many others greatly inferior to him; but, like all true men, he grew in the esteem of others as he became better known; and the longer and the better he was known, the more he was liked.

He was a liberal contributor to all good objects; he was liberal to the full extent of his means. He was an earnest teetotaler; he had been so, I believe, all his life; he used neither alcohol nor tobacco in any form, but cheerfully lent all his influence to assist those who are striving to stem and drive back the fearful flood of intemperance that is desolating both the Church and the world.

"His great moral courage," says Mr. Dickson, "and his extraordinary power of resolution, were accompanied with, if they were not the result of, a simple, and therefore strong, faith in God. His eye was single, and therefore his whole body was full of light. Naturally affectionate, grace made him singularly generous and unselfish. In many little ways, not only among his own kindred, but among others who had no claim on his care, he was ever ready with kind deeds as well as kind words. Along with a sound and able mind he manifested the spirit of meekness and of love. This gave him power even with the poor Eromangans, whose souls he longed after in the bowels of Jesus Christ."

He was fully alive to the duty of using "all lawful endeavours to preserve our own life and the life of others." The mission-house at Dillon's Bay, though an excellent house, stood in, what experience had shown to be, an unhealthy situation. To remedy that, Mr. M'Nair, when at Aneityum during the last Annual Meeting of the mission that he attended, bought from a white man the frame of a cottage of two rooms, which he took with him, intending to erect it immediately on his return home, on another and a more healthy site, that they might at least sleep there. All the necessary arrangements for doing so were made. But this and other schemes, however wise and however well laid, were, in the providence of God, cut short.

Though not a robust man, Mr. M'Nair continued to enjoy a fair measure of good health till within six months of his death, when he was attacked by fever and ague, of an obstinate rather than of a violent character; but under which he finally succumbed. Whether it had become complicated with some other disease or not, it is difficult to say. Most probably it had. He was present at our Annual Meeting in June, attended every sederunt, and took a part, more or less, in all the business; and although he was weak, and suffering a good deal, no one seemed to suppose that he was in any immediate danger. He was appointed to accompany the *Dayspring* in the following month to Auckland and Rarotonga, a voyage expected to occupy about two months, in the hope that the change would go far to restore him to his wonted health. But his strength had been much further reduced than any of us suspected. He had reached home just about a fortnight, when he died. Indeed till the very last no immediate danger was anticipated, although he had stated to some of the brethren on his way home that he felt he had not long to live. On Friday afternoon, the 15th July 1870, after giving a sick native some medicine and a blanket, he went out to the storehouse, and in handing down a bunch of bananas to some natives who had been cutting wood, a severe paroxysm came on. He went in and lay down on the sofa. Mrs. M'Nair asked him if he had much pain. He said, no; but it was his heart, and the difficulty in breathing. The paroxysm passed off, and he was easier during the night; but about daybreak another paroxysm came on. He began to retch, and while Mrs. M'Nair was holding him she felt his head become heavy and a cold clamminess on his hands. She immediately sent for Mr. Smith, a white man who had been there for a few weeks, commencing a whaling station, and who had formerly been second mate in the *Dayspring*. He came in an instant, but all was over. The *Dayspring*, with four of the missionaries on board, had left Eromanga the week before, no one suspecting that his race was so nearly run. But his work on earth was finished.

Though his death was sudden and unexpected, yet he was found prepared—he was, as the old divines would have said, actually, as well as habitually, prepared; his loins were girded and his lamp was burning. He knew in whom he had believed. Mrs. M'Nair wrote us, that the whole of the night before his death he appeared to be in an ecstasy of joy. Grace in habit had become grace in exercise; dying grace was given on a dying bed; as his day was, so was his strength. "Mark the perfect man, and behold the upright; for the end of that man is peace."

He was deeply lamented by the natives. They were both particularly well liked by those about them. To give just one instance. One of our Aneityum teachers and his wife had lived with them for a few months to assist them as servants, but had returned home. When the news of Mr. M'Nair's death came to Aneityum, and this woman heard of it, she cried bitterly, and said, "Oh, they were so good; they were so good to us; their words were so good; and their conduct was so good; yes, both of them were so good; they two never scolded us; they two never spoke angry words to us; no, neither the one nor the other; their words were always soft and good; yes, they two were so good; they two were so kind." His missionary career, though brief, was not in vain. On the evening of Saturday Mr. M'Nair was interred alongside of Rev. G. N. Gordon and Mrs. Gordon, who had fallen martyrs at that station some years before.

On the Tuesday following, Mr. Smith set off in a boat to Port Resolution, and brought Mr. Neilson from Tanna and Mr. Paton from Aniwa, who made every necessary arrangement for Mrs. M'Nair. After his settlement in Mr. M'Nair's station, the Rev. H. A. Robertson, with his characteristic energy, kindness, and good taste, had the hallowed spot, with its granite memorial stone sent out by Mrs. M'Nair, carefully and neatly enclosed; while a tablet, supplied by the Rev. Dr. Steel of Sydney, with an inscription in English and Eromangan, containing the names of John Williams, Harris, the two Gordon brothers, Mrs. Gordon, and J. M'Nair, has been affixed near the pulpit in the wall of the Memorial Church.

Mr. M'Nair left not only a widow, but an infant daughter about a year old, who, when they left the islands, were followed by the esteem and love, the sympathy and prayers, of all who knew them in the mission.

Mrs. M'Nair subsequently became the wife of the Rev. Dr. Turner of the Samoan Mission; and in Samoa, as in the New Hebrides, she has fully realised all the high expectations, as to character and usefulness, that were formed respecting her when she first entered the mission.

CHAPTER XIX.

THE REV. JOHN GEDDIE, D.D.

As Dr. Geddie was the central figure in the New Hebrides mission for a quarter of a century, a brief notice of his life and character will naturally be expected in this volume.

Though brought up and educated in Nova Scotia, Dr. Geddie was born in Scotland; but his parents emigrated to Nova Scotia when he was an infant of little more than a year old. His father was a watch and clock maker in Banff, in comfortable circumstances. Both his father and mother were God-fearing people, and strongly imbued with a missionary spirit. They seem to have come largely under the influence of that revival wave that passed over Scotland, especially in the northern counties—that work of grace which was excited and set in motion chiefly through the instrumentality of the Haldanes and their coadjutors. One of Mr. Geddie's apprentices was converted by their ministrations, and evinced a strong desire to study for the ministry. Both his master and his mistress encouraged the young man; Mr. Geddie even remitted some part of the time of his apprenticeship, to allow him to proceed more advantageously with his studies. This young man proved the reality of his conversion by the history of his after life; he developed into the Rev. Dr. Morrison of London, for some thirty years the editor of the *Evangelical Magazine*, the leading organ of Nonconformity. His daughter was married to the Rev. Dr. Legge, the celebrated Chinese missionary. Mrs. Legge's "Life," written by her father, adds another most interesting chapter to female biography and to our missionary literature. The name of Dr. Geddie's mother was Mary Menzies, who came out of a "pious Secession family, that lived on the banks of the Deveron, about seven miles from Banff, where they were engaged in farming. It may be mentioned, as showing how the family were connected with the mission enterprise, that the Rev. Dr. Milne, the very distinguished Chinese missionary, lived for a time as a farm servant in her father's house."

Dr. Geddie was an only son, but he had three sisters, all eminently Christian women. The eldest was married to the Rev. Dr. Fraser, Clerk of the General Assembly of the Presbyterian Church in Canada, but is dead; the second was married to Mr. James Johnston, for a time merchant in Pictou. Mrs. Johnston sent one daughter into our mission, the late saintly Mrs. Mathieson of Tanna; her son too was preparing to follow his uncle's footsteps, but the state of his health compelled him to abandon his studies. Mrs. Johnston died a short time after her daughter, Mrs. Mathieson. But before the news of Mrs. Mathieson's death had reached Nova Scotia, she had a strong impression borne in on her mind that her daughter was dead. "Mary," she said, "has gone before me, and she will meet me in heaven." Such impressions, though rare, are not unknown. I know a minister's wife in Scotland who had a similar inborn conviction as to her father's death, while she was on a voyage home from India; and Dr. Samuel Johnson relates that Lord Roscommon, the poet, when in France, had some preternatural intelligence of the death of his father, a fortnight before the news came of his being dead. Dr. Geddie's third and youngest sister—a woman of a strong missionary spirit—was married to a Mr. Henderson, a gentleman living and carrying on business in San Francisco; she too is dead. Two of Dr. Geddie's daughters, Mrs. Neilson and Mrs. M'Donald, were settled in our mission in the New Hebrides.

Dr. Geddie was born in 1815; ordained in 1838; left Nova Scotia for the South Seas in 1846; commenced his labours on Aneityum in 1848; and died in Geelong, December 15th, 1872.

The most prominent feature in Dr. Geddie's character— the distinctive, outstanding, governing principle of his life— was his missionary spirit. He was the son, as we have seen, of parents strongly imbued with missionary principles. By them he was dedicated at his birth to be a missionary, should the Lord so incline his heart and fit him for the work; he drank in the missionary spirit with his mother's milk. His father's house was full of missionary books, and was regularly supplied with missionary periodicals; his early reading thus consisted largely of missionary literature. His boyish cravings for literary excitement were gratified, not by the Waverley Novels or the poetry of Scott and Byron, but by the publications of the London Missionary Society, then glowing, month after month and year after year, with the unheard-of triumphs of Christianity in Tahiti and other islands of the South Seas, when the achievements of Nott, Ellis, Williams, and their fellow-labourers were filling Christendom with delighted wonder. Through life his favourite reading was Christian biography, especially the lives of eminent missionaries; he was also, to his dying day, strongly attached to the London Missionary Society, his early reading having made him fully acquainted with the principles, character, and history of that time-honoured Society. He received his classical, philosophical, and theological education at Dalhousie College, and was brought up at the feet of that distinguished Gamaliel, that eminent Master in Israel, the late Rev. Dr. M'Culloch, who did so much to advance the higher education in the Presbyterian Church of Nova Scotia—a man, as was said of the Rev. Dr. Andrew Symington of Paisley, who was a Senatus in himself.

When Dr. Geddie was licensed as a preacher there was no organisation in Nova Scotia by means of which he might enter the mission-field; he therefore, in the meantime, accepted a call from the congregations of Cavendish and New London, on Prince Edward Island, and was ordained as a minister over them. Shortly after his ordination he wrote a series of Letters on Foreign Missions, addressed to the ministers and members of the Presbyterian Church of Nova Scotia, which were published in the provincial papers. The result of all his labours, public and private, was, that the Synod took up the subject, and resolved to commence a Foreign Mission. The Synod put itself in communication with the United Secession Church in Scotland, now with the Relief Synod, the United Presbyterian Church, of which the Nova Scotian Church was a branch, to assist them in the choice of a field. Shortly before this time the United Secession Church had placed £500 in the hands of John Williams, to be employed in opening up for them a mission-field in the South Seas; he had recommended New Caledonia to them, on which the London Missionary Society had placed teachers.

Meanwhile the United Secession Church had given up the idea of a mission to the South Seas, and had fixed upon Old Calabar as the field of their missionary operations. They, therefore, offered to pass over their claim to New Caledonia to their Nova Scotian brethren, which the latter accepted. Having fixed upon a field, the next question was, how to obtain a missionary; and as no one else could be found, Mr. Geddie offered his services to the Synod, which they were most ready to accept.

He lost no time in preparing to depart to the scene of his labours. He had now been seven years a settled minister, and had a wife and three children; but his heart was in the work, and where there is a will there is a way. What time he had he employed in furthering the cause, and in preparing himself more fully for his work. He visited the congregations, to enkindle or foster an interest in the mission. He took lessons in printing, and obtained some instruction in medicine. He tried "his 'prentice hand" in printing a missionary sermon of his own, from Rev. xiv. 6, entitled "The Everlasting Gospel." The printing was creditably executed, and the sermon put into free circulation.

He was a man of a strongly impulsive nature. When any object had taken possession of his mind, his whole soul was thrown into it; it must be carried out then and there, at whatever hazards. It was specially so with him in this case. From the time when he demitted his charge till he was ready to sail for the South Seas he lost two of his children; but, nothing daunted, putting his trust in God, he set sail with the other two, the younger being only six weeks old, having been born in the interval. God accepted the sacrifice, as the missionary's subsequent experience showed. Moreover, instead of waiting a year till he might go direct by London in the *John Williams*, he resolved to go by America. He arrived in Newburyport just in time to catch the last and worst of the whaling fleet bound for the Sandwich Islands. It proved to be a miserable vessel, and going round Cape Horn in the beginning of a Southern winter nearly cost Mrs. Geddie and the two children their lives. In this case, however, his courage is more to be admired than his prudence. Having reached the Sandwich Islands, they had to remain at Honolulu for some two months, till they obtained a passage to Samoa in another whaler. At Samoa they had to remain about eight months, waiting for the arrival of the *John Williams* from England, when they proceeded to the New Hebrides, and were located on Aneityum, under the auspices of the London Missionary Society, that being thought to be a more suitable field than New Caledonia. Their detention at Honolulu and Samoa was by no means lost time. They had thus an opportunity of seeing the working of both the American and the London Society's Missions, and they acquired a large amount of knowledge that was of great use to them when left to their own resources on Aneityum. When the Samoan missionaries held their Annual Meeting, they appointed one of the most experienced of their number, the Rev. T. Powell and his wife, to accompany Mr. Geddie for a twelvemonth, to assist in establishing the mission. The Synod in Nova Scotia wished to commence their mission to the heathen with two ordained missionaries and their wives. But as they could not secure the services of a second ordained missionary, they engaged a catechist, Mr. I. Archibald, and his wife, who accompanied Mr. and Mrs. Geddie to the New Hebrides; but this, like several similar arrangements previously attempted by other missions in the South Seas, proved unsatisfactory and unsuccessful, and at the end of three years Mr. and Mrs. Archibald left the mission and proceeded to New South Wales, where he found employment as a teacher.

To relate what Mr. Geddie accomplished on Aneityum would be to write a history of the mission. All, however, that I can do at present is simply to specify a few traits of his character. He was, in many respects, admirably qualified to commence such a mission. He was enthusiastic in his work; he had a great aptitude for dealing with the heathen; he possessed a kind of intuitive sagacity for treating them so as to gain their confidence. He had a great readiness in acquiring the native language, both in its vocables and its grammar, both in its general principles and in its minute details. He had a very retentive memory; he could remember even minute particulars for any length of time. Hence if he got hold of a word or a phrase, he seemed never to forget it. He had thus very soon a medium through which to communicate a knowledge of Divine truth. In this department of mission labour he was ably assisted by Mrs. Geddie, who acquired an extraordinary command of the language, especially for conversational purposes. The natives used to say of her, that she spoke their language just like a native of Aneityum, and that her words were all the same as theirs, which was the highest encomium on her that they could pronounce.

He gave great prominence in all his ministrations to the primary, vital truths of the Gospel—sin and grace; the fall of man; the love of God; the atonement of Christ; the work of the Spirit; the necessity of a new heart and a holy life. He exhibited Christianity, not as a code of restrictions, but as a religion of privileges, breathing nothing but blessings. He gave prominence to the fact that Christ came not to destroy men's lives, but to save them.

He made early and extensive use of the press. He prepared and printed alphabets, primers, hymns, Scripture extracts, and catechisms. He did not wait till he had scholars before he printed books; he provided the book, and then attracted the readers; and every new book drew in some new scholars.

He was an excellent translator; he had a great facility in discovering how texts of Scripture should be translated so as to be most easily understood by the natives. In general his renderings were clear, simple, elegant, and idiomatic. Perhaps in no department of mission work was his loss more felt than in the translation of the Scriptures. But strange as it may appear, though such an excellent translator, he was by no means a good editor. He wanted that power of patient and continuous application so necessary to secure accuracy in all the multitudinous details requiring attention in the editing of a translation in a new language. This was less felt in the first stages of the mission, when the language, in its printed form, was still in a formative state, but was becoming more seriously felt as the language was assuming a settled and permanent character. Mr. Geddie was a worker, but he was not a plodder, like Dr. Carey, as depicted by Dr. George Smith, whose admirable life of the great proto-missionary of modern times has recently been published. He was always ready to commence and do the main work, but he had not often patience to plod on and finish.

He had a great genius for mechanical pursuits. Although he had had no previous training, beyond freely using the tools in his father's shop, he could turn his hand with great readiness to carpenter's work, mason's work, plastering, &c., as well as printing. He would have excelled as an engineer; he had great inventive power; was fertile in expedients to meet new and unexpected difficulties, where civilisation was as little known as Christianity, and where it was necessary to create the conditions under which work could be done, before he could labour. He had a great command over his hand; had he followed his father's profession, he would certainly have taken a high place among skilled workmen. Had he been a surgeon, he would have been a dexterous operator. He wrote a clear, distinct, beautiful hand, and filled page after page without a blot or a mistake.

He was a man of simple tastes and frugal habits. He was a strict economist; he kept his expenditure always below his income; he was specially careful of the Church's funds, and strove most conscientiously to carry on the mission at the least possible expense to its supporters, not to increase his own salary, but in order that the Church might send out more missionaries, and extend the work to the other islands.

During the first years of the mission he not only wrought hard, but he suffered much from fever and ague. But after the initial difficulties were overcome, and the evangelisation of the natives had fairly commenced,—when doors of usefulness were opening up in all directions,—when all was push on and drive through, and this activity was sustained by the excitement of a daily, continuous, and remarkable success,—he was in his perfect element. For any amount of active exertion, physical or mental, he was always ready and always able; with singular facility, he could turn himself to anything, whether it was to build a mission-house, a schoolhouse, or a church; to translate a gospel, prepare a catechism, or print a primer; to administer medicine, teach a class, or preach a sermon; to traverse the island on foot, sail round it in his boat, or take a voyage in the *John Williams* or the *John Knox* to the adjoining islands. He was ready, ever ready, for all manner of work and every occurring emergency. But he was flesh and blood, and human strength has well-defined, if not also somewhat narrow, limits. He had a remarkably wiry and elastic constitution; but unfortunately for himself, as well as for the mission, he was frequently careless and inattentive as to the state of his health. Like many strong and healthy people, he seemed incapable of realising the sources of danger till the mischief was done, and the remedy came too late. On our return to Aneityum in 1863, we found him quite broken down, and in great need of a change. His visit home at that time had an excellent effect both upon him and upon Mrs. Geddie. Although he had no rest, except during the voyage, and laboured without intermission during the whole time he was at home, yet change of labour was to him, perhaps, better than total rest. The kindness he everywhere received, and the high and generous appreciation of his labours, produced upon his sensitive spirit a powerful and beneficial effect, and, in connection with the bracing atmosphere of the northern provinces, acted like magic in restoring his health. No returned missionary was ever more fully appreciated,—wherever he went he was greeted with a cordial welcome;—the Synod conferred its highest honour upon him, by voting him into the Moderator's chair; an honour which he modestly declined;—an academic degree of D.D. followed him from Canada,—while his visitation of the congregations was a constant ovation.

After an absence of nearly three years he returned to Aneityum a renovated man; the flush of health was again upon his cheeks, his step was again firm and elastic, and his right hand had regained its cunning. But a machine broken and again repaired is seldom, if ever, equal to a new machine; so renewed health is seldom equal to original health. It was so, at least, with him; his improved health did not long continue unimpaired. He was never quite his former self. Those who saw him only during the latter years of his missionary life saw him to a great disadvantage. His buoyancy was mostly gone. The work, too, on Aneityum had changed, and had become of a kind not at all so well suited to his capacity or so congenial to his taste. Formerly it was planting, now it was watering and weeding; formerly it was chiefly evangelising, latterly it was more like pastoral work. Moreover, during the former period the work was carried on under highly exciting and encouraging circumstances; during the latter years, owing chiefly to the depopulation of the island by successive epidemics and the breaking up of the mission on Tanna and Eromanga, it was carried on under very depressing and discouraging influences; the former work required ceaseless activity, the latter was an endless plodding; hence the tone of his correspondence latterly was more desponding.

Had the language of Aneityum been spoken over the whole group, he would have been in his element, following the example of John Williams, visiting other islands, settling teachers, and opening up new stations; but, alas! when he set his foot on Tanna, or Eromanga, or Efate, or any other island of the group, he found his tongue tied and his lips sealed; it was a new language on every island. When he accompanied the *Dayspring* as sailing missionary, the only medium of communication which he had with the heathen natives was a few words of broken English. In this way he was reluctantly "shut up within a single reef," after the labours for which he was best qualified had been accomplished, to carry on another kind of work for which he had less fitness and less desire. He was singularly gifted for dealing with the heathen, and with those newly brought under Christian influences; it was, therefore, very disappointing to him to have his generous efforts so abruptly arrested, and his field of usefulness so completely closed.

But though he had become less vigorous than formerly, there was no very marked debility about him till July 1871, when he had a severe attack of influenza, which was passing over the islands at that time, and from which he never fully recovered; it left him permanently debilitated; and the shock of paralysis which he had in the beginning of June, in the following year, laid him wholly aside from all further labour; it impaired his memory and impeded his speech.

For two years or so before his death I had observed a growing spirituality in his prayers, as if he had some inward presentiment that his days on earth were drawing to a close. Mr. Neilson, his son-in-law, also informed me that throughout the time he lived with them on Tanna, during his last illness, he appeared very frequently as if engaged in mental prayer, while that morbid anxiety and restlessness under which he had previously been labouring entirely left him, and he became singularly calm and contented. The devotional tendencies of his mind appeared very distinctly after his memory began to fail; while he never omitted to ask a blessing before meals, he often, unless prevented, returned thanks two or three times.

For some time before his death he was mostly unconscious. But, happily for us, our salvation does not depend on the condition in which bodily disease may place the soul, or affect its exercises at the hour of dissolution. "The gifts and calling of God are without repentance," and are not reversed on account of any accidents that may befall us on the banks of the Jordan.

Like most men of his temperament, he was not free from constitutional infirmities both of temper and character, which, at times, tended considerably to mar both his usefulness and his happiness, especially during his latter years, when his health began to give way and his nervous system began to be shaken. The strong points of his character were very strong; but then he had weak points as well. Unhappily for himself, as well as others, he was not always aware in what his great strength lay, and in what it did not lie. He was sometimes the victim of strong prejudices, both as regarded men and things. He was prone to indulge unreasonable hopes in the new, the distant, and the unknown; while he was often as unreasonably disappointed with the old, the near, and the well known. He was frequently disposed to draw important conclusions from very slender premises. On subjects which he thoroughly understood, or matters that had come under his own observation, no man could have had more correct views, or express those views more clearly; but on subjects requiring extensive investigation his conclusions were the result of intuition rather than of induction; and hence, on all questions resting on inferential evidence, or requiring a large induction of facts, his opinions were of little value. He was often prone to look on the dark side of things, and, especially after his nervous system became enfeebled, to take up groundless suspicions respecting even some of his best friends.

But he was raised up by God, and qualified to do a great work. That work he did, and did it well. His faults, his failings, his infirmities, will soon all be forgotten; but he will be remembered as the father and founder of the Presbyterian mission on that group; as one who has left his mark, broad and deep, on the New Hebrides, but especially on the island of Aneityum, and whose memory will be long and gratefully cherished by the natives; as one, also, who has increased the usefulness, extended the boundaries, elevated the character, and heightened the reputation of the Presbyterian Church of Nova Scotia; and as one whose example will fan the flame of missionary zeal in that and other Churches for many years to come. Oh that many such as he may respond to the Divine call, and say, "Lord, here am I; send me!"

CHAPTER XX.

MRS. INGLIS.

THE subject of the following sketch was born at Corriefeckloch, in the parish of Minnigaff, Kirkcudbrightshire, on the 15th of April 1821. Her father, John M'Clymont, was a well-known and much-esteemed farmer, and for long a leading elder in the Reformed Presbyterian congregation of Newton-Stewart. Her mother, Jane Murray, who was a model wife, mother, and mistress, was the daughter of a highly respectable elder in one of the Secession congregations in Stranraer. Jessie M'Clymont was the eldest of a family of eleven, of whom eight were daughters and three were sons; of these, only four are now living—one of her brothers and three of her sisters. Corriefeckloch is situated in one of the highest of the upland districts of Galloway, on the borders of Ayrshire, near to the Merrick, the highest hill in the South of Scotland. The district being pastoral, the population was sparse, and the educational advantages were very unsatisfactory. After utilising what the locality could supply, she had to be sent to Newton-Stewart, Stranraer, Ayr, and Manchester, to supply what was lacking at home. When her education, so far as it went, was completed in one of the best ladies' schools in Manchester, she returned home, at the age of fourteen, a precocious girl, both physically and mentally, and for the next nine years of her life, till the day of her marriage, on the 11th of April 1844, she was her mother's right hand in the upbringing of the younger children of the family, and in assisting her in all household duties. It was for her an admirable training—better than that found in most boarding-schools. She became a thorough expert in domestic economy, both theoretical and practical. It was a family training that went far to fit her for the place she was called to fill as a missionary's wife. The family at Corriefeckloch had a large circle of intelligent Christian relations and friends; and while they practised a strict economy, they used hospitality without grudging. Theirs was a house often visited by ministers, not only of the Reformed Presbyterian Church, but of all denominations. It has been observed by some, that in those families where a prophet's chamber is provided, and often occupied, where ministers of the Gospel are frequently entertained when discharging their duties, there is among the children a greater intelligence, a higher culture, and a more earnest and enlightened piety than is to be found in families of the same status where there is no chamber on the wall for the passing prophet, and where no Elisha or other holy man of God is constrained by the mistress of the house to go in and eat bread as he passes on his way.

It is often a difficult matter to fix the date of any one's conversion; a more important matter is to be certain that it has actually taken place. It is stated in the Life of the late eminent Dr. Wardlaw of Glasgow, that he could not fix the time when he was converted. He was surrounded with healthful religious influences from his earliest childhood, and through these the Spirit of God had operated silently but surely, and in such a way as left no doubt of the efficacy of

His work, if the child was not sanctified from his mother's womb. The subject of this sketch, being the eldest child of pious parents, was carefully instructed in Scriptural knowledge, brought up in the fear of the Lord, and trained up in the way she should go; was a staid, thoughtful child, and had always the appearance of one living under the powers of the world to come. The Rev. Dr. A. Symington, in his admirable Memoir of the Rev. T. Halliday of Airdrie, quotes with approbation the following sentence :—" In a regular state of the Church, and a tolerable measure of faithfulness and purity in its officers, family instruction and government are the usual means of conversion, and the public ordinances of edification;" and Samuel Rutherford says :—"I mean not by this that all the children of God can tell the very first mathematical point of the time of their conversion; for there be some with whom the Lord has dealt from their youth, and with some the Lord deals more smoothly in their conversion than He deals with others."

But however the Spirit of God may have been working in her young heart, it was the reading of John Angell James's " Christian Professor," the gift of a friend, through which the Spirit either produced a change of heart, or quickened into new activity a feeble spiritual life, which led her to come to a decision, and make a profession of her faith in Christ. At that time there was a vacancy in the congregation of Newton-Stewart, in which, as I have said, her father was an elder. Dr. Symington of Stranraer was Moderator of the Session *pro temp*. Along with some other candidates, she was carefully examined by him, and on his report was admitted by the Session to the full fellowship of the Church, in 1839, I think, when eighteen years of age. The family lived thirteen miles from their usual place of worship at Newton-Stewart. For a number of years, during three or four months in summer, the members of the Secession and Reformed Presbyterian Churches maintained a preaching-station for the benefit of their own families and the inhabitants of the district generally; but for about eight months in the year, including the entire winter, there was no preaching nearer than Newton-Stewart. But a gig and a cart were called into requisition every Sabbath, and the bulk of the family were always to be found at church. Those who remained at home improved their time by the reading of good books. A favourite book with her on these days was Brown's "Dictionary of the Bible"—a book found then in almost every well-instructed family, in the South of Scotland at least, and which is well fitted, from its contents, historical, doctrinal, and practical, to attract, instruct, and impress the reader. She was always a Bible student. When out in the islands, as a kind of light reading at odd times, she read through the whole of Kitto's "Pictorial Bible."

Three months after our marriage we sailed from London to New Zealand, and joined the Reformed Presbyterian Mission to the Maories. After eight years we removed to the New Hebrides, in which mission she laboured for twenty-five years. On our return home she spent four years—three in London and one in Kirkcowan—assisting me to carry through the press the Aneityumese Old Testament and some other native books, including the Aneityumese grammar and dictionary. She was thus publicly employed in mission-work for thirty-seven years. During the last four years of her life she lived retired in Kirkcowan; but she always felt herself as being identified with the New Hebrides mission, and did everything in her power to promote its interests both at home and abroad. She kept up a regular correspondence with all the missionaries' wives, also with a good many ladies, both in Australia and New Zealand, who were warm friends of that mission; her interest in the mission was unabated till the day of her death.

It is not my intention to give a full account of her life, or a full delineation of her character; to do so would be to write a history of the mission—she was so identified with all its operations. All that I intend is simply to sketch the outstanding facts of her life and the more prominent features of her character. She entered the mission with the full conviction that God had called her to that work, and she threw all her energies into it. Having put her hand to the plough, she never thought of looking back. Although strongly attached to her father and mother, to her brothers and sisters, yet, during all the long and lonely years which she lived on the islands, often not seeing a white face but our own for five or six months at a time, she never gave way to the feeling of home-sickness; she never repined; she cheerfully recognised the principle, "He that loveth father or mother more than Me is not worthy of Me." But while thoroughly missionary at heart, she was no fanatic; she took a common-sense view of the situation. She recognised herself as being first a wife, and next a missionary. She felt that her household duties were her first duties; that she was bound, in the first place, to use all lawful endeavours to preserve her own life and that of her husband; to attend so to food, clothing, and domestic comfort as would secure the highest possible health in the circumstances, in a place where the climate was debilitating, and where every convenience and every comfort had to be created before it could be enjoyed; where every violation of the laws of health was followed by the inevitable penalty; and this policy went far to secure the subsequent success of the mission.

From various causes our views on almost every subject were very much the same, from the dogmas of theology down to the minutest details in the arrangement of mission-work. This similarity in our views and sentiments was not caused, but it was greatly fostered, by our general reading being nearly always the same. Shortly after our marriage we happened to read an anecdote of Mrs. Taylor, wife of the author of the "Additions to Calmet's Dictionary of the Bible," and other works. When Mrs. Taylor had been married about a year or so, a lady friend called upon her one day, and in the course of conversation asked her what books she was reading. "Books!" said Mrs. Taylor, "I read no books; the housework and the baby occupy all my time." "Read no books!" said the astonished lady; "and what do you think you will become? Your husband is a great reader; he is reading daily; and if you read none, will you be any companion to him ten years hence? No; do what you like, but you must read. Offer to read with him and for him; read aloud for him while he eats his meals, and get him to read aloud to you while you nurse the baby and do your work. See that you read or hear him read as much as he does." Mr. Taylor was in business at that time, and it was only when his work was over that he had time to read. Mrs. Taylor took up the suggestion, and carried it out; and the woman who became known as the mother of Isaac and Jane Taylor and their sisters must have read to good purpose. My wife caught up the idea, and carried out the principle, in its spirit at least. We arranged that I should read all my strictly professional reading by myself, while she was engaged with her own especial duties, but that we should read together all our general or popular reading, especially in the evening. In our particular circumstances, having the arranging of our work mostly in our own hands, it was easier for us than for most people to make such an arrangement. In this way we read together our newspapers, magazines, quarterlies, and books of general interest. Sometimes I read while she was plying her needle, and at other times we read time about. On this plan we read the writings of the Symingtons, and most of the literature of the Reformed Presbyterian Church, ancient and modern; for, while the reverse of sectarian, we wished to possess an intelligent knowledge of the principles of our own denomination. We read together the Life and most of the practical writings of Chalmers, the Life and the whole of the theological works of Principal Cunningham, also the writings of Hugh Miller, of Moffat, and of Livingstone. We read a considerable amount of missionary biography and books on missions, especially on missions in the South Seas. We made remarks on all these books as we read them, and in this way, our knowledge being drawn so much from the same sources, the tendency was to bring our views and feelings into harmony, and lead us to aim at the same ends and to seek to accomplish them in the same manner; and union here was strength.

From the very first she set herself, as a duty, to acquire a knowledge of the native language, both in New Zealand and in the New Hebrides. She had a considerable knowledge of the Maori language; but as we never succeeded in obtaining a satisfactory field of labour in New Zealand, owing to the arrangements of the other missions and the unsettled state of the natives, her knowledge of it was limited compared with her knowledge of the Aneityumese. She never thought of speaking to the natives in broken English, or "pigeon" or sandalwood English, as it is called. This is easiest at first, but accuracy is longer in being attained, and the result is far less satisfactory. She began to speak to the natives on Aneityum with some two or three words, and supplemented these with signs, and wrought away as she best could, but continuing to add to her vocabulary and improve in the knowledge of the language, till there was not a word in common use the meaning of which she did not know; and before long she spoke it with great readiness and fluency, if not always with strict grammatical accuracy or with a perfectly correct pronunciation. How few speak a foreign language exactly like a native! but she spoke it so that the natives always understood what she said to them, and she always understood what the natives said to her.

She never waited for some great opportunity to arise, or till some great work was to be done; she cheerfully accepted the day of small things, and always undertook the work that lay nearest to her hand. When we went to Aneityum, as she knew nothing of the language, she went to the morning-school, and commenced a class of ten or a dozen little girls in the alphabet, as she could teach them that with the least possible knowledge of the language. By the time these knew the alphabet and could read a little, she was able to speak to them. She continued this class till they were all good readers. She then, in addition to reading, taught them to commit Scripture to memory, and they went on all learning some parts; but a number of them committed to memory gospel after gospel as fast as they were printed—about one in the year—then the Acts, and then Paul's Epistles, from Galatians to Philemon. What they learned daily during the week they repeated in whole on Sabbath. By-and-by, as the work grew upon her, she had to give up her attendance at the morning-school, and confine herself to a Bible-class on the Sabbaths and on the Wednesdays. She instituted a forenoon sewing-class for the women on certain days of the week, which was largely attended. She also established a boarding-school, or a school of industry, for girls and young women. She began with two, but they went on increasing till she had at times as many as sixteen. They lived on the premises, under the immediate care of a responsible man and his wife. For twenty years at least they were under the care of Lazarus and Esther, two natives well known in the mission. My wife undertook to clothe the girls and teach them, but their parents or friends were to supply them with food. Not infrequently, however, she had to feed a portion of them as well. This school proved a great success; the girls were well instructed and carefully protected. The most of them became teachers' wives, and in after years exercised a salutary influence on the community.

When Mr. and Mrs. Geddie came to Aneityum, they were accompanied from Samoa by an experienced missionary and his wife, Mr. and Mrs. Powell, to assist them in establishing the mission. The Powells brought with them a knowledge of the best modes of conducting female education, as carried on in Samoa. After their departure, Mrs. Geddie first, who had seen the system in operation in Samoa, and three years afterwards my wife, carried out those principles and plans that had been found to work so successfully by the missionaries' wives in Samoa, utilising their experience, and working on the same lines, simply varying their modes to meet different circumstances among an entirely different race of people; and to this they owed much of their success.

My wife was an excellent teacher. In the language of the Educational Code, she was strong in drill. For in its order her Sabbath Bible-class exemplified the Italian proverb—it was "as round as Giotto's circle;" and her week-day sewing-class, often numbering from forty to fifty, was equally well arranged. At first she had to supply the scholars with needles, thread, thimbles, scissors, and all sewing material. If the natives had cloth of their own, she cut it for them as required; if they had none, she supplied them also with seams. Her aim, like Dr. Chalmers's, was to multiply herself. She trained so thoroughly the girls living on the premises, that they were able to act as monitors under her; and when these large classes were collected, she divided them, and set one of her own well-trained girls over every class of four or five to teach them; and in this way female education and a knowledge of sewing was extended.

But by-and-by, as scholars increased, she restricted this kind of teaching to a class for the teachers' wives, which met once a week; and as clothing became more plentiful among the natives, she caused the teachers' wives to bring with them all the cloth the natives possessed, and she, assisted by the most skilful of her own girls, cut out the garments for the owners of the cloth, and sent the teachers' wives back to their respective localities to keep schools with their own women, and teach them to sew. If they had no cloth of their own, she supplied them with garments, cut out and tacked together, to be sewed in the district schools, and brought back to her when finished, a week, or a fortnight, or a month afterwards, as distance or other circumstances might render necessary.

In another respect she was a great help to me among the women. In heathenism the women were so down-trodden by the men, that they would never have come to me, being a man, to speak about anything. But she, being a woman, was recognised as their friend, and in proportion as they came to know her character their confidence increased. Hence they came to her to explain all their ailments and unbosom all their griefs and sorrows. In this way through her I gained a great amount of valuable information respecting the social condition of the community, which guided me in many important matters, and enabled me often either to remove or to prevent many serious evils, which, if allowed to go on, might have resulted in disastrous consequences. But with knowledge thus acquired, which was always power, without any one suspecting it, I could often bring about either the prevention or cure of evils, as the case might require. I was able often to ameliorate the condition of the women, and at the same time do no harm to the men, but the very reverse.

She possessed the administrative faculty in a very high degree. She had order both as to place and time. She laid out her work beforehand; she saw clearly what was to be done; she knew well how it was to be done; she ascertained what labour she could command; and she gave her instructions so distinctly that the work was invariably well done, and the workers were never oppressed. Whether the helps were few or many, she divided the work equally among them; it was felt also to be so reasonable, and comparatively so light, that it was hopefully undertaken and cheerfully performed. The natives during her busiest times felt that they were never burdened. There was no hurry, no bustle, no fuss. Things invariably went on almost like clockwork, meals were served up to the very minute, and every other arrangement was as exact. A gentleman from Sydney, who was staying with us for a short time, was so struck with the punctuality of the meals as got up by the natives, of course under her directions, that he said one day, "Well, I have lived on board a man-of-war, and in many places where order reigned, but I never saw punctuality like this. Why, the meals are all to a very moment." At meetings of the Mission Synod we often sat twenty for dinner and all other meals for a week or ten days at least; yet so thorough were her arrangements, that on one occasion a lady of the party wrote to one of her friends that there was not even a salt-spoon either awanting or out of its place. The captain of the *Dayspring* said that she could have conducted the commissariat department of a man-of-war. Some visitors were of opinion that the natives at our station were of a different race from the others, they seemed so docile and so easily managed. They were possibly not aware, however, that at such times she was up every morning at four o'clock; that she had at her back from twenty to thirty of her best-trained natives, mostly teachers and teachers' wives, whom she had trained herself and brought there for the occasion. She had every one of them told off for some special duty, that every one might know his or her work, and that they had to do nothing else. Before breakfast, which was at seven o'clock, owing to the heat, everything had been arranged for the day, and to the uninitiated it seemed as if the whole organisation was some self-acting machine that required no guiding; they did not know how much thought, and planning, and arranging, and hard work had been done before all these agencies had been put into such working order, and the mistress of the house could accompany her lady visitors for two hours daily to the meetings of the Mission Synod, as if she had had as little to think of as they had. There was work—hard work—but there was no worry; for thought and timely arrangement had prevented all that. It was not mere mechanical drill on the part of the natives that wrought these results; it was intelligent, well-directed principle. On one occasion there was an unusual number of children—some twelve or fourteen. To meet this demand an apartment was curtained off with mats in the Teachers' Institution; a temporary table was provided for the children and their nurses, and their meals were served up to them there; and every morning a different missionary and his wife were appointed to take charge of the juvenile table, to see that the children had their meals properly, and that the nurses did their duty to all parties. This proved a satisfactory arrangement. To provide food during that time for missionaries and their families, to the number of thirty or more, and an equal number of native servants, required some forethought. Accordingly for two or three weeks previously she advertised for fowls, and bought every one that was brought to her, till her coops were all full. She spoke to every fisherman on the shore to keep her supplied with fish during the meeting; she had spoken to eight or ten of the chiefs to supply her daily with so many baskets of taro, each man on his day; and she had pigs and goats ready to be killed as they might be required. On such occasions, in addition to these, she provided in abundance yams, bread-fruit, bananas, cocoa-nuts, pine-apples, sugar-cane, oranges, &c., according to the season. She bought everything that came. If the missionaries could not eat all that was provided, the servants could; or if the servants could not, there was an overflow meeting outside that

s

could utilise the fragments; and with whom it was always desirable to be on good terms, not knowing when their help might be required for some purpose; so that nothing was ever lost. She had two kitchens—one of them a temporary erection—with an American stove in each, the one new, the other old. She had a cook and his assistant in each kitchen, with other help. She prepared a dozen bedrooms, the majority of them extemporised, as a matter of course, but all of them supplied with everything necessary. In these circumstances, with guests all agreeable, and all willing to be pleased, the meetings proved very enjoyable, and to the most of the visitors the only regret was that their stay could not be further prolonged.

She took a great interest in the native children, especially the female children, who were sadly neglected in heathenism; male children were highly prized, but female children were nothing accounted of. You would see the fathers often carrying about and nursing their sons, but you would never see a man nursing his daughter. On one occasion, shortly after we went to Aneityum, a woman near us gave birth to a daughter, that being the third daughter she had born in succession. When she learned that it was a daughter and not a son, as she wished and hoped for, she cried out to the women beside her, "Oh, kill it, kill it!" The natives around her were Christian, and hence her request was refused; but the utterance showed how little value was placed upon girls. My wife set herself to save the infant girls, and the first step she took was not to denounce the poor mothers, but to draw them into her plans. She told the women that she had a great love for the little girls, and that from this time forward she would give a nice dress to every little girl whose mother would bring it to her as soon as she was able after the child was born. She therefore set to work, and, with the help of her own girls, got a number of little garments prepared; and whenever a mother brought to her a newly-born girl, she dressed it with one of these garments, kissed the baby, praised its clear, bright, black eyes, spoke kindly to the mother, urged upon her the importance of nursing the child carefully and keeping it clean, and asked her to bring it back often that she might see it. From that day to this there has not been a girl killed on Aneityum, or yet seriously injured. It was the influence of Christianity that was the great cause, but this also helped. The children were brought to me for medicine, but she supplied medical comforts; and, either directly or indirectly, she saved many an infant's life.

During the first year of our residence on Aneityum, a man and his wife brought their sick child to the mission-house. The mother was a young wife about eighteen, connected with one of the best families in the district; she was professedly Christian, and very good-looking. The husband was one of the most glum, sullen, and forbidding-looking savages that I ever looked upon—an avowed heathen. The child was to all appearance dying; but my wife got a tub of warm water, bathed the child carefully, dried it, and wrapped it up in a piece of a soft blanket, then gave the poor mother a cup of tea and a biscuit. The child by-and-by got a little medicine. They stayed for a few days, partly on our premises and partly in the house of an uncle of the mother's, a Christian man, who attended to the mother and the child. The treatment was successful; the child fully recovered, and grew up to be a fine young man. My wife always professed to claim him as her child, seeing she had saved his life. The father was never so terribly glum afterwards; a slight gleam of grateful sunshine lit up his dark countenance, and by-and-by he abandoned heathenism and avowed himself a Christian. On another occasion a man and his wife had come with a sick child, and stayed in one of the little hospitals at the mission station. One morning the man came to me to borrow a spade. I asked him what he was going to do with the spade. He said he was going to dig a grave in which to bury the child. I said to him, "When did the child die?" "Oh," he said, "it is not dead, but it is dying." On hearing this my wife said to him, "Go quickly and bring it to me." He went off at once and brought his wife with the child. It was a cold morning, at least for Aneityum, and the cold was telling on the poor child. It was not dead, but would certainly have died if nothing had been done for it. My wife got a warm bath ready, bathed the child, and afterwards wrapped it carefully in an old soft shawl that had been sent to her from New Zealand in a mission-box, and gave the poor sorrowing mother a cup of tea and a biscuit. When the child revived and began to suck vigorously, the poor father was in an ecstasy of delight, and seemed to forget entirely everything about the spade and the grave. She sent him off to gather wood and keep up a good fire in the hospital. In a few days the family returned home, the mother and child both quite well. By acts such as these, which were often repeated, she saved many an infant's life and alleviated a great amount of juvenile suffering, and at the same time she gained an amazing influence for good over the mothers and the female population generally; so that there was nothing at all reasonable which they were not willing to do for her if she only asked them to do it. They were docile as children, and would have refused her nothing.*

She was the first to introduce the making of arrowroot on Aneityum. When we went to the island, all the arrowroot that was used was got from Samoa, and was of very inferior quality, owing to the way in which it was made. After a time she said to me one day, "What a pity it is, when we have the arrowroot growing on the island, that we should not make it for ourselves." We had at that time a Rarotongan teacher and his wife living with us for a year, till they should be settled elsewhere. When the arrowroot was ripe, my wife said to the Rarotongan woman, "Tutau could you teach me to make arrowroot?" "Oh yes," said Tutau, "if you get me the arrowroot." The raw material was procured. "Now," said the woman, "how do you wish

* I had just finished this sketch when I received a copy of the *Toronto Presbyterian Review* of September 17th, 1885, containing a notice of Mrs. Inglis's death, by the Rev. W. M'Cullagh, formerly of the New Hebrides mission, who occupied Dr. Geddie's station on Aneityum for three years, from 1864 till 1867, in which he says:—"Of her it may be truly said, 'Blessed are the dead which die in the Lord,' &c. She was in every sense the model missionary's wife, for piety, prudence, energy, tact, and skill. Few could surpass her in the duties of practical housekeeping, whilst the mission premises, both inside and out, furnished abundant proof of her superintending care. Mrs. Inglis knew how to utilise the products of the island, so that visitors were at once surprised and entertained by her simple yet varied hospitality. She was indeed a true helpmeet to her husband, and though she had no family, her spiritual children were numerous. Her trained domestics would have done credit to any first-class hotel in the Dominion, and her influence over the female portion of the island was magical. No doubt this contributed in no small degree to her husband's success in that part of the island. Her death will be deeply felt by her husband and the Church, and by all who knew her; and yet their sorrow is not without hope, for assuredly hers will be the reward recorded in Daniel xii. 3: 'They that be wise shall shine as the brightness of the firmament, and they that turn many to righteousness as the stars for ever and ever.'"

it to be made? Do you wish it to be made as we make it for the missionaries, or as we make it for a contribution to the London Missionary Society?" "What is the difference?" said my wife. "Oh," said Tutau, "there is a great difference. When we make it for the missionaries, we make it far more carefully; we wash the bulbs first, and scrape the skin all off, and then wash them all again, and make them as clean as they can be made, before we grate them down and strain the pulp through a thin cloth; but when we make it for the Society, we just wash the bulbs and then grate them down, skins and all. The arrowroot," she said, "is just as good, but it is not so pure and white." My wife said, "Oh, I want you to make it as you do for the missionaries—the very best that can be made." Tutau set to work, and made fifteen or twenty pounds, the first arrowroot ever made on Aneityum. My wife watched the process, and treasured up in her memory the knowledge thus acquired. The next year she offered to buy all the unprepared arrowroot which the natives might bring. They accordingly brought and brought, and she got our own natives to make it under her direction, till, when finished, instead of twenty or thirty pounds, as she intended, she had from two to three hundred pounds. This was taken by our steadfast friend, Bishop Selwyn, to Mr. Archibald Clark of Auckland, who sold it, the one-half to the Hon. Mr. Shepherd, Colonial Treasurer, the other half to the Hon. Dr. Sinclair, Colonial Secretary—gentlemen who knew thoroughly the difference between genuine and adulterated arrowroot. Mr. Clark sent the proceeds in clothing for the natives, and also some suggestions as to how it might be improved in the making of it for the market, and offered to take half a ton next year. On the New Hebrides the natives have never learned that there are two ways of making arrowroot; they know only the best way. The industry was now established, but simply as a contribution to the mission, not as an article of commerce. The difficulty is in finding a market. The natives of Aneityum have contributed upwards of £2000 for Bibles, books, and missions — the proceeds of arrowroot. Other islands, viz., Tanna, Aniwa, Eromanga, Efate, and Nguna, have all followed the example of Aneityum; the work is going on, and extending year by year. The arrowroot has uniformly realised a shilling a pound. What is wanted is a steady market, and, to secure this, it would be well if each Church connected with the mission would appoint a small active committee to attend to the sale of the arrowroot. Hitherto our best agents have been the wives and daughters of our ministers and elders—wise-hearted and willing-handed Christian women. But these must be sought out and their services engaged; and it would be the work of these committees to discover and enlist them. In this age of enterprise the sale of every manufactured article must be pushed, and why not push " mission " arrowroot?

Her great familiarity with the language was of very important service to me in translating, revising, and editing the Scriptures. She never translated any of the Bible herself, but she was an acute and a sound critic. I always read to her every chapter that I translated. She often objected to words and phrases, and she often suggested improvements; and both her objections and her suggestions were generally correct, or were at least worth attending to. She listened attentively always to the last revision of every chapter, and approved of all the final corrections. Every final proof she attested at least twice. After I had corrected the proofs till I thought them perfect, she took the Authorised English Bible and read it over slowly word by word, naming also every stop, while I watched the translation to see that no word was omitted, and that no word was added. When this was done, I took the English version and she took the translation, and read it over in the same way, and I checked it. At times we reversed the process : I read, and she watched and checked the errors, if any. I may here remark in passing, that, owing to the different idioms of the two languages, the points are not always inserted in the same places in the sentences. Nevertheless it was always useful to compare the punctuation of the two versions. Those unacquainted with such work can scarcely comprehend the labour and the close attention required in such a task. There are nearly a million words in the Aneityumese Bible, and perhaps more than 120,000 stops. Now, to read twice through the entire Bible, name these million words each time, and be certain that each word is correctly spelled, and also name twice over each one of those 120,000 stops, and see that each is inserted in its proper place, that a period should never take the place of a comma, a colon of a semicolon, or a point of exclamation be placed for a note of interrogation. This is the drudgery of literature, wanting all the inspiration and all the pleasure of original composition, and where, as Dr. Johnson says of the compilers of dictionaries, the utmost that can be expected is to escape censure. In this department of mission-work she laboured conscientiously and successfully for twenty-nine long years, from the time she went to Aneityum till four years before her death, when the entire Bible, the first part of the Pilgrim's Progress (abridged), the Hymnal, the First Catechism, the Shorter Catechism, and the Grammar and Dictionary were all printed.

She had an excellent constitution, and throughout her whole life enjoyed a fair measure of good health. On Aneityum, and also after her return home, she suffered a good deal from fever and ague of a mild type; however, she never had any violent attacks. The most serious ailment from which she suffered was sunstroke in 1858, which was followed by several slight attacks of paralysis, but from which she always completely recovered in a few days.

On our return to this country in 1860, we were introduced by Dr. Goold to Dr. Patrick Heron Watson of Edinburgh, who was just then commencing his brilliant medical career, by which he has taken his place in the front rank of the profession, and gained for himself a European reputation. He examined her very carefully, and after hearing the history of the case and learning all about the symptoms, he pronounced it to be sunstroke. It was the first case of sunstroke we had known, although we knew of several afterwards. Dr. Watson's treatment was very successful; she had no more paralytic symptoms, although there was a tenderness left in the brain, and she had to be cautious in exerting herself; she never durst strain the eyes by writing, reading, or sewing, especially white seam. Any long close application of the eyes was felt on the brain. On one occasion on the islands she did not write a letter for eighteen months, and by exercising due caution she suffered very little. On account of this weakness, I was always afraid she might be cut off by paralysis or apoplexy, but never apprehended that heart disease, as it turned out, was likely to be the cause of her death. Although she did not reach the extreme limit of human life; although, like Jacob, she did not attain unto the days of the years of the life of her fathers—her mother died at seventy-six, her maternal grandmother at eighty-six, and her paternal grandmother at ninety-one—yet the time of her working life was above the average. For more than half a century, from her fourteenth year to her sixty-fifth, every day of her life she had done a full woman's work. During all the twenty-five years of our mission-work on Aneityum, she wrought to the full extent of her strength, often greatly beyond it, especially during the first eight years. There were at that time, on our side of the island, 1900 natives; of that number little more than a hundred professed Christianity when we went there, and wore any European clothing. Before the end of those eight years all those 1800 heathens had renounced heathenism, were professing Christianity, and were wearing more or less of European clothing; and almost every one of those 1800 garments worn by the natives had passed through her hands. The demand for clothing was urgent and almost unprecedented in extent. She wrote to her friends at home and in New Zealand for clothing, new or old, and they responded nobly. But the planning as to how to clothe the greatest number of people with the smallest possible quantity of cloth was a problem difficult to be solved. But it was solved in some way. Some would say, "Why not let them do with their native clothing?" as none of them were absolutely naked; for throughout all those islands the dress of which Adam and Eve's girdles were the original patterns is still universally worn. But as it was then, so it is now. As soon as Adam and Eve received and embraced the promise of Christ, as soon as they became professedly Christian, the Lord clothed them with coats of skins, which became a badge of their Christianity; so as soon as those natives renounced heathenism and professed Christianity, the wearing of some portion of European clothing became a recognised badge of Christianity, as well as the first step towards their civilisation. European clothing had, therefore, an important bearing on the progress of Christianity on the island, and we did our utmost to utilise the demand.

But these severe and long-continued strains on her strength in a debilitating climate, as well as the effects of the sunstroke, were telling on her system; and when we returned home, after eight years' labour on Aneityum—after sixteen years' mission-work altogether—although her health was comparatively good, she was so changed in appearance that her friends could scarcely recognise her. Indeed, on the night of her arrival, her youngest brother and her second youngest sister really doubted her identity. When she went away to the mission, they were children of six and eight years of age respectively; but that night, before retiring to bed, they said to one another, "That lady is never our sister; but we will say nothing about it till the morning." Next morning, when the fatigue of the journey and the excitement of meeting had passed off, and when a refreshing night's sleep had restored her to something like herself, the doubting brother and sister said again to one another, "Yes, that must be Jessie after all; the old life and fire are still in her." But after remaining in this country two years and a half, assisting me, along with Williamu, a native of Aneityum, to revise the New Testament and carry it through the press, her health and strength became quite reinvigorated, and she never broke down afterwards.

She had good conversational powers; she spoke with ease and fluency, but she never attempted to give any public address. At tea-parties or similar gatherings, however, especially if questions were put to her, she could pour forth interesting information about the natives and the mission. During one of our visits to Victoria, we were staying with a family very deeply interested in the mission; a few friends were invited to meet us. During the evening the gentleman of the house got beside my wife and began to question her about the mission. A good part of the company gathered round them, and an animated conversation was carried on till a late hour. I was doing what I could to entertain another part of the company. Next day this gentleman said to one of the party, "What a pity it is that Mrs. Inglis would not go through among the friends of the mission, and explain things to them as she did to us last night; it would do so much good to the mission. I assure you that she told us more about the islands, and the natives, and the mission than I ever knew from all the lectures I ever heard or all the books I ever read; and the beauty of it was, that she told us so distinctly and so clearly all those things I wanted to know, and that is what the lectures and the books seldom tell you."

She never wrote anything for the press. She was always kept so busy making history that she had no time to write it. But, on the other hand, I scarcely ever wrote anything for publication which I did not first read to her for her criticism. Many a line and many a sentence she made me score out, and many a one she made me alter. "I think," she would have said, "you had better put out that sentence. It is very good, and I daresay it is all true; but there is rather too much about yourself in it." Again she would say, "Read that sentence again. I think you could make it clearer if you would rewrite the sentence, and put in a word or two of explanation near the end of it." She seemed to have an intuitive perception of what was right and proper both in sentiment and language.

She took a special interest in the newly arrived missionaries' wives. She gave them the benefit of her experience, and assisted them at their settlement, and afterwards in every way she could; and they, on their part, were never slow to acknowledge their gratitude.

She took the Bible as fast as it was translated and printed, and taught it to the women and girls as earnestly as ever missionary's wife taught it. She taught them first to read it, and then to commit it to memory, and left the Spirit of God to apply it to their hearts and consciences in His own time and way. The Bible was thus the basis of their religion, and also the basis of their civilisation, and the fruit appeared in due time.

The Lord blessed her in her basket and in her store. She had a great aptitude for creating plenty around her; she managed so successfully with her cows, her goats, her poultry, and her garden, that she had always abundance; so that when visitors came, and, as it sometimes happened, unexpectedly and in considerable numbers, she was never taken aback. In the islands, in the first years of the mission, a twelvemonths' stores had always to be ordered at once, and they had to be ordered always six months, sometimes twelve months, before they were received; on one occasion two years' supplies had to be ordered at once. But she invariably calculated so carefully, that it was a rare thing that she ever ran out of anything by ordering too little, or that she lost anything by having ordered too much. She never grudged any expense or any labour that was necessary for carrying on the mission successfully, and she aimed at nothing else. With her it was, "This one thing I do." She was thoroughly unselfish. She was a rigid ⁻economist; put her foot firmly down upon all extravagance. "Waste not, want not," was one of her principles; hence she had always plenty; but she was neither penurious nor greedy. She was a thorough manager, unsurpassed as a housekeeper; she was neatness itself in her person, her dress, and her household arrangements. She knew what her income was, and she not only always kept within it, but left a large margin for contingencies. She was charitable to the poor, but she was discriminating; she was kind to the deserving poor, and even to the undeserving she was not hard. She would rather have been imposed upon by two undeserving tramps than that one deserving person should have been sent away hungry. The blessing of him that was ready to perish came upon her, and she caused the widow's heart to sing for joy. In the cause of God she was always liberal, especially in support of the Bible, missionary, and temperance claims.

She was naturally shy, diffident, and reserved. This was at times, by those who did not know her well, set down for pride; but it was quite the reverse. It was her humility, not her pride, that often made her appear to be stiff and distant. She looked upon all her equals as cleverer and better than herself. It was generally only when she was forced to act that her superiority appeared. It was always where she was best known that she was most appreciated. She had a **very large** circle of general acquaintanceship, arising from the circumstances of her position in connection with the mission; but she had also among these a great number of warmly attached friends; and she never lost a friend except by death. But her friendships could hardly have been said to be made; they rather grew, and grew insensibly, from some mutual suitability in the parties. She hardly ever remained in any locality for any length of time without contracting some permanent friendship. She was never demonstrative, either in her feelings or in her profession; she always felt greatly more than she expressed, either on religion, friendship, or personal suffering; but she was always true, generous, and sincere; was always prepared to do more than she promised, and was more ready to confer a favour on others than to ask one for herself.

She never thought of herself but as of an ordinary woman doing an ordinary woman's work—doing nothing but what any one might do. She never did anything for show, or to be seen, or to be spoken about. In her character and in her life-work there was nothing at any time, as she judged herself, or as she appeared to the world generally—there was nothing remarkable, nothing brilliant, nothing romantic, nothing out of the way. She was not specially clever, not specially talented, not learned, not accomplished; was just, as she judged herself to be, an ordinary commonplace woman, to whom the Master had given one talent to occupy till He came; and she certainly did occupy to good purpose. She left her mark very distinctly behind her wherever her lot was cast. One of the great lessons of her life lay in this, that she was in no way extraordinary herself, and did no extraordinary work; she was nothing but what any ordinary woman may be, and did nothing but what any ordinary woman may do. Hence she could be easily imitated. She aimed at nothing that was out of the way, nothing that was unattainable, nothing that was romantic, nothing that was heroic; she held on the even tenor of her way. She was quiet, undemonstrative, plodding, and persevering. She was never fussy, and never did anything for the sake of effect. With her work meant work. Whatsoever her hand found to do she did it with her might. She put everything into its proper place, and did everything at its proper time, and was herself always up to time. I do not think that she ever lost either a railway train or a steamboat in her life. She laid all her plans in good time beforehand, and always carried them out with quietness and decision.

She was a woman of a strong independent mind. She had more faith in my opinions than perhaps any one else, but she would never accept of my opinions simply because they were mine, unless she was convinced by the arguments which I adduced that the opinions were correct; but she was specially quick in apprehending the force of an argument, and yielded at once the moment she was convinced. When we came home in 1877, the views of Dr. Robertson Smith were moving ecclesiastical society in Scotland to its lowest depths. She read largely of the popular literature on the subject, both Dr. Smith's and his supporters. But she refused to accept his views as correct, simply because his arguments failed to convince her, and to satisfy her judgment that he was right; and she returned with increased satisfaction to what has been called the traditional view of the Mosaic authorship of the Pentateuch, and the generally accepted views respecting the other books of the Old Testament, because all the arguments put forth in behalf of the advanced views failed to convince her that the new views were better than the old.

She did not care about speculative or controversial divinity; her mind was far too practical for that. Her creed was embodied in the Shorter Catechism. She believed in the equity of the Divine government and the sovereignty of Divine grace, in the plenary inspiration of the Bible and the efficacy of Christ's atonement, and the doctrines that cluster around these.

Nothing was so distasteful to her as a Christless sermon, or one in which the atonement was ignored. Her religion was of the strong Puritanical type; there was nothing feeble or sentimental about it; she had no craving after the new and the sensational. She was a great admirer of the Henrys, both Philip and his son Matthew; she admired both their writings and their character. Born and brought up, as she was, in one of the outstanding centres of the Scottish persecution, the moors around her being "flowered with martyrs," within four miles of the birthplace of Margaret Wilson, one of the Wigtown martyrs, personally acquainted with all the present descendants of the Wilson family—in a locality where the memories of Peden and Renwick are still fragrant, where the places at which Renwick preached are still pointed out as if the conventicles had been held only yesterday—in childhood and youth poring over the "Scots Worthies" and the "Cloud of Witnesses," as well as the "Pilgrim's Progress"—no wonder, in these circumstances, that the spirit of the Covenanters was strong within her. Her religion made her earnest, truthful, devout, and practical. She was hopeful, cheerful, joyful; there was about her nothing gloomy, nothing fanatical, nothing frivolous. Her religion was healthy. Accepting life as a good gift and a great trust from God, her aim was to know, obey, and submit to the will of God in all things, as the angels do in heaven. She regarded her chief end as to glorify God and to enjoy Him for ever.

She knew nothing of despondency or depression of spirits. She required no company or no amusements to keep her from being dull. She never thought of seeking to enjoy herself; that was what she could do anywhere and everywhere. She strove to maintain a conscience void of offence towards God and towards man, and she found that, in so doing, Wisdom's ways were ways of pleasantness and all her paths were peace. She was a woman of a good understanding; she feared the Lord from her youth, and feared the Lord above many. She was energetic rather than impulsive, and was actuated by a sense of duty rather than impelled by feeling. She was a Martha rather than a Mary; an active rather than a meditative Christian; strong in character rather than tender, in manner firm rather than fascinating. She was more ready to serve others than seek her own enjoyment in reading and devotion while neglecting them. Her greatest happiness was in making others happy, though it often involved much toil and trouble to herself. She would have served like Martha rather than sat like Mary. She would have gone forth with Martha to meet Jesus rather than have sat in the house with Mary till her sister came and called her. She, like Martha, would have been cumbered with much serving, and been anxious and troubled about many things when preparing an entertainment for the Lord; but I do not think she would have complained to Him about her sister, and in this way might have escaped the rebuke. But Martha must have accepted the rebuke meekly, for Jesus loved Martha apparently better than either Mary or Lazarus, as the Apostle John places her name first in the list of the three beloved ones, and says, "Now Jesus loved Martha and her sister, and Lazarus." But whatever eminence she attained, it was the result of a long, slow, well-sustained process, not of any daring, rapid, brilliant, successful enterprise. She never attempted anything extraordinary, but her excellence lay in always doing ordinary things well.

Next to the mission, which was her life-work, her heart was in the temperance movement. She was practically a life-long abstainer, but she was a pledged teetotaler from her marriage till her death, and she was no half-hearted adherent. She did not sign the pledge to please her husband or any one else. With her it was the result of a strong personal conviction. She firmly believed that the great outstanding evil of the present day in this country is intemperance, and she resolutely took her place in the front rank of reformers. She believed, and therefore it was easy for her to practise. She never either tasted intoxicating drinks herself or offered them to others. During the more than forty-one years of her married life, while she exercised hospitality considerably above the average, she never once placed upon her table either wine or any alcoholic liquor. Some complain that they cannot dispense hospitality without using these beverages. She began family life on the temperance principle, and never felt any difficulty. She has entertained at her dinner-table missionaries and ministers of all denominations, and a large circle of private friends. Her guests have been as numerous and of as varied a class as almost any person in her position has been required to entertain; and yet, so far as is known, she never gave offence to any of them on that account, or caused them any disappointment. Her guests all knew always what to expect. Her principles and her practice were so well known that nobody could take offence. And whether she herself were dining with high or low, with a missionary or a minister, or any one of her acquaintances, her temperance principles were always avowed and acted upon. Her fearless example often strengthened the courage of feebler natures and animated the hearts of younger adherents to the cause. But while she was ardent and firm, she was never either rabid or intolerant.

She made it a point never to introduce the subject for discussion into any public company, either in her own house or elsewhere. Her own example of abstaining, and the badge of blue ribbon, which for the last four years of her life she had invariably worn, generally led some one, especially if the company was new, to start the subject; and, as she was well read up on the question, she was never taken aback. She was quite familiar with the Scriptural, the scientific, and the legislative aspects of the subject. She had such a knowledge of the facts and the arguments that she could carry on a discourse or a discussion in such an interesting and profitable manner as never to excite the slightest ill feeling on the part of those who differed from her on the subject.

She was a generous contributor to the funds of the Scottish Temperance League and other temperance organisations, and she ever welcomed to her house and to her table the agents of all the temperance societies. Some abstainers have been accused of penuriousness, of giving up drink simply to save their money, and that their teetotalism was simply a cloak to cover their stinginess. No such charge could be brought against her. When exercising hospitality, she was careful to provide liberally of substitutes for alcoholic drinks. She always supplied tea, coffee, or other non-alcoholic drinks in abundance. To persons working for her, doing jobs or running errands, she never gave any intoxicants; she gave them other refreshments or a money consideration, or both, according to circumstances. She knew well that the saving effected by total abstinence could easily bear those expenses. She was careful that her good should not be evil-spoken of, and that the influence of her total abstinence should not be marred by any charge of niggardliness.

She had enjoyed more than a full average of good health during her whole life. About two years before she had a severe attack of the complaint of which she died—*angina pectoris*—but from that attack she completely recovered, and she had no symptoms of it ever after; and during that last summer her health was unusually good. But on Monday the 3d of August, about two in the afternoon, while she was finishing her dinner, she felt a spasm go through her chest, of the same kind as before, but not nearly so severe. Her sister, who lived close beside us, was with her at once. An intimate lady acquaintance, who happened to be at dinner with us, was also present. The doctor arrived in a very few minutes, and injected morphia into the arm, and examined her carefully. The pain gradually became less, and the doctor went away.

During the afternoon she suffered from sickness, but that also gave way to suitable remedies, and sanguine hopes were entertained that a night's rest would put her all to rights. But about six o'clock in the evening, after she had drank a little tea, she said to me, "I am afraid it is coming back." I caught hold of her at once. She gave a slight quiver, and all was over. She moved her lips, as if wishing to speak, but although she was repeatedly spoken to, "there was no voice nor any that answered." Help in abundance was immediately at hand. Everything that medical skill and friendly assistance could do to restore animation was done, but without avail; life was gone. The symptoms had been so mild that neither the doctor, the attendants, nor the patient herself had the slightest apprehension of any fatal result. But the end had come. It was so sudden, that it was not like a death; it was like a translation; she was not, for God had taken her. The voice from heaven had said to her, "Behold, I come quickly," and continued saying to the survivors, "Be ye also ready." But to the believer sudden death is sudden glory.

"BLESSED ARE THE DEAD WHICH DIE IN THE LORD, THAT THEY MAY REST FROM THEIR LABOURS, AND THEIR WORKS DO FOLLOW THEM."

CHAPTER XXI.

SIR GEORGE GREY, K.C.B., EX-GOVERNOR-IN-CHIEF OF THE NEW ZEALAND ISLANDS.

My reminiscences of the New Hebrides mission would be incomplete if I did not insert three names—all three important links in the history of the mission—viz., Sir George Grey, Admiral Erskine, and Bishop Selwyn—three men who thoroughly understood native character, fully sympathised with missionary effort, and did everything in their power, in their respective positions, to promote the elevation of the native races. Sir George Grey enjoyed exceptional educational advantages. He was a pupil of the late Archbishop Whately, and imbibed largely the enlightened principles of that scholarly, philanthropic, and statesman-like prelate. He was first known to the public by a remarkably well-written and interesting volume of travels in Western Australia. His first public civil appointment was to be Governor of South Australia. He found it a *chaos*, and left it a *cosmos*. He was next appointed to be Governor of New Zealand. At that time the natives were everywhere in a state either of open or veiled rebellion. In the days of ancient Rome there were military roads all over the empire. "Starting," as Dr. Wylie says, "from the golden milestone of Augustus, in the capitol, they traversed the empire in all directions." The one end of each commenced at Rome, the other terminated at the outer extremity of every province. Along those roads Roman legions could be marched to every point where their presence was required, and the result was the tranquillity of the empire. Sir George adopted the imperial policy. He began road-making at Auckland, and pushed the roads forward as fast as possible into all the leading centres of native population. He offered good wages to all the natives who would work on the roads. This secured the support of all the friendly natives; by-and-by the waverers joined them, and finally many of the rebels deserted their party and joined the roadmakers. In this way the Government party, like the House of David, waxed stronger and stronger; while the rebel party, like the House of Saul, waxed weaker and weaker. Sir George also erected two villages, Howick and Onehunga, to be inhabited by pensioners and their families, who were to be sent out from home, each family to be supplied, not with Mr. Chamberlain's "three acres and a cow," but with ten acres and a cottage. In this way the city of Auckland was protected by two garrisons of veteran soldiers. The result of these measures was the security of life and property, and the speedy development of prosperity in the colony. Sir George was afterwards promoted to be Governor of the Cape Colony, and was also a second time brought to be Governor of New Zealand. After this he retired into private life, bought a small island called Kawau, on the Thames, below Auckland, on which he built a beautiful mansion, where he still resides. After a time he returned to public life, and entered the New Zealand Parliament as one of the Members for Auckland, and has been either Premier or leader of the Opposition nearly ever since. He is, as might be expected, a man of high culture and fine literary taste. When he first came to New Zealand, my friend Dr. Logan and I used to read with great interest Sir George's speeches at the opening of the Legislative Assembly—not for the political principles which they expounded, but purely for their literary merits; they read like the orations of Burke, *mutatis mutandis*. He was a first-rate Maori scholar; in addition to his volume of travels, he published two volumes of Maori songs and traditions, of great value for ethnological and philological purposes.

It was in 1850, while I was fulfilling a temporary engagement at Auckland, that I made the acquaintance of Sir George Grey, through my friend the late Dr. A. Sinclair, at that time Colonial Secretary, with whom I was staying. I had met him before, but simply officially. He thanked me very cordially for information that I had supplied to the Government, some two or three years before, respecting the movements of the rebel Maories, while we were living on the Manawatu. The Government had thanked me officially at the time. It was then, as I have elsewhere stated, that he obtained from Captain Erskine a passage for me to the South Sea Islands in H.M.S. *Havannah*, which led to our settlement in the New Hebrides, and which was of such importance to me during all my subsequent missionary life. On my return to New Zealand, at Sir George's request, I drew up a report of my voyage, from a missionary point of view, which he printed in the *Government Gazette*, and also afterwards in small pamphlet form. He took a deep interest in my missionary prospects, and has been my steadfast friend ever since. At that time it was thought by Bishop Selwyn and those best acquainted with the New Hebrides, that the climate was so unhealthy that European missionaries would not be able to live on the islands more than seven or eight months in the year, and that they would require to spend the hot months in New Zealand or Australia. If I had chosen, as some advised me, to open an institution near Auckland for island youths, after Bishop Selwyn's plan, Sir George would have given me a grant of Government land for a site, &c., and assisted me as far as he could. In my circumstances, however, the plan was impracticable. And it was well that nothing was done; as we subsequently found that the climate of the New Hebrides, though debilitating, was as healthy as the average of tropical islands; but his kind offers were no less appreciated on that account.

When he was Governor at the Cape I received three letters from him. In the first one he said that he intended to make a voyage in his yacht among the islands of Western Polynesia, and hoped to call on us at Aneityum. But before he was ready to sail the Indian Mutiny broke out, and the next two letters had reference to delays and disappointments. Troops had been ordered from the Cape. Sir George sent five of his own horses, as a present to the Government, to strengthen the Indian cavalry. The voyage to the islands was never accomplished. A previous attempt ended also in disappointment. Accompanied by Bishop Selwyn, he was proceeding to the islands in the Government brig. They called at the Isle of Pines, but while entering the harbour they were informed that a French man-of-war was lying at anchor, that the French flag was flying on shore, and that the French had annexed New Caledonia without consulting the British Government. Astounded with this intelligence, and not wishing to commit themselves in any way till they should have official information from the Government at home, they put the ship about, and sailed back direct to Auckland. It was understood that Sir George was distinct in counselling our Government to disallow the action of France; but we were then in the very thick of the Crimean war. Inkerman, Balaklava, the Redan, and the charge of the 600 were words on everybody's lips; hordes of Goths and Vandals were pouring in from the frozen North, and we were leaning upon France and Italy for help. In these circumstances Lord Aberdeen, Sir James Graham, and the other members of the Government thought that, although the French had stolen a march upon us, they could not at the time afford to have a quarrel with France about a barren island in the South Seas, the very name of which not one person in ten thousand had ever heard pronounced; so the unscrupulous conduct of the French was overlooked and condoned.

Since the *recidivist* and annexationist policy of the French was made known, Sir George has been distinct and emphatic in denouncing it. He has long pleaded for the annexing of the New Hebrides to New Zealand, and thus to become a part of that province. This would both secure those islands from the French and effectually protect them from the kidnapping system and the labour traffic, as New Zealand has all along been entirely free from the slightest taint of slave-holding proclivities.

Sir George still takes a warm interest in the New Hebrides mission. After my wife's death I received from him a very kind, sympathetic letter, and at the last meeting of the General Assembly of the Presbyterian Church in Auckland, he invited the members to meet him at his residence on Kawau. When there he spoke with great cordiality about the New Hebrides mission, and with what interest he had read the sketch which

I had prepared of Mrs. Inglis; he also showed them the books in the Aneityumese language which Dr. Geddie and I had sent him, and explained the value these would be to the future historian of the South Seas.

The latest notice that I saw of Sir George Grey was that of a great demonstration made to his honour on his last birthday—his 74th, I think—in which, at a public meeting in Auckland, his friends presented him with an address, to which was appended more than 11,000 signatures; a clear indication of the estimation in which he was held, after more than forty years of public life, spent chiefly in New Zealand.

CHAPTER XXII.

ADMIRAL ERSKINE, R.N., EX-M.P. FOR STIRLINGSHIRE.

IN 1850, through the influence of Sir George Grey, I obtained from Captain (now Admiral) Erskine a passage in H.M.S. *Havannah*, from Auckland to the New Hebrides, and thence to Queen Charlotte's Group, the Solomon Group, New Caledonia, and thence to Sydney. The voyage occupied three months. I was the captain's guest, and as such enjoyed every comfort, and possessed special advantages for acquiring all the information that could be obtained respecting the islands and the natives.

Admiral Erskine belongs to an ancient and honourable Stirlingshire family. He is a grand-nephew of Dr. John Erskine, the leader of the Evangelical party in the Church of Scotland in the end of last century, and the colleague of Principal Robertson, the leader of the Moderates. When I sailed with Admiral Erskine, he brought vividly to my mind the description given by Lord Brougham of his distinguished relative, Lord Thomas Erskine, whose "movements," he says, "were firm, easy, and graceful as those of a blood-horse." He possessed the natural eloquence of the Erskines; if he had gone in for the pulpit or the bar, he would have been an eloquent orator. He was an excellent linguist; he pronounced the native words with great ease and accuracy. One of his officers told me that they never met a foreign vessel at sea, French, German, Dutch, Spanish, &c., but Captain Erskine could speak to them in their own language. He was a born ruler of men; the order on board of his ship was perfect, but there was little or no punishment. During the three months that I was on board I saw only one case: a sailor by some means had got drunk, and was made to sit for twelve hours on the main-deck in irons, to make him feel ashamed. The order on board was the result of that latent power possessed by the captain, which was always felt but was never apparent. He was remarkably careful of human life; when among heathen islands he would allow no one on board to go ashore till he was morally certain that there was no danger to life; and then they went all ashore unarmed, to show the natives that we had confidence in them, and that they might have confidence in us. He was equally careful about the health of the seamen. I never saw him angry but once, when the officer in charge of the ship, a young man, had neglected, when a squall was coming up, to take in sail soon enough, and allowed the men to be partially wet. "If you were sailing in the West Indies," he said, "and acted in this careless way, you would soon have the half of the men on the sick-list"—a proof, moreover, by the way, that he looked upon the West Indies as being far more unhealthy than the New Hebrides. He was equally careful of the men's comfort; he saw that they never missed their meals at the regular hours. One day, perhaps, he would be going ashore in the forenoon, but on discovering that it was 11.30, within half an hour of the men's dinner-time—he dined himself at four, when the vessel was at anchor—he would say to the midshipman in charge of the boat, "Stop just now; let the men have their dinner, and then we shall go ashore." On another occasion, perhaps, he would be on shore, and wished, on some account, to remain longer; but discovering that they had not time to do what he wished and be on board at twelve, he would say, "Oh! never mind; let us go on board at once, that the men may be in time for their dinner." In this way the work of the cooks and the stewards was never deranged, and the health and temper of the men were never tampered with; they were healthy and they were happy, hence able and willing for their work, and it was easy for them to obey.

He always treated the natives with justice, kindness, and courtesy. Whenever he came to an island he at once sought out the chief or chiefs, and got them on board. If any native could be found that could speak English, he got him to interpret. He showed them through the ship, caused his steward to give them some food, inquired into any grievances they might have, explained to them the objects of his visit, gave them some small suitable presents, and parted with them fast friends. On two occasions only did anything disagreeable occur—in the one case by the action of the seamen, in the other by that of the natives; but in both cases amicable relations were immediately restored by the tact and good sense of the captain. The one case occurred at Aneityum, the first island at which we called. Two boats went ashore to water; at the watering-place a number of cocoa-nut trees were growing temptingly near to the place where the boats went ashore, and the sailors helped themselves freely to the nuts, without asking leave from the natives. The owners naturally felt aggrieved, and had it been a purely heathen island, they would have found ways and means of obtaining redress, though probably not ending pleasantly for either party; but as the natives were partly Christian, wiser counsels prevailed, and they went to the missionary, and asked him to tell the captain. On the following day, when Captain Erskine went ashore and called at the Mission-House, Mr. Geddie told him what the natives had said. When he went on board, and found on inquiry that the complaints were well founded, he summoned the whole ship's company to the quarter-deck, imposed a fine of so much tobacco on the crews of the two boats, and delivered to them a very solemn and convincing address. They expected, he said, to be three months among those islands, where the natives were all savage cannibals, and the success of the expedition depended largely on their maintaining peaceful relations with the natives; he told them of other expeditions becoming complete failures owing to the seamen stealing from the natives, getting into collisions with them, and lives being lost on both sides. On the following day he went ashore. His steward took the tobacco. Mr. Geddie sent for Nohoat, the chief. The captain caused the tobacco to be given to him. Both the chief and the natives were delighted beyond measure; it was the first time in their lives that they had received payment for stolen cocoa-nuts; and from that day to this, on Aneityum at least, the men of war, as well as the missionaries, have been regarded as their best friends; in the language of the island they and the missionaries are called *Nup u Beritani* (British); other white people are called simply *Nup u Tonga* (foreigners).

The other case occurred at Yengen, a harbour on the south-east side of New Caledonia. Two boats were ashore watering. All went on harmoniously for some days; but on the afternoon of our last day on shore, the men were washing some of their clothes, and had them spread out to dry, when the natives began to be impudent and troublesome, and finally they stole some of the seamen's under-shirts. On seeing this, the officer in charge of the watering party ordered the men to cease their work, pick up everything belonging to themselves and the boat, and return to the ship; this they did, and he reported the affair to the captain. He at once sent for the chief, and told him what the natives had done. The chief immediately sent off his brother after the thieves. As fast as he could run he went over a hill and down to a valley on the other side, and in less than an hour he was back with the stolen property. Captain Erskine commended the chief highly for his honesty and energy. Thus, by the exercise of a little patience, prudence, and forbearance, a collision was averted, a misunderstanding was prevented, and peaceful relations were maintained; and when we weighed anchor on the following morning, the best of feeling existed between the ship and the shore.

The previous year Captain Erskine had visited Samoa, Tonga, and Fiji. Wherever he went he employed his influence to strengthen the hands of the missionaries, but especially in Fiji, where heathenism was still strong. At Mbau, the capital, King Thakambau was still a professed heathen, but Christian influences were beginning to tell upon him; and a captain of a man-of-war, coming in the name of Queen Victoria, confirming all the teaching of the missionaries, could not fail to influence the king and chiefs of Fiji. He was specially strong in speaking against murder, and cannibalism which was often the incitement to murder. One day he invited some of the principal chiefs, along with the missionaries, to dine with him on board. After dinner he began to expostulate very earnestly with the chiefs for their canni-

U

balism, showing them that it was not the missionaries alone who were against this horrid practice, but every white man; that even soldiers and seamen were as much shocked at it as the missionaries. "Here am I," he said, "a warrior by profession, a fighting chief like yourselves, a captain of a fighting ship, with nothing but fighting chiefs and fighting men on board, all sent by the Queen to protect her subjects, and fight against her enemies, if they attack or injure any of her people; and yet I and every fighting chief and fighting man in the ship are all as much shocked by your cannibalism as any of the missionaries can be; and were the Queen to know that I have been dining with men that eat human flesh, she would be so shocked that I doubt if she would ever let me into her presence or allow me to touch her hand again." The chiefs could bear the reproofs of the missionaries alone, and reply to them, but remonstrance in this style, broadsides poured in hot and heavy from such a quarter, so confirmatory of all that the missionaries had urged, was more than they could well bear. At last one of the most noted among them for his cannibal propensities, apparently ill at ease under such expostulations, grumbled out in defence—"It is very well for white men to talk in this way; they have plenty of *Bull-ama-cow* (beef); we have none; and unless we eat human flesh, we have nothing else." It was not long after this till Thakambau and some of his chiefs professed Christianity; and when he did so it was at the risk of his life. The first Sabbath that he appeared in church avowedly a Christian, the missionary had to abridge the service, afraid lest the heathens should attempt Thakambau's life; but he held fast to his profession; and when his death was reported in London a few years ago, at a public meeting of the Wesleyan Missionary Society in Exeter Hall, Sir Arthur Gordon, ex-Governor of Fiji, bore the strongest testimony to the high Christian character of Thakambau. Captain Erskine's influence told largely for good on King George of Tonga, King Malietoa of Samoa, as well as on King Thakambau of Fiji. His influence was the same in the New Hebrides, on Aneityum, Tanna, Eromanga, and Efate. Mr. Geddie was the only missionary on the group at that time, but there were Samoan and Rarotongan teachers on Tanna and Efate, whose hands he strengthened. On Eromanga we landed unarmed, both at Dillon's Bay and at Bunkhil. So far as is known to me, with the exception of Bishop Selwyn, we were the first white men that went ashore on Eromanga after the murder of Williams and Harris, and that was eleven years after the event. So horrible was the character borne by the Eromangans at that time, that our action in going among them unarmed was deemed heroic by the outside world, but the merit was all due to Captain Erskine for his admirable arrangements.

Captain Erskine was always a friend to the native races When he was a young officer in command of a small Government gunboat in the West Indies, before the emancipation of the slaves, he was a strong supporter of the anti-slavery policy, and wrote a number of articles in the emancipation newspapers in Jamaica—all anonymous of course. When the Kidnapping Act for Western Polynesia was passing through Parliament he was Member for Stirlingshire. The Rev. Dr. Kay, the secretary for our mission, wrote me out to the islands, saying that one of the best clauses of the Bill, introduced by Admiral Erskine, had been thrown out while passing through the House of Lords. When I saw him in

London six years ago I referred to the Bill, and said I was sorry that his clause had been thrown out by the Lords. "So it was," he said, "but when it came back to the House of Commons Mr. Hugesson said, 'Oh, never mind, we shall watch our time and try to get it inserted again;' and we did so, and succeeded, and when the Bill received the Royal assent the clause was again in its original place."

He is a member of the Committee of the Aboriginal Protection Society; and the last time I was in London the Secretary of that Society said to me, "Oh, Admiral Erskine is an excellent man—one of the very best members of our Committee; he is, I think, the very best 'Old Salt' I ever knew."

Admiral Erskine's chief literary work is a "Journal of a Cruise among the Islands of the Western Pacific," an exceedingly well-written and interesting volume, the style clear, natural, and vigorous. Lord Nelson's and Captain Cook's were the two portraits that hung in his cabin, and they seemed to be his professional models. Nelson's famous watchword, "England expects every man to do his duty," was conspicuous on the wheel at the helm.

It was thirty years from the time I saw him last in Auckland, immediately after that voyage, till I again met him in London. I was then able to show him the whole Bible printed in the language of Aneityum, and some other books in the same language, and to explain to him, as I have elsewhere stated, what an important service he had rendered to the New Hebrides mission by granting me that three months' voyage in H.M.S. *Havannah*. He was much gratified with my visit, and with hearing of the progress of the mission. I subsequently sent him a copy of my Aneityumese Dictionary. "To the righteous *good* shall be repaid."

CHAPTER XXIII.

THE RIGHT REVEREND DR. SELWYN, BISHOP OF NEW ZEALAND.

BISHOP SELWYN, the name by which he was best known, was a man to whom the New Hebrides mission was much indebted during the earlier years of its history. In 1852, at considerable inconvenience to himself, he gave my wife and me a passage from Auckland to Aneityum in his mission schooner, the *Border Maid;* he also took our house, boat, goods, and live stock, and hampered himself much to accommodate us. Had we been missionaries connected with his own Society, he could not have been kinder to us or more attentive. He was on a three months' exploring cruise among the islands, and on his return home to Auckland he came considerably out of his way to call at Aneityum and ascertain what kind of a reception we had met with. Parties connected with the trading establishment had led him to understand that the natives were in an unsettled state, that their feelings towards the mission were at best very doubtful, and that but for their restraining influence on the natives Mr. Geddie would hardly be able to remain on the island, and what the future might be was very uncertain. He told me, on his return, that although he said nothing about it, he was very anxious on our account all the time he was away, and that he felt quite relieved when he came back and found that we had met with such a cordial reception, that our prospects were so encouraging, and that on both sides of the island the feelings of the natives towards the mission were so favourable; and that, instead of the safety of the mission depending on the influence of the traders, the balance of parties was, if anything, inclining to the other side. Afterwards either he or Bishop Patteson paid us a visit year by year, as they passed our island, up till the time that we had a vessel of our own, the *Dayspring*, when their visits became unnecessary. During all that time he did everything in his power to promote the interests of our mission.

On one occasion my watch became dry and dirty, and refused to go. When the Bishop next called at our island I asked him to take the watch with him to Auckland, to be cleaned. This he cheerfully undertook to do. But not content with this, he made me take his watch, and wear it for a twelvemonth till his return. This I did; it was a silver watch, as like my own as might be; for he was simplicity itself—utility and not show was his principle. When he came to Wellington that year, he called upon an intimate friend of mine, Mr. W. Lyon, a bookseller, but an eminent geologist, and a man of good literary taste and high scientific acquirements, showed him my watch that he was wearing, and asked him if he had no new scientific book to send me; if he had any one, he would be happy to be the bearer of it. Hugh Miller's "Footprints of the Creator" was just out, and Mr. Lyon gave the Bishop a copy of it to bring to me, which he duly delivered, and which I read with much interest. He also brought back my watch, cleaned and in thorough repair.

When we got the *John Knox* we had no difficulty in procuring a native crew; but we had to engage a white man to take charge of the little vessel. We got a suitable man out of the *John Williams;* but his salary and other expenses raised our outlay to nearly £100 for the first year. No provision had been made to meet this expenditure; but just as Mr. Geddie and I were casting about in our minds what we were to do, Bishop Selwyn came in one morning from New Zealand, and brought me £103, 16s. 4d., to expend on the mission as I thought proper. He received it in this way. "When I was at Dunedin," he said, "while pleading for my own mission in the English church there, I saw some Scotch friends present, and I said that on Wednesday next I would be leaving Dunedin and going almost direct to the New Hebrides, and if any of them wished to send any contribution to the Scotch mission there, I should be happy to take charge of it. On Wednesday morning, when I came to the wharf, I found three gentlemen waiting for me, who placed £34, 16s. 4d. in my hands to be given to you for your mission;—and mind you, I got only £13 for my own mission. When I came to Wellington, I told your friends, Mr. M'Donald, the manager of the Union Bank, his brother-in-law, Mr. Wallace, and others, what your Scotch friends in Otago had done, and if they wished to follow their example, I should be happy to be the bearer of the gift. When I left Wellington I was made the bearer of £30. When I came to Auckland, I told your friends, Mr. Shepherd, the Colonial Treasurer, and Mr. Clark, the ex-Mayor, what had been done in Dunedin and Wellington, and before I left Auckland they brought me £39, making in all £103, 16s. 4d." This money, so providentially sent to us, Mr. Geddie and I appropriated for the support of the *John Knox.* On the following year the Bishop brought us £60 from New

Zealand, viz., £30 from Dunedin through Dr. Burns, and £30 from Auckland through Mr. Clark. So far as I remember, he did not call at Wellington that year. In this way, greatly to our relief, our first two years' financial liabilities were provided for.

When he brought my wife and me to Aneityum, he said to me, "Now, Mr. Inglis, you know that, owing to the different principles of our respective Churches, I cannot hold any ecclesiastical fellowship with you; but in everything secular, I shall be always happy to do anything in my power to assist you and your mission." I thanked him cordially for his kind offer, and I assured him that I would gladly reciprocate it, as far and long as I was able. I have indicated how faithfully he fulfilled his promise; and he continued to do so till the day of his death; while, on the other hand, neither I nor the Reformed Presbyterian Church ever failed to recognise our obligations to Bishop Selwyn. In 1860, when, in answer to my appeal, the children of the Reformed Presbyterian Church raised £300 to assist in the repairs of the *John Williams*, Mr. Kay, the secretary of our mission, made an appeal to a select number of our people for a pound each for Bishop Selwyn's vessel, and transmitted him £50, as a recognition for the services he had rendered to our mission. He was much pleased with this contribution towards the support of his mission ship, as evincing the feelings entertained towards him by the Reformed Presbyterian Church. When I was leaving the island with the translation of the Old Testament, to get it printed in London, the Mission Synod appointed the *Dayspring* to visit New Zealand; Mr and Mrs. Watt were also allowed a furlough of four months to be spent in that colony. Mr. Watt and I were also appointed by the Synod to accompany the vessel for three months, and bring the claims of the mission before the Presbyterian congregations in New Zealand. As the *Dayspring* was going to New Zealand in ballast, at the expense of the ship I bought 14,000 dry cocoa-nuts at 10s. a thousand, and filled the vessel with them, to make presents of them to the children of the Presbyterian Sabbath-schools who had annually contributed to the support of the *Dayspring*. When we came to Dunedin I found there the Rev. John Selwyn, the Bishop's son, with their mission vessel, the *Southern Cross*. On the Sabbath I heard him address the Episcopal Sabbath-school children, and afterwards went up and spoke to him. On the Monday following my wife and I met him on the street, along with the Bishop of Dunedin. After speaking a few words I said to him, "Your father once said to me that, owing to the different principles of our respective Churches, he could not hold any ecclesiastical fellowship with me, but in all secular matters he was willing and ready to help us, and I assured him that on these grounds I was equally willing and ready to reciprocate. Now," said I, "we have the *Dayspring* here, filled with ripe cocoa-nuts, and Mr. Watt and I shall be delighted if you will allow your Sabbath-school children to come down to the wharf, come on board, see through the vessel, and get a cocoa-nut each, and I hope there is no canon in your Church to prevent this form of reciprocity." He laughed, and said he thought not; but, continued he, "I am in the Bishop's hands, and we shall see what he says." I turned to the Bishop, who was speaking to my wife, and repeated the same words to him. He also laughed at my reference to the canons, and said he thought there would be no such restriction. "But," said he, "it is Mr. So-and-so "— one of his clergy—" who has charge of the arrangements connected with the children; we will speak to him on the matter, and he will communicate with you." On the following day I received a very polite note from that gentleman, saying that he and the teachers would gladly accept of our offer, and if such a day—naming one—would suit us, it would suit them. On the day fixed the children were brought down; they were shown through the vessel, got a cocoa-nut each, and went home well pleased, cherishing the best of feelings towards the *Dayspring* and the New Hebrides mission. To produce the invisible feeling of goodwill between members of different churches is one of the surest ways of bringing about the visible bonds of outward union. In this way even a dry cocoa-nut, if placed in the right soil, may in due time grow up and bring forth the freshest and the sweetest of living fruit.

When we left the islands the labour traffic was annoying us very much, and the attitude of the French was anything but reassuring, and when we settled in London I was anxious to consult Bishop Selwyn—at that time become Bishop of Lichfield—and see how his influence could be got to tell in high places, and how the Government could be best approached on these subjects. I wrote to him, offering to take a run out and see him at Lichfield. He wrote me back a very kind letter, inviting my wife and me to spend a few days with Mrs. Selwyn and him at the episcopal palace at Lichfield. Circumstances occurred which prevented us from accepting his invitation. But he subsequently wrote me, saying that he expected to be in London for a few days at the opening of Parliament, and inviting us to breakfast with him at the Lollards Tower, his town residence, and we would talk over these matters then. In the letter containing the invitation he not only described the way I was to go, but also drew a sketch of the route I was to take in crossing the Thames at Westminster Bridge, and the stairs where I was to leave and at which I was to arrive. I went, and found him alone, his sister, Miss Selwyn, keeping house for him that morning. After prayers and breakfast, we talked over the matters affecting the New Hebrides. He purposed seeing the Earl of Carnarvon, an intimate personal friend of his own, who was at that time either Foreign or Colonial Secretary. Afterwards he showed me through the old venerable antique building. On the topmost storey is the apartment that was used as a prison, with eight strong rings, to which were bound those pre-Reformation confessors and martyrs, the Lollards, from which the tower took its name. History and tradition are both silent respecting the inmates of that apartment, and the meaning of the rudely-cut letters that remain on the walls is not known; but the name of the tower and these old rusty rings bear distinct testimony to the spirit cherished by Rome before the tenth part of the city fell by the revolt of Henry VIII., and what it will continue to be till the other nine parts fall also, and the cry shall be heard, "Babylon the Great is fallen!" He also showed me the church close by, in which he had been consecrated as Bishop of New Zealand. It was about fifteen years since I had last seen him; he was then sixty-seven years of age, but I knew scarcely any change in his appearance. He was fresh, healthy, and vigorous; and, looking at his strong well-knit frame, coupled with his strictly temperate habits, humanly speaking, one might have predicted that he had still more than twenty years of active life before him. But, alas! "the race is not to the swift nor the battle to the strong," for in less than two short months, after only a few days' illness, he was laid in his grave; and the New Hebrides mission and all the natives of those seas had lost one of their oldest, best, and truest friends.

He was a great favourite among the Scotch in New Zealand, and he took very kindly to them, although he sometimes learned that the motto under their national emblem, *Nemo me impune lacessit*, was not an obsolete phrase, but still imbued with vitality, and that the thistle required to be handled very gently. On the first visit that he made to Dunedin he called upon the Rev. Dr. Burns, who was the nephew of our national bard, and the first Presbyterian minister in Otago, and one of the two founders of the settlement. Bishop Selwyn was accompanied by another colonial Bishop and some clergy. After the usual salutations and a little general conversation Bishop Selwyn addressed himself to Mrs. Burns—a lady, by the way, of great beauty, and as ready in reply as she was beautiful. "I am afraid, Mrs. Burns," he said, "that in this quiet, strictly Presbyterian settlement of yours, you will be startled by such an irruption of Bishops and Episcopal clergy." "Oh, not at all," she said; "I have been accustomed all my life to Bishops and all grades of the clergy; my father held two livings in Essex. No number of Bishops or clergy would startle me." "Oh, indeed!" said the Bishop, "I was not aware of that; but how, then, did you happen to leave us and come here?" "Oh, I just thought better of it, sir," she said; "my mother was a Scotchwoman, and one of my uncles was a parish minister in Scotland. I knew both Churches; I decided for myself, had the courage of my convictions, left the Church of England, and joined the Church of Scotland; hence I am here." The Bishop was taken somewhat aback; he was more startled than the lady. This was not thistle *down*, which he thought he was handling; but his self-possession enabled him to conceal his surprise. Dr. Burns sat still and said nothing; but he felt inwardly pleased with the patriotic demeanour of his wife. There was, however, too much principle and too much politeness on both sides for the incident to leave any disagreeable feeling in the minds of either party.

As a missionary Bishop Selwyn stood unsurpassed for his self-denial, his energy, and his enterprise. His modes of operation did not, however, commend themselves to the majority of other South Sea missionaries; his new modes were in general not successful, and his successful modes were in general not new. The greatest services that he and Bishop Patteson rendered to the South Sea missions was their example, by which such an ardent missionary spirit was created. While, from their social position, their talents, their acquirements, and their character, they were in circumstances to command the highest ecclesiastical appointments in the National Church, they cheerfully resigned those advantages, and chose the obscurity, the privations, the perils, and the drudgery of missionaries to the most degraded of savages. Their example sent a thrill of enthusiasm through the hearts of all the students at both the great English Universities. At both these seats of learning it elevated and ennobled the whole missionary enterprise; it evoked the eulogiums of the public press, and converted at their death even the humour and the irony of *Punch* into the deepest pathos. The verses written on the death of Selwyn were in the same strain as those previously written on the death of his great African compeer, the last line of which, contrasting the plain slab over his grave with the gorgeous monuments around, ran thus—

"*Dead marble that*,—but *this* is LIVING STONE."

Bishop Selwyn was avowedly High Church; but if his head or his intellect was distorted with mediæval notions about apostolic succession and kindred dogmas, his heart was all right; it was largely imbued with the spirit of apostolic love and charity. He said to me on one occasion, "People accuse me of being a Puseyite, but to whatever extent I am High Church, it was my mother that made me. She was a good Churchwoman, kept all the fasts and all the festivals, and I followed her teaching and example; and hence, to whatever extent I am a High Churchman, I owe it not to Dr. Pusey, but to my mother." This is a very encouraging example to good mothers as well as to good sons.

CHAPTER XXIV.

ANEITYUM IN 1876.

THE following is the substance of the last report on my station which I read in the New Hebrides Mission Synod, which met on the island of Nguna, June 12th, 1876, and which was published in full in the *Reformed Presbyterian Magazine* for November and December of the same year. I said—

As I fully expect this to be my last report here, I shall endeavour to lay before you as complete an account of the condition of my station as the limits assigned to our Synodical Reports will properly admit.

RELIGIOUS SERVICES.

Our Sabbath and week-day services have been conducted in the same way as in former years. I preach twice every Sabbath, and always give an address at the weekly prayer-meeting on the Wednesdays. We have public worship regularly on Sabbaths and Wednesdays at three out-stations. These are conducted generally by the natives themselves, although I visit them as often as I can, and regret that I cannot visit them oftener. But to render these services as efficient as possible, I invariably appoint to each station two men in rotation every Sabbath, selected out of our elders, deacons, and teachers, to take charge of these services; and I employ four natives every Sabbath at the principal station, two to read a chapter each, and two to pray. In this way we have a chapter read and a prayer offered up by natives at the beginning of each service, and I do the same at the Wednesday prayer-meeting.

Mr. Spurgeon condemns, in no measured terms, the practice of some ministers who employ inferior men to conduct the first part of the service, and reserve their chief strength for the sermon; he considers the reading of the Scriptures and the prayer to be as important as the sermon. From his point of view I have no doubt but there is much truth in his remarks. But in my circumstances I feel myself standing wholly beyond the reach of his strictures. I follow this course, not so much to save my own strength—although that is an important consideration in this debilitating climate—as to instruct the natives in the mode of conducting public worship, where so much of it has to be done by the natives themselves. By bringing elders, deacons, and teachers, in rotation, from the out-stations to take a part in the services at the central station, they are stimulated to improve themselves; and they have the benefit, on these occasions, of hearing my discourses. Moreover, by sending others from the central station to the out-stations, or occasionally from one out-station to another, the worshippers have the benefit of a constant variety of gifts all ministering to their edification; and by this constant mutual intercourse the people at all the stations come in contact regularly with all the best of our men, and these come in contact with one another; so that, as iron sharpeneth iron, their intercourse one with another is calculated to quicken them mutually in the exercise of faith, love, and good works. A number of them read the Scriptures very well; their prayers are always earnest and devout, and also more or less edifying, though often largely susceptible of improvement; but their addresses or exhortations, while they now and again contain striking remarks, and are in general quite sound as to doctrine, are, upon the whole, rambling, feeble, and by no means very effective. Scripture truth comes forth from their lips so much diluted that the instruction conveyed is very limited, and the impressions produced are anything but powerful. I have much more confidence in the Word of God which they read than in the expositions of it which they deliver. Still, I consider it of such great importance to have the public worship of God conducted on Sabbath at these out-stations, that I am fain to employ even this feeble agency. In order to have the praises of God sung, prayer publicly offered up, and the Scriptures read, all in their own tongue and in the hearing of all, I feel content to put up with addresses, poor, feeble, and unconnected, when the speakers, as our old Scotch divines would have said, are *minting* after what is good.

I have never opened any strictly theological class, nor yet supplied our teachers with outlines of sermons to assist them in conducting public services, as is done by most of our brethren in the older missions. More than the half of them hear me preaching or expounding three times every week. I thought they might extract as much matter out of these as would supply a substratum for their own observations. My chief reason, however, for doing so little in this direction has been the want of time. We cannot do everything. But as my successor is likely to have less labour of some kinds than I have had, I trust he will be able to overtake work of this kind, and various other kinds besides, which I have been obliged to leave undone.

I have dispensed the Lord's Supper three times on my side of the island since this time twelvemonth, and once at Mr. Murray's station—he and Mrs. Murray being absent in Sydney. I admitted no new members during the past year, but I have at present sixteen candidates attending my weekly class; the most, if not the whole, of these I hope to admit at our next Communion. I have baptized twenty-one children. On our Communion Sabbath we have no service at our out-stations; the people are expected all to attend at the principal station. On these occasions, besides the Wednesday prayer-meeting as usual at all the stations, we have public worship on the Friday afternoon, and a public prayer-meeting on the Monday morning. On the Friday a sermon is preached, new members, if any, are admitted, baptism is administered, and tokens are distributed to the Church members. We have generally a very good attendance on the Friday. At each of our Communions during the past year the attendance was large and the deportment of the worshippers all that could be expected, almost all that could be desired; and our belief is that much good was done as the result of all the services.

The late Rev. J. Angell James of Birmingham, in common, I believe, with most of the English Congregationalists, used to test the vitality of spiritual religion among his people, not by their attendance at public worship on Sabbath, but by their attendance at prayer-meetings during the week; and he complained sadly in his latter years—looked upon it as a bad omen—that while his Church members and the general congregation had largely increased during the course of his ministry, there had been no corresponding increase in the attendance upon the weekly prayer-meeting, which led him to infer that their prosperity had been more outward than inward, more visible than vital. Now, if this test could be applied with safety to our Church members here, we might "lay a very flattering unction to our souls," and think that with us matters stood very well.

While attendance on public worship on Sabbaths at our four stations may be about four hundred, the attendance at the prayer-meetings on Wednesdays may be set down at about two hundred. But alas for Aneityum! Weekly afternoon prayer-meetings, attended by half the Sabbath-day congregations, family worship evening and morning in every household, and twenty-eight morning schools opened and closed with praise and prayer—good as these things are in themselves, they will prove a very fallacious test if they are accepted as proof that there exists on Aneityum a very enlightened, vigorous, self-sustaining Christianity. The Church there is still in the feebleness of infancy. We trust that there is life, and that widely diffused; but the strength in that life is small and feeble, and must not be severely strained. Our people require much of the care, watchfulness, guidance, and support of the missionary to direct them to the chief Shepherd and Bishop of souls, and, through no special fault of theirs, will do so for a long time to come.

It is Andrew Fuller, I think, who says that there are two classes of Christians in the world—the one in which the devotional element prevails, the other distinguished by their higher and stricter morality. Each class, he says, are disposed to judge the other too severely; the devotional class look upon their moral neighbours as cold and lifeless in their religion, if they have, indeed, any vital religion at all; while the rigid moralists look upon their more devotional neighbours as a set of psalm-singing, canting hypocrites. Now, both these judgments, he says, are wrong. Both these classes may be intentionally honest. The devotional feelings and exercises of the one class are not a cloak of hypocrisy, and the stern and apparently cold morality of the other is not self-righteousness. Constitutional differences, physical or mental, or different modes of religious training, may have produced these different phases of religious life. Be these things as they may, I feel certain that it is far easier among the Aneityumese to develop devotional habits than high and strictly correct moral character. It is far easier to get them to pray, sing hymns, hear sermons, and read the Scriptures than to be truthful, honest, chaste, and unselfish. It is true this is simply what we might expect—the former are the means, the latter is the end; and it is always easier to put the means into operation than to secure the end contemplated by these means. But the longer we live among these natives, the more are we convinced of the awfully degrading effects of heathenism, and how slow and difficult must be the process of obliterating its baneful effects. We see more and more distinctly the depth of that pit out of which their Christianity has to be dug, and the hardness of that rock out of which it has to be hewn.

Education.

I visited all my schools, twenty-eight in number, in the end of last year. The condition of the schools was, upon the whole, satisfactory. The London School Board complain of three primary difficulties which they have to grapple with—first, how to get the children into the schools; second, what to make of them when they have got them in; and third, how to obtain efficient teachers. Our experience is much of the same kind on Aneityum. Our system of education is national, unsectarian, Scriptural, and free,—no school fees,—but it is not compulsory; and hence our attendance, though as good as we could reasonably expect, is not at all so regular as we could wish. Happily we have neither Papist nor Secularist in our community, and hence, though the Bible is our principal school-book, we require no conscience clause in our school regulations.

The only new book we obtained last year was the Almanack, 800 copies of which were supplied gratis from the mission press on Tanna, through the kindness of our brother, Mr. Watt—a much-prized kindness, which he has shown us for several years in succession. These Almanacks I distributed on both sides of the island in the beginning of the year. Mr. Murray edited a new edition of our psalter and hymn-book, adding three new hymns of his own, which he got printed in Sydney. The edition, consisting of 1500 copies, and delivered to us in sheets, cost nine pounds (£9). All small books of this kind the natives themselves fold, stitch, cover, and cut, the missionaries and their wives supplying the binding materials, training the workers, and superintending the work. The binding of these books would cost nearly as much as the printing; and where we cannot raise the whole of the money by selling the books, as they do in most of the older of the South Sea missions, we think it well to save the half of it, by making the natives bind them themselves; and if there is any truth in the proverb that "a penny hained is twopence gained," the saving is as good as the selling would be. With a slight exception, all our former hymn-books were printed by Dr. Geddie, assisted by the natives. I am suggesting to Mr. Murray that he raise the one moiety of the £9 among his friends in New South Wales, and I will undertake to raise the other half among mine, as I am unwilling to draw upon our arrowroot fund, which is being raised solely for the payment of the Scriptures.

I opened our Teachers' Institution this year for about three months, during February, March, and April. The attendance was very good; I had eighty-two names on my list, and the average attendance in good weather was from sixty to seventy. The progress, especially in writing, was very satisfactory; there was no want of capacity and no lack of application. We call this our "Teachers' Institution" because it was begun primarily for the instruction of our native teachers; but we open it to all the better class of scholars who choose to attend. Our object by this school is to promote what in these latitudes we call the "higher education," but which elsewhere would be considered sufficiently elementary. Our main strength is expended in teaching what is known, in modern educational terminology, as the three R's; although we do attempt to introduce our pupils to the knowledge of the very simplest elements of a few of the higher branches of education, including the English language. But I have always made it my principal object to get them well grounded in the art of reading, so as to open to them intelligibly the Word of God. It is of little use to supply them with Bibles unless they are able to read them; and I teach them writing, arithmetic, and other things chiefly for the bearing of these on the art of reading. Good reading lies at the foundation of all scholarship. Till the art of reading is fully mastered, nearly all other branches of learning are difficult; but the art of reading one's mother-tongue being fully mastered, almost everything else becomes comparatively easy. With natives especially it is of primary importance that they be taught to read well. But this is an arduous task, and requires on the part of the missionary much labour, a good deal of administrative capacity, constant supervision, and unwearied perseverance.

Dr. Chalmers, in one of his inaugural addresses to his students, as Principal of the New College in Edinburgh, calls attention to the obvious distinction between the *powers* of the mind and the *acquisitions* of the mind, and shows that certain branches of learning—mathematics, for example—are of far more value to ministers, from the strength and culture which they impart to the mind, than from the acquisition which preachers make to their knowledge by means of these studies. In like manner, I value writing, arithmetic, and some other things learned by the natives, more for the mental training they supply than for the addition made to their knowledge by these acquirements, although the direct advantages of these studies are not to be despised. When Williamu was in Britain he wrote a number of interesting and instructive letters which I forwarded to his friends on Aneityum. The natives have for a long time corresponded among themselves;* and now, not only the missionaries, but even the traders, are beginning to conduct their business with the natives, when necessary, by means of letters. And as for arithmetic, its value is indisputable to a people who had names for numbers only up to five, and who could count objects up to twenty only by repeating these five numbers on their twice five fingers and their twice

---

* Scarcely ever a mail arrived in this country from Aneityum since the time we left the islands but my wife and I had letters from some of the natives.

five toes, and then giving the sum total for twenty by saying, "My two hands and my two feet." Moreover, as they had no characters to represent even these five numbers, we introduced both the English names for numbers and the Arabic numerals. Hence, so far as our natives learn arithmetic, they become acquainted, not only with the science of numbers, but with the vocables and the structure of the English language.

Translating and Correcting.

Since the last meeting of the Mission Synod I have employed all the spare time at my command in carrying forward my corrections of our translation of the Old Testament. I have gone over the latter half of Exodus, the whole of Leviticus, the last eighty Psalms, the last forty-seven chapters of Isaiah, the whole of Jeremiah, Lamentations, and Ezekiel, embodying Mr. Copeland's corrections of these four prophetical books; his corrections of the Psalms I have yet to embody. I may also mention that when I received Dr. Geddie's unprinted MSS., which had been in the hands of the printers in Melbourne, the last eight chapters of Leviticus were awanting. I wrote to the Secretary of the Bible Society in Melbourne, under whose direction the printing was executed, but I have received no answer as yet to my letter; I have, therefore, translated these chapters. Mr. Copeland has revised the translation, and I have embodied his corrections. When I shall have embodied Mr. Copeland's corrections of the Psalms, I shall have finished all that I consider necessary to be done to render the translation ready for the press, as far as corrections are concerned; but considerable portions of the corrected translation will still require to be copied out. I have gone over every part of the translation twice, a very large portion three times, a considerable part of it four times, and many portions of it still oftener. But as one of the senior missionaries in Samoa—one of the highest authorities on such a subject in the South Seas—remarked to me in a note sometime ago, "There is no end to revising and correcting." And I daresay the learned companies of revisers who meet respectively in the Jerusalem Chamber, Westminster, and the Chapter Library, Winchester, to improve our English version, would say the very same thing.

In his "Essays in Ecclesiastical Biography" Sir James Stephens says of the Benedictines, the oldest and best of the monastic orders: "Their rule assigned an eminent rank among monastic virtues to the guardianship and multiplication of valuable manuscripts. It taught the copyist of a holy book to think of himself as at once a pupil and a teacher,—as a missionary while seated at his desk—using each finger as a tongue—inflicting on the Spirit of Evil a deadly wound at each successive line—and as baffling with the pen the dread enemy, who smiles at the impotent hostility of every other weapon grasped by the hand of mortal man." Now, the principle, true in the main, underlying this somewhat exaggerated language, is certainly more applicable to the translator of God's own Word than to the copyist of any holy book, especially in our days, when we are so aided by the printing-press in multiplying copies that we can meet the demand to any extent and supply every reader with a Bible for himself.

But some seem to think that to supply a community so small and insignificant as the Aneityumese, a community of less than 1500 people, with a translation of the whole Bible, is involving an amount of labour and expense altogether out of proportion to the good likely to be accomplished; an idea, the like of which has not been propounded since the canon of Scripture was closed and the work of translating the Bible into foreign languages was commenced. In reply to such an objection I would say, as for the labour of translating, that, as I have said, is finished, and it was all accomplished during what may be looked upon as the spare hours of the missionaries. I speak from experience when I say that the work of translating, as a whole, has stimulated rather than retarded our other missionary labours. Moreover, it was in this way that we obtained our mightiest lever for the elevating and the evangelising of the community. As for expense, there has seldom been less ground for such an objection. The natives paid the full price, about four shillings a copy, for 2000 copies of the New Testament, and about one shilling and sixpence a copy for 2000 copies of the Psalms; and there is every probability of their being able to pay for 1250 copies of the Old Testament as soon as they are printed. It is true there will be some two years' labour in editing the Old Testament, and the expenses connected with that work; but I am entitled to a furlough about this time, and would be obliged to take it; and I know not in what labours my time could be more profitably spent than in carrying this translation through the press. Now, if the National Bible Society of Scotland grants supplies of the Scriptures gratis, or at reduced prices, to the inhabitants of the Old Hebrides and other parts of the Highlands—to a people who have had the Gospel among them for centuries; and if the British and Foreign Bible Society supplies Bibles to the natives of some parts of India at the reduced price of *tenpence* a copy—to a people whose civilisation goes back to the ages of hoary antiquity; would it be generous, would it be just, to the natives of the New Hebrides—to the poor Aneityumese, who twenty-five years ago were the lowest of savages—to deny them the Old Testament in their own tongue, when, if they go on as they are doing, every man, woman, and child on the island will be prepared to pay, not *tenpence* a copy, like their brethren in India, for the *whole Bible*, but *ten shillings* a copy for the *Old Testament alone*, and that before the books have left the Bible Society House in London? I am glad, however, to say that the British and Foreign Bible Society have no such narrow views of economy. Every letter that we receive from their Secretary encourages us to go on translating, and they will print for us. The President of the Society, the Earl of Shaftesbury, said, in October last, at a public meeting in Glasgow: "There might be some insignificant languages which they had not reached yet, but they trusted, by the blessing of God, to reach them, and that they would not leave a single corner of the world to which the Bible had not penetrated, or a single dialect of importance into which it had not been translated."

The Public Health.

I have, as usual, opened my dispensary daily, and supplied medicine to all comers. I have attended, as far as lay in my power, to the wants of the sick; and my wife has supplied tea and other medical comforts to all within our reach, in many cases with very beneficial results. Beyond ordinary colds, there has been no sickness; there has been no epidemic during the year. Food has been plentiful, and the public health has been generally good; yet, without any assignable reason, the death-rate for 1875 was exceptionally high, and at the same time the birth-rate was exceptionally low; the deaths being forty-six, about one-third above the average, and the births only twenty-one, being about a third below the average. The measles and the subsequent epidemics from 1861 till 1866 completely disorganised society on Aneityum, and left it in such an abnormal state that it has not yet recovered itself. We have, as a rule, a high birth-rate; and if we could only diminish the death-rate, the state of things would soon improve; and I have still good hopes that, as Christianity develops its strongly conservative, life-preserving influence, the tide will turn in our favour, as it did in Rarotonga, Huahine, and other islands to the eastward, whose history in this respect was much the same as our own. This year, thus far, the births and deaths are about equal. During the first four months of this year there were twelve deaths, viz., ten males and two females. There were also twelve births; and, strange to say, ten of these were males and only two females! In India, with its 250 millions of people, the population increases annually at the rate of one-half per cent. Every 200 at the end of the year becomes 201. Leaving out 1875, the average of the previous seven or eight years showed a decrease of population on my side of the island of about one-half per cent. annually. Every 200 became 199. Aneityum would therefore be equal to India if we could shift the balance between life and death just one per cent.—not a formidable undertaking, one would think, in these days, when sanitary principles and sanitary regulations are accomplishing so much in arresting disease and prolonging life. One encouraging circumstance is, that within the last few years there has been a slight increase in the female population.

Our own health has been much as it was in former years. With the exception of about three weeks, during which I was laid up with influenza, my own health has continued very good. My wife's health has been better than she expected—she has never been laid up; she has always been able to attend to her domestic and missionary duties, but she has suffered much from intermittent fever, a mild form of fever and ague, especially at night; and she is longing very much to escape from the influences of the subtle malaria, which is weighing her down like a nightmare, depriving her of refreshing sleep, and literally killing her by inches. A furlough of a year or two, either at home or in one or other of the more bracing of the adjoining colonies, would, I doubt not, humanly speaking, set her up fully for several years more of mission labour; but our present plans, in connection with the printing of the Old Testament, do not admit of such an arrangement, and will, indeed, render it unnecessary.

Native Contributions.

Last year the natives on my side of the island prepared and contributed 2065 lbs. of arrowroot, all of first-rate quality, towards the payment of the Old Testament. This is the largest contribution they have ever made. The contributions which they made both for 1874 and 1875 I have still beside me. These I intended to take with me last year, but as arrowroot, when well made, will keep for any length of time, having altered my arrangements, I retained them with me till I leave the islands, when I shall take with me the whole of what may be contributed up till that time, and endeavour to dispose of it, as advantageously as I can, either in the

Colonies or at home, or both, as the case may be. We have had no other contributions for mission purposes. The natives, however, make plantations for the teachers; they send large presents to the teachers on the other islands, and they keep up all their own school-houses. During the year they have built or repaired several school-houses which had been destroyed or injured by the earthquakes or the tidal wave; and they have done the average amount of thatching and other repairs needed on the mission premises. We have had no fencing done since this time twelvemonth, because we have needed none. There was no hurricane this year, and our fences were all put up twice last year—once before and once after the destructive ravages of the tidal wave. They, however, put up one piece of heavy wooden fencing, for which I paid them, and which may require a word of explanation. It has always been necessary for us to have our cows and goats herded, and this was always now and again a source of difficulty. Four years ago I got a park made. I had attempted the same thing ten years ago, but it did not succeed. On this last occasion the natives gratuitously enclosed the park on three sides with a strong close fence of upright posts, all of hard wood; the sea formed the fourth side. That fence cost them a great amount of heavy labour. This was a great improvement; but, nevertheless, at low water the cattle had no difficulty in getting round the end of the fence, and they were still now and again getting out and doing mischief to native plantations, and that even when we kept a herd with them. I saw plainly that the value of the fence would be more than half lost unless the side next the sea were also enclosed. Moreover, I saw that unless this were done the cattle would be a constant source of annoyance to my successor, especially during the first year. The natives, however, had wrought so much and so well for me in the early part of the year, repairing the damages of the sea and the earthquakes, that the resources of voluntary labour were for the time being nearly exhausted; besides, the planting season had now commenced. I could, under a strong pressure, have got them to do it for nothing; but as I had no wish that what I expected to be my last demand upon them for labour should savour of oppression, I thought it best to pay them for this piece of work. I selected forty men, consisting of the strongest of our teachers, and others whom they approved of. They wrought the first three days of each week, for three weeks—nine days in all. The usual wages for natives on Aneityum is sixpence a day without food; but as they were picked men and the work heavy, and as they worked with a will, I gave them eightpence a day each and their dinner. I killed a few goats and pigs to *kitchen* their taro; by a happy coincidence I had got several presents of taro at the time, so that these dinners for forty men for nine days were not, after all, a burdensome affair. I paid them £12, being six shillings each, all in white silver coins— "current money with the merchant"—and they went all home well pleased. Some authorities estimate the *denarius* or penny of the New Testament which the labourers in the vineyard received at *sevenpence halfpenny*, so that the wages which I paid were very nearly the same as those that had the sanction of Scripture. This fence has been a great boon to us; we have had no trouble with our cattle since. As the fence was at first intended for the benefit of my successor and not myself, I might, on the principle of the new "Agricultural Holdings Act," have asked the Synod to authorise me to apply to the Treasurer of the Reformed Presbyterian Mission to repay me the sum of £12 for unexhausted improvements; but as we are likely to have the benefit of these improvements for a year, and as we have all along been liberally supplied with mission-boxes, which have enabled us to obtain supplies of native food and native labour, the expense of which I should otherwise have had to pay out of my own pocket, I consider it would be not only ungenerous, but unjust, in me to make any such claim at present.

Native Help to the Mission.

There are at present twenty natives, male and female, from my side of the island living on the other islands, either as teachers or as servants to the missionaries. One of our teachers on Tanna died during the past year, and two teachers and their wives, after several years of faithful service, returned home invalided; one native servant returned from Eromanga. We have, however, sent out nine other natives during the year, viz., three to Futuna, one to Eromanga, and five to Nguna. We also supplied the *Dayspring* during the most of the season with five or six natives, as a boat's crew, and we supplied parties of workmen for some months on Eromanga and Nguna, to assist in house-building and other labours, for the benefit of the missionaries. Of course these have all been paid fully and fairly for their work; but, nevertheless, such supplies of reliable semi-skilled labour are of great importance to the mission.

The Labour Traffic.

The so-called labour traffic has shown an unwonted audacity this last year on Aneityum. The *May Queen*, from Queensland, of which Mr. James Underwood is labour agent, took away several natives from the other side of the island. The Government agent might be satisfied that the natives were all lawfully and honourably obtained, but Mr. and Mrs. Murray did certainly not think so. The vessel came in after dark, and was off again by morning light. During the night some five or six natives had been got on board, and among others a young man whom Mr. Murray had engaged as cook. When Mrs. Murray went into the kitchen in the morning to give directions about the breakfast, she found that the fire was not kindled, and that the cook was on his way to Queensland. On a subsequent occasion the same vessel, after coasting along my side of the island all day, and sending in her boats at every point to lure away the natives, but without effect, sent in a boat to my station near midnight, well supplied with liquor, to try and get hold of some of the young men, possibly our cook among the rest. We were in bed, and heard nothing of it till the morning; but Williamu got notice of what was going on, came down to the beach, and the object of the labour agent was defeated.

The *Laura Lind*—Captain Lind—from Noumea, sailing under German colours, with which Mr. Joseph Underwood is connected, has no labour license; nevertheless, she took away several natives from our island to New Caledonia. It is said that the French authorities were unwilling to let them pass into the labour market, but passed they were; self-interest outweighed legal objections, and they are now in Noumea, working out their three years' term of servitude. History, it is said, repeats itself. "When Hadad heard in Egypt that David slept with his fathers, and that Joab, the captain of the host, was dead," the courage of the Edomite revived. So is it now. Commodore Goodenough is gone, and the traffic lifts up its drooping head.

Absence from Home.

We have been about four months absent from our station during the past twelvemonth; half of that time in connection with the meeting of the Mission Synod and our visit round the mission stations, and the other half at Mr. Murray's station during his absence. When the *Dayspring* left the island in December last, my wife and I went round to Anelgauhat, as we generally do, to see the vessel off. We had previously arranged to stay some time there, partly for the sake of the change to ourselves, and partly to take charge of the work in the absence of Mr. and Mrs. Murray. We stayed eight weeks, during which time I conducted the public services on Sabbaths and Wednesdays. I attended the Sabbath-school, held meetings of session, baptized children, dispensed the Lord's Supper, solemnised marriages, visited the sick, dispensed medicine daily, and did whatever other mission work required to be done. My wife did all in her power among the women. We had great satisfaction in our visit. The natives over the whole district manifested towards us even more than their wonted cordiality and kindness; they brought us large presents of food, and performed cheerfully whatever work we required them to do. They re-thatched several houses and covered every house on the premises with cocoa-nut leaves, to protect them from hurricanes.

Since the *Dayspring* arrived from Sydney, and we were informed that, in consequence of the state of Mrs. Murray's health, Mr. Murray is resigning his connection with the mission, and is not returning to Aneityum, my wife and I spent four days on a visit to their station. We found everything in excellent order; everything had been put in order for the return of the mission family, and much disappointment was felt because they had not returned. As requested by Mr. Murray, I packed up all his books and papers; we also packed up all the clothing, bedding, &c., and the smaller articles belonging to the house, and left six cases ready for shipment. We likewise made arrangements that the premises and the property should be carefully looked after till another missionary take charge of the station, and the sooner that is done the better. All has been peace and quietness since Mr. Murray left them, but the absence of the missionary is felt at every point. When Mr. and Mrs. Murray left the island they had just so far acquired a knowledge of the language and of the people that they were beginning to be really efficient, and the people were just beginning fully to understand and appreciate their real worth. That station has suffered much within the last twelve years from the changes and absence of missionaries. During that time the station has been occupied for longer or shorter periods by no fewer than five missionaries, and, adding one absence to another, it has been vacant for as good as two years. A great, real, and substantial work has been effected on that station, but that work will be in a great measure lost unless an efficient missionary is speedily and permanently settled for that side of the island.

Statistics.

The following statistics will be sufficient to show the state of the mission on my side of the island at the present time, viz. : — Total population, 713 : males, 446 ; females, 267 ; married men, 169; married women, 169; unmarried males, 277; unmarried females, 98; church members at present, 354; church members admitted since commencement of mission, 664; baptisms since commencement of mission, 1168; marriages since commencement of mission, 475; elders, at present, 13; deacons, at present, 12; teachers, at present, 28.

Within the last eighteen months we have lost by death one of our elders, two of our deacons, and twenty-one of our church members. The whole population are professedly Christian, are supplied with books, and attend church and school. On our island, therefore, we have no room for aggressive work or church extension. Our work is confined to instructing, improving, elevating, and building up a professedly Christian population — a work, however, in which there is ample scope for tasking the energies of the most earnest and devoted of missionaries.

Church Discipline.

The venerable Thomas Boston, of Ettrick, says somewhere in his Memoirs, if I remember his words aright, "Satan has been raging terribly in the lower end of this parish; three cases of adultery have come to light." If in his sequestered parish, and among his well-instructed and carefully superintended flock, such flagrant immoralities were from time to time breaking out, we need scarcely be surprised, however much we may be grieved, that scandals to a much greater extent should, from time to time, break out among a people like ours, so recently brought out of the lowest depths of heathen degradation. Satan has indeed been raging terribly on my side of the island this year. Before our last Communion the session suspended no fewer than sixteen of our members. Seven had been suspended last year; of these we restored four, thus leaving nineteen under suspension, the largest number by far that we have ever had suspended at one time. I feel thankful that it was under myself, and not under a newly-appointed successor, that such a painful event occurred; otherwise it might have been thought, and with some show of reason, that I had been concealing the real state of the mission and the true character of our church members, and that our church fellowship was nothing better than a mass of hypocrisy and corruption. Instead of this being the case, I am happy to say that with our church members as a whole we have all along had all the satisfaction that could be reasonably expected.

Of the sixteen members last suspended, fifteen were suspended for adultery; the remaining case was that of a woman striking the wife of one of her neighbours with an axe while under the influence of a fit of jealousy. Happily the jealousy was groundless, both on the part of her husband and the woman whom she struck, and the injury inflicted was not severe; but the case in itself was too serious to be passed over; human life has been held so cheap among these islands that, whenever it is endangered, as in this case it was, I do my best to impress the natives with its value in the sight of God.

While here, as everywhere else, we have every form of human depravity to fight against, yet breaches of the seventh commandment form the one great class of evils with which we have chiefly to contend; nor need this be much wondered at when we remember that there are only sixty-three females for every hundred males, and only thirty-four unmarried females for every hundred unmarried males. This evil is a legacy bequeathed to us by heathenism, when every widow was strangled on the death of her husband, and female infants were often killed; and the evil was aggravated rather than mitigated by the successive epidemics that passed over the island from 1861 till 1866, inasmuch as the female portion of the population suffered more severely, in proportion, than the male. In this respect—that is, in the disproportion of the sexes—Aneityum is not unlike a garrison town in England. The state of morals in these towns was largely revealed last year in the House of Commons, in the discussion on Mr. Stansfeld's motion for the repeal of the "Contagious Diseases Act." And certainly, bad as things are with us, Aneityum morals, even at the worst, will not suffer much, if anything, by comparison with the morals of these towns, even after all the reforms effected by the rigid and revolting restrictions which the collective wisdom of Parliament and the Government has brought to bear on them. Our Aneityum Government has no statutory enactments on this subject—no registers in which to record the names of every erring sister—no medical superintendence under which to place them—and no hospitals in which to imprison them as often as the law requires. But Church and State do what they can. Marriage receives every encouragement; but owing to old notions, customs, and traditions, all of heathen origin, but still possessing much vitality, especially the principle, so rigidly carried out, that young women must be married in their own tribes or within their own districts—owing to these things, many of their marriages are ill assorted, and often aggravate these evils instead of removing them.

Sin, like disease, is largely preventible; and we do all that we can to facilitate such family and social arrangements as may best promote both the purity and the peace of the community. To prevent or restrict this evil, the Church plies all the moral means at her command, while the State employs penal inflictions, and tries to strike terror into the hearts of evil-doers. We preach the Law of God and the Gospel of His Son to all; publicly and privately we warn and exhort men to beware of this sin. We admonish, reprove, rebuke, and suspend our church members. Our chiefs, as a punishment, impose hard labour—they fine, they banish, they tie, and they flog offenders, according to the different aggravations of the offence. And, bad as things are, they would doubtless be much worse if these influences were in abeyance, and we may safely hope that, if they are diligently and perseveringly employed, a better state of things will ensue. Life and property have been for a long time safe on Aneityum, and those things that are pure, lovely, and of good report are steadily following. If we continue sowing we shall reap in due time. God is faithful. When Paul planted and Apollos watered, God gave the increase.

CHAPTER XXV.

CONCLUSION.

A BOOK, like a sermon, should have some practical application; and the lesson which I am especially desirous to impress upon my readers and the friends and supporters of our mission is the great need of increasing the number of our missionaries. For years we have been striving to raise the number to twenty, but we have rarely been able to raise it above twelve. We have oftener been two below than one above that number. Owing especially to the great number of languages spoken in the New Hebrides, we require a much larger proportion of missionaries in our group than in the eastern islands, where the languages are so much fewer in proportion to the population, where one translation of the Bible suffices for so many more people, and where native agency can be so much more easily trained, and made so much more extensively useful, and can be also largely employed for a much higher service. A much smaller number of missionaries is sufficient to accomplish the same work there than with us. In Samoa, and the islands on which the same language is spoken, the population is estimated at about 40,000; and there one translation of the Bible is sufficient for the whole, and one Institution, conducted by two missionaries, supplies native teachers and native pastors for the entire population. The Hawaiian

Islands and their dependencies in Micronesia, containing probably 100,000, are supplied by one translation of the Bible and by one Institution; while the Fiji group, with a population of 150,000, requires only one translation of the Bible and one Institution for the training of teachers and pastors for the entire group; whereas the New Hebrides, with a population of perhaps not more than 70,000, with their twenty languages, all so distinct from one another, will require twenty translations of the Bible and twenty Institutions for the training of a native agency, to supply the whole mission. It is thus seen at a glance how many more missionaries proportionately, and all men of high scholarship, we require, than was needed by those older missions in the eastern groups. How wisely the Lord guided the first missionaries to the South Seas, to select the eastern and not the western groups—the easier and not the more difficult races, to begin with! But the easier fields being all fully gained, we are now committed to the more difficult. And we cannot draw back; we must not stop, be the cost or the labour what it may, till every island in that vast ocean is won for Christ.

One reason why we are so anxious to increase materially the number of our missionaries at present, is the new *Dayspring*, with auxiliary steam power, that we are so soon to obtain. The Lord has granted success to Mr. Paton far beyond our most sanguine expectations. He came home avowedly to raise £6000 for a new *Dayspring*—a Quixotic attempt, as many of his friends thought; but, after clearing all expenses, he returned with £9000, for a vessel and for the taking out of new missionaries. We expect soon to be able to reoccupy our two stations on Espiritu Santo, the largest and most northern island of the group. In going to Santo the vessel has to traverse the whole group, so that an increase of missionaries does not involve an increase of sailing to the mission vessel, and the new ship will possess a great increase of carrying power. In this way, the more missionaries that we have on the field the relative expenses of the vessel will be reduced.

There is much to encourage us in making this proposal, both within and without the mission. The Lord has, to a large extent, graciously blessed our efforts for the evangelisation of the natives. One island after another has been won over to Christianity. We have churches organised on six islands, and we occupy stations on as many others. We have printed the whole Bible in one language, and we have printed portions of it in eight languages more. A great amount of preparatory work has been done, and experience has been acquired which will facilitate our progress in time to come, especially if the work be carried vigorously forward.

Without the mission, too, the encouragement has been marvellous and striking. Thirty-four years ago, in the providence of God, two missionaries met on the island of Aneityum, representatives of two of the smallest Presbyterian Churches in Christendom—the least of the many thousands of Judah. Now those two small Churches have been joined by others in Scotland, in the Dominion of Canada, and in Australasia, till they number more than 2000 congregations; these have all adopted the New Hebrides mission as their own, and that with a cordiality and unanimity that is as surprising as it is gratifying. Moreover, the *Dayspring* was obtained, and has been supported in a manner equally remarkable. The finger of Providence has been conspicuous in the history of this mission from first to last. In the way in

CONCLUSION. 347

which these agencies have been brought together, and in the way in which these various Churches have been led to co-operate, there has been so much of the doings of the Lord, and so little of the doings of man, that I cannot but regard it as an earnest of what the Lord intends to do for us and by us, unless we become criminally slothful.

It is true there are formidable difficulties to be encountered, and much in our position and prospects that is fitted to discourage. But is there not something, yea much, of this in every mission? Of these the savage and degraded character of the natives is one of the most apparent; it strikes you the moment you land on their shores. But it has been fully shown that the Gospel can overcome this difficulty. Another formidable obstacle is the number and diversity of the languages—nearly as many languages as there are islands, sometimes two or three on the same island, and all very widely different. But that is not an insurmountable difficulty; it is being overcome, and will always yield to patient, persevering labour and the blessing of God; only you must send out scholarly men for this work—men who have an aptitude for acquiring new tongues, men who know something of the principles of language, and who have been drilled into such studies. It is said that in the Wesleyan ministry the failures have been chiefly among the less educated. At one time the acquiring of a new, especially a barbarous, language was looked upon as an almost insuperable barrier in the way of missionary effort, and learned men employed illiterate interpreters; even men of such mental powers as Jonathan Edwards and David Brainerd, preached to the North American Indians through interpreters. But such ideas are now utterly exploded. No missionary now ever thinks of preaching regularly through an interpreter; and those of us who have grappled with the difficulties involved in the acquiring of new and barbarous languages know that there is nothing formidable in this task; nothing but what average ability and average scholarship, with a fair amount of application, followed by God's blessing, may readily accomplish. The Lord is now doing by His ordinary providence what He did by a special miracle when the lambent tongues sat on the heads of His servants in the day of Pentecost. Tongues were then a sign, as well as a gift; one of the credentials of apostleship, the token of authority to preach the new faith. Now they are only a gift, the means and the medium of announcing salvation through Christ; and they are to be acquired by ordinary means, and by taking advantage of the many facilities which God in His providence has provided for this end.

The climate is certainly the most formidable of all our difficulties; its demands have been so heavy upon physical energy, upon health and life, that people feel alarmed. It would be unwise and unsafe either to ignore or underrate this danger. I certainly regard it as the most formidable difficulty we have to contend with in the mission—more formidable, perhaps, than all others put together. It must be recognised, calculated upon, and provided carefully against in every step that we take. But from what we know now, we can see that, beyond a fair, or at most a high, average, the causes of sickness and mortality in the group are to a great extent preventible. None, however, should be sent to our mission but persons in good health and of a sound constitution, and who would be able to "rough it." Experience has led the London Missionary Society and others to adopt a rule that both missionaries and their wives should be subjected to a medical examination as to their health before being sent out. On the islands much can be done to preserve life and secure health by the careful selection of a healthy locality to live in, the proper construction of houses, attention to food, clothing, exercise, medicine, and the laws of health in general. These are important everywhere, but especially so there.

It is admitted on all hands that ours is a very difficult mission field. The Rev. A. W. Murray, formerly of Samoa, subsequently the pioneer of the New Guinea mission, one of the oldest, most successful, and most experienced missionaries connected with the London Missionary Society in the South Seas, and who knows more about the New Hebrides than any man outside of our mission, in a letter I had from him just before I left the islands, said:—"In judging of the New Hebrides mission and its results, we need always to bear in mind that it is a field of very special difficulty. What the difficulties are it would be useless, of course, to specify to you; but they are greater, I think, and more formidable, than those that are found in any other of our South Sea missions. We rejoice to think, however, that they are not insuperable; 'prayer and pains, with God's blessing,' as John Eliot used to say, 'will surmount all difficulties in due time.' 'In due time we shall reap, if we faint not.'" We have now a much clearer view of our difficulties than we had twenty years ago, and we have no wish to underrate them. Still, in reading the reports of other missions and other mission fields—and every missionary, and every one connected with the management of missions, will find it highly advantageous to make themselves as extensively acquainted as possible with the history and proceedings of other missions—I feel satisfied that, while our mission field has its own special difficulties, there is nothing in ours calling for special despondency. We have special difficulties, but we have also special advantages and special encouragements. God has set the one over against the other. I really see few mission fields that I would exchange for our one. We have already set our feet on the necks of some of our most formidable difficulties, and have overcome them, and time, and patience, and perseverance, and well-directed effort, with the blessing of God, will accomplish the rest, and, like Joshua and Zerubbabel, we "shall bring forth the head stone thereof with shoutings, crying, Grace, grace unto it."

In appealing to parents for their children for this work, one almost invariable answer we receive is this: We would willingly give them up, but they do not show any inclination for the work themselves, and we do not like to influence them or urge them against their will. But why not influence them so as to bring about a willingness? This, as appears to me, is the very point where parental duty fails. Every parent is expected to influence his child to give his heart to God, and make a profession of his faith in Christ. Why not, then, if they evince sufficient capacity, influence them in the same way to become ministers or missionaries? They are not to force them; but surely it is their duty to influence them, as far as possible, by their prayers, their example, and their conversation; by putting suitable books into their hands; by bringing them within the range of such other influences as might operate favourably upon them; and by keeping them as far as possible out of all contrary influences. Many of our best missionaries have been led to devote themselves to this work from reading the lives of other missionaries who had gone before them. It was the pondering over the first question in the Shorter Catechism that was the initiatory step in Lady Glenorchy's conversion, and in that noble life of Christian usefulness which she afterwards led. Dr. Chalmers has well shown in one of his lectures (the 11th of Romans) that when God requires us to forgive and love our enemies, He does not intend us, by doing so, to contravene any part of our mental or moral constitution. Christ's injunction is, "If he repent, forgive him." The repentance is to precede the forgiveness, which removes all the difficulty to a Christian spirit. We are to love our enemies, but it is not with a love of complacency, as we do our friends, but simply with a love of benevolence or pity; and the consideration of the retribution that awaits them, if fully realised in our minds, will produce this pity; so that loving them in this way will be natural and easy. So, in influencing young people to become missionaries, there is no need of contravening any part either of their mental or their moral constitution—of leading them to engage in a work to which they would have no heart. If the right influences are brought to bear upon them, and prove efficacious, these will give them heart, love, and life for the work. Let Christian life, ministerial character, and missionary labours be presented fully and forcibly before them, as bearing on the glory of God, their own usefulness and happiness, and the present and future well-being of their fellowmen; let them feel that in becoming missionaries they are not like those engaged in secular occupations, however useful and however honourable, operating on perishable materials; they are operating on the imperishable—the immortal—on mind and spirit; they are affecting directly the highest interests of humanity; the effects of their labours are not confined to time, they will extend into and throughout all eternity.

From whatever cause, there can be no doubt that those influences which would lead young men to become missionaries are brought to bear far too lightly on the rising youth of the Churches. Every Church and every Missionary Society is crippled for want of agents. Why is this, while every other profession is crowded? Parents are at a loss what profession to choose for their sons. Every profession is over-supplied with candidates—the medical, the legal, the literary, the mercantile, the agricultural. The missionary staff alone is under-supplied; and why should it be so? Surely there is nothing in the life of the missionary in these latter decades of this nineteenth century, as seen even from a worldly standpoint, nothing in his labours, his perils, his poverty, or his reproaches, that should stagger any brave, earnest-hearted Christian youth. On the other hand, as seen from the same point of view, there seems to be now falling to his share a pretty fair portion of both earthly rewards and worldly honours; while the crowning promise from another standpoint is: "They that be wise (*marg.* teachers) shall shine as the brightness of the firmament; and they that turn many to righteousness as the stars for ever and ever" (Dan. xii. 3).

THE END.

ERRATUM.—Delete lines 7 to 15 inclusive on page 38. The information, relied upon as trustworthy for the statement in these lines, has been found to be incorrect. The teachers were not left on Tanna, and the missionaries never afterwards saw cause to change their views as to the dangers of their situation.

www.ingramcontent.com/pod-product-compliance
Lightning Source LLC
Chambersburg PA
CBHW031424230426
43668CB00007B/423